COLLEGE

We Make the Road by Walking

margit misangyi watts

UNIVERSITY OF HAWAII AT MANOA

Prentice
Hall

Upper Saddle River, New Jersey
Columbus, Ohio

Library of Congress Cataloging-in-Publication Data

Watts, Margit Misangyi
    College : we make the road by walking / Margit Misangyi Watts.
      p. cm.
    Includes bibliographical references and index.
    ISBN 0-13-098756-5
    1. Education, Humanistic.   I. Title

  LC1011 .W29 2003
  378.1'98—dc21   2002070387

Vice President and Publisher: Jeffery W. Johnston
Senior Acquisitions Editor: Sande Johnson
Assistant Editor: Cecilia Johnson
Production Editor: Holcomb Hathaway
Design Coordinator: Diane C. Lorenzo
Cover Designer: Jeff Vanik
Cover Art: Corbis Stock Market
Production Manager: Pamela D. Bennett
Director of Marketing: Ann Castel Davis
Director of Advertising: Kevin Flanagan
Marketing Manager: Christina Quadhamer

for tom

This book was set in Scala by Aerocraft Charter Art Service. It was printed and bound
by Courier Kendallville, Inc. The cover was printed by Phoenix Color Corp.

Pearson Education Ltd.
Pearson Education Australia Pty. Limited
Pearson Education Singapore Pte. Ltd.
Pearson Education North Asia Ltd.
Pearson Education Canada, Ltd.
Pearson Educación de Mexico, S.A. de C.V.
Pearson Education–Japan
Pearson Education Malaysia Pte. Ltd.
Pearson Education, Upper Saddle River, New Jersey

10 9 8 7 6 5 4 3 2 1
ISBN 0-13-098756-5

Contents

We tell ourselves stories in order to live.

JOAN DIDION

SECOND JOURNEY | SCHOLARLY NARRATIVES 102

CHAPTER FIVE

Reality and Truth 105

CHAPTER SIX

Ways of Knowing 125

CHAPTER SEVEN

Information and Knowledge   145

THIRD JOURNEY   UNDERSTANDING SCHOLARSHIP   166

CHAPTER EIGHT

Discourse   169

CHAPTER

Research   189

FOURTH JOURNEY   CONTRIBUTING TO SCHOLARSHIP   212

CHAPTER
TEN

Beyond the Classroom   215

Acknowledgments

Try not to have a good time. This is supposed to be educational.

CHARLES SHULTZ

This has been both educational and a good time! Writing a textbook has pushed my limits in numerous ways, and I am certain that I have learned as much, if not more, in the process than I have imparted to others. Of course, this kind of undertaking is never a lonely one. Many people have contributed in unique ways both to help shape my thinking and to simply get the manuscript to the publisher.

College: We Make the Road by Walking had a beginning. There is always a beginning, isn't there, even if we don't know it at the time? I'd like to thank Dean Richard Dubanoski for getting me started in the early 1990s. He challenged me to initiate a new first-year program, supported me when I was putting it together, and continued to mentor me over the years as the program matured. Not only did he help secure funding, pave the way through the thick and thin of bureaucratic nightmares, and secure a position for me to run this new program—he also gave me his greatest gift: his time. We spent hours talking about educational philosophy, the needs of students, the beauty of a liberal education, and the opportunities to create new models for first-year students. It is for this time that I thank him most.

Once the program was under way, my learning stemmed from two sources—my students and my staff. If you pay attention, you can learn a great deal from your students. Daily contact in and out of class with first-year students honed my thinking, helped my development of a foundational course, and led me, finally, to write this book. However, as my contact with students shaped my ideas, the constant conversations with my staff and colleagues in turn helped me derive meaning from my experiences. In particular, my assistant, Megumi Taniguchi, helped clarify the actions of our students. She had incredible insight as to their motivation and needs, and in our daily chats, my understanding grew. She took the time to reflect with me on our daily work with these first-year students, and in that reflection we were constantly able to react accordingly. Again, my thanks are for that gift of time.

Speaking of time once again, it plays well into this story. Dick Dubanoski introduced me to a new librarian on campus, Randy Hensley, in the hopes that we might connect and collaborate. This meeting was incredibly fortuitous. Randy and I "connected" immediately. He was interested in integrating library skills, or what we now call information literacy skills, into the learning community I was running. His contribution far exceeded either of our expectations. Over the years, Randy became a co-instructor in the program and helped shape the curriculum.

His contributions can be found throughout this book in subtle and not so subtle ways. Randy wrote each "Travel Essential" section. These valuable essays are his musings on the importance and integration of information literacy, with special focus on the topic at hand. Many of the activities throughout the book are products of conversations with Randy, and the instructor's manual is full of Randy's input as to teaching strategies and pedagogy. He has devoted a great deal of time to the development of our first-year program and, consequently, to the thinking in this book. There is no simple way to thank him for his priceless contributions.

Timing is everything. I visited southern Maine in the summer of 2001 to meet with my colleague Steve Romanoff and further discuss collaborative efforts between our respective learning communities. Little did I know that I would find the title of this book while travelling. Steve played a tape of his new solo album and offered the lyrics of his first song as something he thought was close to the meaning of my book. (The lyrics can be found inside the front cover of the book.) Steve took the time to listen to what I wanted to accomplish and then asked me to listen to his song. The match was perfect. The gift of his song was more than the music—it was validation.

I also want to thank all those who helped get this book into the publisher's hands. Marilyn Myers worked endless hours acquiring permissions to use the various articles. She was a tireless sleuth when trying to find long-lost student addresses in order to get their signatures. She was meticulous in keeping records; contributed ideas for journal entries, activities, and writing assignments; and spent hours talking over the general structure of the book. Marilyn became a daily sounding board and contributed greatly in both organization and creativity.

The support of my editor, Sande Johnson, and assistant editor, Cecilia Johnson, was necessary to make this all come together. It was gratifying to work with two professionals who truly understood where this book was going. Sande picked up on the unique focus from the beginning, and our work together was seamless. Cecilia tirelessly answered the questions I raised as the book went into production. I wish to thank them and the other Prentice Hall professionals who assisted me—I can't imagine better people with whom to work.

I also wish to offer my sincere thanks to those who reviewed this material and offered constructive comments toward its improvement: Dan Angelo, San Bernardino Valley College; Colleen Boff, Bowling Green State University; Mack Caldwell, University of Oklahoma; Jane Eddy, Viterbo University; Angeleque M. Hill-Reynolds, Pensacola Junior College; Mary Stuart Hunter, University of South Carolina; Barry Maid, Arizona State University; Mary K. Pepe, Valencia Community College; Mary Jane Petrowski, Colgate College; Stephen J. Romanoff, University of Southern Maine; and Susan Barnes Whyte, Linfield College. The book is better as a result of their efforts, and I appreciate their help.

My student assistants, Carol Hasegawa, Ronson Ibarra, and Lori Okimoto, were always helpful in running down citations and doing last-minute copying and other clerical tasks to help me complete this book.

As in all endeavors, it is those closest to you who shape your work and who are impacted the most by it. My sons, Jameson and Nicolas, were very helpful once they took off for college. They showed me in a most personal manner what it was like to be a first-year student. I treasure their willingness to talk with me about their experiences. Finally, I'm back to time. And thus, this book is dedicated to Tom, my husband of over 30 years, who has supported my academic and creative endeavors in immeasurable ways. Thank you.

Introduction

MAKING THE ROAD

With word and deed we insert ourselves into the human world, and this insertion is like a second birth, in which we confirm and take upon ourselves the naked fact of our original physical appearance. This insertion is not forced upon us by necessity, like labor, and it is not prompted by utility, like work. It may be stimulated by the presence of others whose company we may wish to join, but it is never conditioned by them; its impulse springs from the beginning which came into the world when we were born and to which we respond by beginning something new on our own initiative.

—Hannah Arendt

BEGINNING THE WALK

Entering college is "beginning something new," and it is your own initiative, or walk, that will enrich your experiences. A passion for learning is not something we should be inspiring in you; rather, it is what we must keep from being extinguished. Human beings are by nature passionate, curious, and intrigued, and they seek to connect, find patterns, and make sense of things. Therefore, learning is more effective when new information is made meaningful and is linked to personal experience or prior knowledge. *College: We Make the Road by Walking* should help you explore and express your own ideas as well as allow you to make your own tacit knowledge explicit. Additionally, when given time to reflect on your learning and to make associations between units of knowledge, you will connect in meaningful ways.

This book is not intended to teach you *what* to think; instead, it aims at helping you learn *how* to think and, more importantly, *why* bother to think at all. It addresses ways of knowing, how and why scholarship is created, and how you, as a student, can contribute to the creation of knowledge. In fact, it is when you discover your own ability to contribute to scholarship that the answer to *why* becomes apparent.

WHY THIS APPROACH?

Let me give you some background as to why this book is relevant to you as a first-year student. At lunch one day, I was telling a colleague about my experiences that morning with my students. I was annoyed by their blatant lack of interest or passion—the "I don't really care" attitude. The students were thinking, "What's in it for me?" My colleague suggested that perhaps I was frustrated because we sometimes expect too much from students; we expect their agendas to match our own. He proposed that not all students come to college to "learn" or to be "liberally educated" or to be "involved in intellectual pursuits." He suggested that many students attend college for other reasons, such as parental pressure, an athletic scholarship, not wanting to begin working full-time, or some vague notion that a college degree can later be traded for a successful career.

Faculty and students often have agendas that don't quite match. I couldn't help but wonder what exactly we did need to offer a first-year student to make for a mutually satisfying experience. My own teaching experiences helped me realize that students need to connect with learning and to understand that their contributions are important to the process. In other words, learning should be viewed as a journey, but not one with a full itinerary, set plans, or stops along the way. It is you, the student, who is responsible for making the trip interesting, meaningful, and significant. Thus, the subtitle *We Make the Road by Walking* supports the structure of this book, which is flexible, open, and useful in multiple ways to all kinds of students. You, with some guidance, will be making your own road.

STRUCTURE OF THE BOOK

The book consists of a number of readings, activities, writing assignments, connections to service learning, words from the business community, student writing, journals, technology tips, and essays on the value of information literacy. Explanations of each of these facets of the book can be found in the "Guide to the Book" section on page xv. You will also find a "map" of the book, and a discussion of the value of journal writing.

The book is meant to be used as a workbook, so please make it your own. Pages have been perforated for ease of use and journal pages are included for your convenience.

CONTENTS OF THE BOOK

You will be asked to consider and share what you bring to the educational experience. Who are you? How do you learn? What kind of intelligence do you have the most of? Do you understand your own values and perspectives and how you might have gotten them? How do you deal with change? Do you comprehend how valuable your education is to the rest of your life? Throughout the making of your road, you will explore personal narratives and eventually understand how to make the connection between these and scholarly narratives.

Let me speak a little about the concept of *narrative*. A narrative is a story. Simple. But what is not so simple is that narratives, or stories, come in many varieties and serve many functions. You grew up with stories—from your grandmothers or aunts, your kindergarten teacher, your friends and parents, and television, radio, magazines, and other media. All of these were telling you stories—sometimes to give you family history, others to entertain, and others to lure you into buying some product.

Your life is made up of stories. If you were to tell anyone about your life (which you will be asked to do in this book), you would probably fashion the details and facts into stories. What you probably have never considered is that scholars also write stories. Their stories just happen to be fashioned from intense research or study in a particular field. But they are still stories.

College: We Make the Road by Walking is divided into five journeys, each with a specific goal and arranged in chapters that build on one another. The First Journey is called "Personal Narratives." The purpose of this journey is to help you to discover your own stories and how they inform your learning, your knowledge base, and your perceptions and values. It is also designed to help you begin to understand the values and perspectives of others.

In the first chapter in this journey, "Learning," you will do some reading on the concept of change and how it affects people. You will also encounter part of the autobiography of Malcolm X and be asked to contemplate what role you play in your own education. Finally, you will respond to a speech given to freshmen at Yale about the value of a liberal education. Is this speech something you've heard before? Does any of it make sense to you? Bore you? Ring a bell? The speech is intended to engage you in lively discussion about the ideas presented.

The second chapter, "Your Story," includes several personal stories written by others. It is replete with activities and assignments that lead up to your crafting your own autobiography. You will examine your past—the events that brought you to this place now—and will speculate about how knowing this information might help you learn about scholarship.

The third chapter, "Styles and Intelligence," introduces you to multiple intelligences to help pinpoint your strengths and weaknesses. What is your learning style, and how can your learning habits be adjusted to accommodate your style? Knowing about both style and intelligence will be useful as you navigate your way through this new academic environment. It will also help you understand the various teaching modes you will encounter throughout your college career.

The fourth and final chapter of this first journey, "Values and Perspectives," will enable you to discover things about culture and gender, perceptions about the United States, and perspectives about the world. This chapter includes lively activities and will prepare you to move from the personal into the scholarly realm.

The Second Journey focuses on "Scholarly Narratives." You will learn how to make comparisons between what you know on a personal level to how information becomes knowledge on a scholarly level. In Chapter Five, "Reality and Truth," you might question the concept of reality. Beginning with an exercise in perspectives offered by the allegory of Plato's Cave, you will understand how easily perspectives can be skewed. Then, by looking at the new technologies that take us into cyberspace and the proliferation of reality television, you might stretch your definition of reality even further.

The sixth chapter, "Ways of Knowing," asks several questions. What is the purpose of knowledge? What are the ways we actually "know" something? What is the difference among knowing something through experience, observation, authority, or reflection? Getting a handle on how you know what you know will help you discern the difference between information and knowledge, the topic of Chapter Seven. This chapter, "Information and Knowledge," introduces you to types of knowledge products and will help you discover the parallels between personal and scholarly narratives and focus on what makes knowledge important.

The Third Journey, "Understanding Scholarship," will introduce you to how scholarship is created, by studying the concept of discourse, a conversation over time, or another way of telling a story. In the eighth chapter, "Discourse," your introduction to question analysis, the creation of a hypothesis, and the concept of critical thinking should broaden your understanding of how scholarship is constructed.

"Research," the ninth chapter, will help you learn how to retrieve information and evaluate sources once you've found them. This chapter also focuses on writing a research proposal. You will select a topic, construct a hypothesis, learn how to write a review of the literature, develop an annotated bibliography, and produce a final product that contributes to the discourse of your particular topic.

The Fourth Journey, "Contributing to Scholarship," is where all of your skills and new understanding of why one pursues knowledge come together. Why study at all if in the end you don't have somewhere to share your work? In the tenth chapter, "Beyond the Classroom," you will learn the many ways you can contribute to your community by sharing your knowledge. The possibilities range from participating in museum exhibits to putting on a student conference. On a smaller scale, you can display your learning through school publications or newspaper articles. Whatever outlet you choose, viewing your work as useful to the wider community gives it a new focus and meaning. A section on internships helps you see the value of extending your learning outside of the college arena. If you understand the notion of *making the road by walking,* then you will want to expand your journey and create a more interesting and relevant path for yourself. One way is to participate in opportunities within your community and elsewhere—whether this be a paying internship for a semester or apprenticing with a firm to learn the ropes. Either way, the experience can be invaluable to your overall education. In addition to exhibiting your work, you can become involved in service learning. Chapter Eleven defines the concept of service learning and gives suggestions on how it might be useful in your studies.

The Fifth Journey, "Further Travels," concentrates on reflection. The final chapter suggests that you look back on your path, see what kind of road you have begun to design for yourself, and note what you have learned. One way to understand anything is through reflective practice. This portion of the book helps you to take stock of your experiences while using this text, perhaps causing you to redirect your educational efforts, and prepares you for whatever steps you will take next.

Good luck on these journeys. Remember, each individual's path will be different—that's the beauty of learning. May the making of your own road challenge and engage you.

margit misangyi watts

Guide to the Book

When you follow an idea, it could lead anywhere.

CARL ENGLISH

Comparison of me before and after my first year in college:

Very narrow-minded and
with a fear of failure

Open-minded and willing
to try new things

MAP OF THE BOOK

This book uses a number of terms that allude to travel. These expressions should remind you that learning is a journey. Of course, you have a choice about which kind of journey your college experience might reflect. Much like a trip to Europe could be spent seeking out American fast-food restaurants or listening to someone else's version of what you are to think, your time in college could mirror the

Do not follow where the path may lead. Go instead where there is no path and leave a trail.

MURIEL STRODE

security of your high school days. Or, your college journey can open your mind to many new discoveries and adventures, such as tasting that strange-looking food in South America or puzzling over a sculpture on the steps of some ancient ruin and figuring out for yourself what it might mean. The choice is yours.

In this book, you will encounter words that encourage you to value your experience in college as a journey toward the creation of your own education. You are the driver; the text is but a guide.

- **Snapshots.** These entries that begin each chapter are written by first-year students. The topics range from lessons learned to personal experiences and reflections. Each entry was chosen specifically to highlight the topic of a particular chapter. They give you a "snapshot" of stories told by students like you.

- **Souvenirs.** You will find five souvenirs, one for each journey. These are stories that come from my personal experiences teaching first-year students. Each souvenir reflects a profound lesson I learned by being a teacher. I offer these reflective pieces to you as "souvenirs" of another's journey to help you understand the concept of "making the road by walking" for yourself.

- **Travel Essentials.** For your journey through college and beyond to be significant, you will need to become information literate. At the beginning of each chapter, you will find an essay by Randy Hensley on how to connect the concept of information literacy to the topic at hand. As you move through the five journeys in this book, you will discover how "essential" it is to know when you need information, where to find it, how to make certain it is credible, how to use it and, finally, why you might use it after all. Your journey will be more complete as you develop your information literacy skills.

- **Compasses.** Each journey begins with an introduction and then reminds you to set your course while keeping in mind your ultimate responsibility to the wider community. Each compass serves to reorient you to the true meaning of education. The compasses are reminders that, in the final analysis, your contributions to your community will be the most important product of your becoming an educated person. Service learning (a concept explained in detail in Chapter Eleven) is central to your ability to connect theory to life. Thus, at the beginning of each journey, you will find hints, suggestions, stories, and advice about how to infuse your college experience with even more purpose.

- **Quotations.** Many people over the years have had insight into the way the world operates. They have written books, composed songs, painted murals, built buildings, and created new products. Whatever their life's work, these people discovered meaning in their lives; through the quotations interspersed within these chapters, they share their ideas with you. Don't quickly gloss over these quotes—take the time to see how each quote might enlighten you.

- **Cash In on Education.** Students are concerned about the application and relevance of their college educations to their lives, especially their future employment opportunities. Thus, at the end of each chapter, you will find a short essay by a college-educated individual who is a member of the working community. Each individual has been asked to comment on the value of education. This is a bit like exchanging currency on a trip. At some point, you will have a degree, and you probably want to know what it will get you in return. These sections highlight the skills professionals think you need and will gain during your years in college. Sometimes, what they think is most important might be surprising. These essays should help illuminate for you how the wider community views higher education as well as help you see more clearly how you might exchange your investment in a higher education for future success.

JOURNAL WRITING

A journal captures how each of us sees, understands, reacts to, and makes meaning from our experiences. Most of you have had the opportunity during your years in school to write in a journal of some kind. Perhaps you have also kept a personal journal for your own reflection. Educators widely believe that keeping a journal helps you to remember, to understand, and to gain perspective.

What does this mean exactly? It appears that when we write down our thoughts, whether these are in response to a reading or lecture or perhaps to some activity, we seem to do a better job of making sense of it all. Writing helps us to:

- contemplate the relationship among ideas
- consider the connections
- study the contrasts
- understand possible implications
- see the significance
- make meaning

Let's go over these reasons for personal journal writing. Pretend that you are asked to read an article and then are given a few questions to answer in response to your reading. Journal writing will give you the opportunity to organize your thoughts more carefully, and you will begin to *contemplate the relationship among ideas*. Most

---

Writing, like life itself, is a voyage of discovery.

HENRY MILLER

likely, you will find that in the process of writing your thoughts down you will see patterns emerge. All of a sudden, you can *consider the connections* between ideas within the reading and discussions held in class. You can also *study the contrasts* between what you read and what you have experienced. This will help you *understand the possible implications* inherent in your thinking. You will see the significance of the article more clearly and be able to make meaning of your reading.

For purposes of this book, which is a journey into the world of scholarship and learning, you will find journal entries dispersed throughout. These are to be your place for journal writing. However, you will see that the pages are a bit different than what you might expect. They are divided into lined and unlined sections to give you an opportunity to fully express your ideas.

Lev Vygotsky, a theorist who was convinced that learning is done symbolically, suggested that when people figure things out (or think), they do so in systems of language, music, mathematics, pictures, and so forth. This means that you figure out the meaning of things in multiple ways. Thus, the prompts for the travel logs will not only ask you to write your responses, reflections, and thoughts but will suggest that you draw pictures, maps, symbols, or whatever comes to mind to help you work out your ideas and concepts.

So, the purpose of your journal is to:

- keep an ongoing dialogue with yourself about things that interest you
- keep a record of your progress
- evaluate and review your learning
- practice personal writing
- explore theories, concepts, and problems

Journals can also be a place to ask questions or do some personal reflection.

Please remember, though, that journal writing is not meant to be stressful. These journals are excellent practice for writing, thinking, reflecting and, most of all, learning. If learning is a journey, then keep a record of your travels.

CONCEPT MAPPING

Concept (or mind) mapping is a tool for making connections between and among ideas. These ideas could be from a reading, a lecture, or your own creative brainstorming. The general rule for making such a map is to go from the general to the specific. You can be very structured about your map and begin with a key idea and then have straight lines take you out to the more specific ones. Take a look at this example. You would put the key concept in the larger box—let's say health issues—and then in the smaller boxes you might put the phrases, eating disorders, sleep deprivation, and substance abuse.

In this way, you have created a "map" that outlines the beginning of your thinking on the topic of health issues. Of course, you can go further by drawing lines from one of the smaller boxes and getting even more specific on one of the subtopics.

If you want to do a more open-ended map that details every thought you might have on a subject and visually keys this information to your memory, make a mind map. In this form of mapping, you can be creative and go all over the page, following your ideas as they flow. For example, if you had just read an article on rain forests, you might create the following map for yourself:

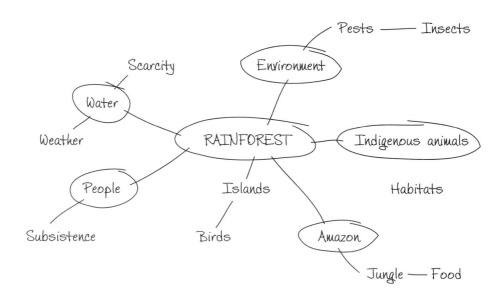

Use this manner of organizing your thoughts whenever possible. It will be useful not only for your journal writing but also for any brainstorming you might be doing to write a paper, keep track of a lecture or a reading, or make plans for a project.

COLLEGE

We Make the
Road by Walking

SOUVENIR

A Teaching Moment

For me, one of the most important aspects of teaching is creating learning opportunities for students with diverse backgrounds, abilities, and interests. In all my classes, I design projects that allow students to shine.

Several years ago, my classes were working furiously on their capstone museum exhibit project. They worked in groups that had been together throughout the year and had developed a sense of trust and collaboration. Each group had a particular focus and a piece of the exhibit to complete.

Of course, in all group projects there tend to be students who don't pull their weight. This particular year I had a student, let's call him Bill, who really didn't do his part and had made everyone in his group angry. Bill didn't do well in general and appeared to lack any motivation or interest in learning.

One evening his group, about five students, stood outside the dorm looking at their enormous unpainted canvas. (They had sewn a canvas large enough to cover a 12-foot teepee.) I brought them a small 8.5 x 11 book with Plains Indian designs from which to choose. They thought I was crazy! How in the world were they going

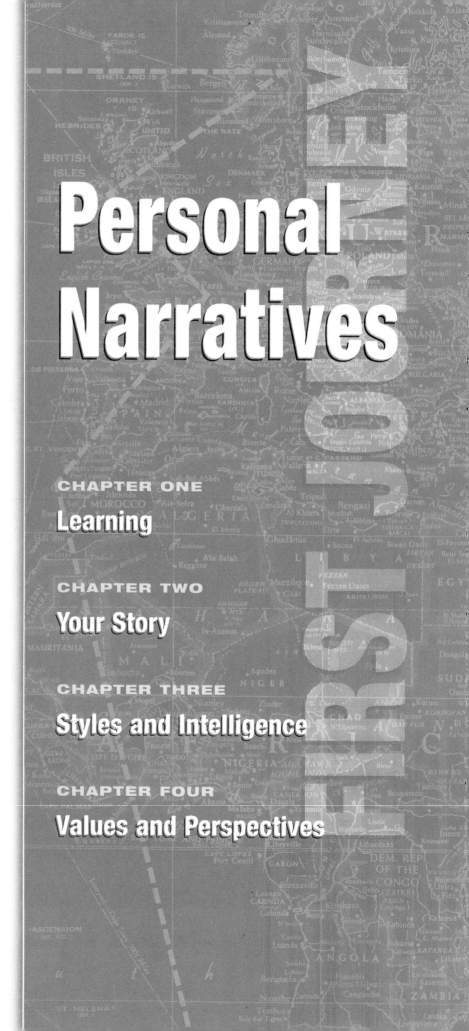

Personal Narratives

Introduction to the First Journey

Peter Senge begins his book *The Fifth Discipline Fieldbook* by describing a common greeting of the tribes of Northern Natal in South Africa. They greet one another by saying "sawu bona" and "sikhona." The expression *sawu bona* means, literally, "I see you," and the reply *sikhona* means "I am here." This exchange is important because its inherent meaning is clear: your greeting acknowledges my particularity, and my reply confirms the success of your acknowledgment. If one goal of education is to develop self-sufficient, curious human beings, we must teach the value of each individual. Thus, you are about to explore personal narratives as a first step toward participating in building your communities. Because you are a unique individual, your educational process—the road *you* are making—must validate what you bring to your academic experience.

Learning has affective and subjective dimensions. Your intellectual development includes both learning to articulate your own point of view and listening to the views of others. In this manner, you become responsible creators of your own knowledge and meaning. After all, not only is education defined by specific measures, such as exams, grades, and statistics, but it is the process of developing your mind. Because each mind is different, your educational experience needs to recognize your uniqueness and should confirm you in the manner of *sawu bona* and *sikhona*.

Many educators agree that you should acquire a depth and breadth of knowledge, develop the ability to communicate, think critically, be acquainted with important methods of inquiry, secure lasting intellectual and cultural interests, gain self-knowledge, and learn how to make informed judgments. In fact, most educators agree that your undergraduate experience must lead to your becoming a more competent, more complete and concerned human being. In other words, you are to develop the ability to become involved in life on visual, verbal, and auditory levels and you are to gain an understanding of history, science, and the arts, along with an understanding that knowledge is essential for a fulfilling, responsible life. Going to college is supposed to make you an *educated person*.

What is an educated person? Part of the answer to this, surely, is that there is no single answer. On the contrary, the whole notion of *sawu bona/sikhona* suggests that there must be as many answers as there is diversity among us in our natural endowments and worldviews. Later in this First Journey, you will read a speech by A. Bartlett Giamatti, who is convinced that you should be learning just for the *sake* of learning. However, we know that today's

to translate something that small onto this huge canvas?

After about 20 minutes of silence—very uncomfortable silence—Bill came up to me and asked to see the pictures. He studied them for a few minutes and then asked me if I had any duct tape. Nodding yes, I headed for the office and brought him a large roll.

With the rest of his group looking on with expressions of "now what is he going to do?" Bill proceeded to outline two eagles and chevron decorations around the entire canvas. When he was finished, the students could see that painting inside the duct tape would give them an incredibly beautiful canvas for their teepee.

Jaws on the ground, mine included, the students congratulated Bill. The next day, all of the other groups asked Bill to paint the backgrounds for their exhibit pieces. His spatial intelligence was excellent, and he finally contributed something of substance in a way recognizable by everyone. And I was validated for offering the students this kind of experience.

students desperately cling to the hope that a college education will give them a ticket to a better future.

Therefore, if we, as educators, neglect the importance of enabling you to make connections across the curriculum and to your lives, we fail miserably in our mission to educate. Not only have we then ignored your very real need to see your education as a commodity to be traded for a better life, but we have undermined our own ability to foster the intellectual engagement that is at the foundation of higher learning.

A liberal education need not be useless if we adhere to the notion of *sawu bona/sikhona*. This First Journey pays attention to your variety of learning styles, values, differing attitudes toward education, various levels of motivation, cultural backgrounds, and skill levels. In each of the four chapters within this journey, you will be asked to bring yourself fully into your academic experience. Only then will you be able to appreciate your role in your own education.

COMPASS

I have interacted
I have maintained a positive attitude
I have had fun
I have learned
I have contributed
I have helped
I have nourished the minds and bodies of children
I have changed

—First-year student

Have you ever wondered what it really means to say, "When I get out in the real world I will . . ."? Why aren't your educational experiences considered part of the real world? What makes everyone accept the notion that time in school is somehow separate from what will go on afterward? If we can all agree that the mission of higher education is to foster learning, discovery, discussion, and the creation of knowledge about the world, shouldn't time spent in college be deemed the "real" world? How else do you bridge the gap between theory and practice?

One way is to participate in *service learning,* community service that is aligned with your course work. When you are involved in a service learning project, the opportunity to be a creative problem solver, a member of a team, a decision maker, and a part of the community arises. More importantly, making the connection between class content and the work of your community is a valuable bonus to your learning. Enrich your education.

CHAPTER ONE

Learning

Objectives

- to understand the concept of learning

- to review your own experiences with learning

- to be open to change

- to set goals for yourself as a learner

- to understand the notion of a liberal education

"We make the road by walking, Farther than the eye can see, . . ."

5

I Am What I Am

I am what I am. I am Chinese.

My eyes are slanted. So what? Who cares?

I am what I am. I am German.

I am haole. Yet, my skin is not pale.

I am what I am. I am Filipino.

My brown skin. I am perfectly colored.

My light brown skin matches my light brown eyes.

I am what I am. I am Hawaiian.

Who cares if it is not by blood?

I am Hawaii. I am the Aloha Spirit.

Yes, I am in college.

You can hear the educated English when I speak.

You can also hear my pidgin. I love that language.

From my first day to my last,

I will arrive with a "Howzits Brah!!" and

Leave with one loud and happy, "Kay den kuz!"

I am the country.

I am Ewa Beach, Waipahu, and Pearl City.

I am what I am.

If you don't like it, then who cares?

I am the metal that was poured from the melting pot.

A Chinese man loved a German woman and

A Filipino man loved a Chinese woman.

Their children brought forth a new American.

They brought forth me.

The local, the American, the Teen-Ager, and

The Future of This World!

I am what I am.

And that is what I am.

—Jared Keoni Chun

TRAVEL ESSENTIAL

Information Literacy and Learning

"I learn something new every day." Somebody has probably made this statement to you at least once in your life. You have also probably been asked, "What did you learn today?" You were probably asked this question a lot when you were younger, more than you wanted to be. Sometimes it was used as a test by your parents to see if you paid attention at school. Other times it was meant to start a conversation between you and another adult about your day and the events that comprised it. What's the deeper reality behind these seemingly casual, unimportant conversation starters?

First, they assume that you can, in fact, learn something, that you are capable of experiencing something new. Second, they imply that learning something becomes a part of you, changes you, adds to who you are, to what you can do, to how you are. Finally, the use of the word "learn" indicates a process in which something you did or that was done to you occurred through a series of events, actions, or activities that you were a part of in some way.

Learning is creating. It is a process whose components are information and connection. Learning occurs when information, or "data," is connected to who we are or, in other words, to what we already know. The connecting transforms the information into meaning for us, making it useful, important, exciting, or fun. For example, I listen to a new song and I decide that I like that song because it has a great melody.

Go deeper. The actual song that I hear is information. When I decide that I like the melody,

I have made a connection to how I feel about music or other songs I already like or to what I think about the performer or type of music. I have made the song a part of what I already know, what I have already experienced or think or have liked before. You can come up with hundreds of examples of this process happening every day, in all kinds of ways with all kinds of things. That's learning.

Information literacy is about making the process of transforming information into learning more deliberate. It is about being able to recognize information, to find the information you want, and to decide the best information for the learning you want or need to do. Information literacy is about knowing when you need information for the best learning possible and knowing where to find the best sources for that information to ensure quality learning. Is the best source of information a person? Is it a book? A website? A television program? Being information literate is knowing how to decide, where to find, and when to look.

There is no learning without information, and there is no quality learning without a conscious effort to get the most relevant raw material (information) possible. Learning, then, is making connections between your internal understanding of yourself in the world and external factors that can influence that internal world. Information is an external repository of influences. By making this process of connecting the internal to the external deliberate, focused, and efficient, we create our own definition of being a learner and being information literate.

LEARNING

A few years back, first-year students were asked to brainstorm words that describe education. The words that came up most often were *knowledge, learning, thinking, open-mindedness, expanding perspectives, career,* and *success.* One of the main objectives of education is to help students learn about themselves and the world in a coherent manner. Thus, it was interesting to note that all of the

---

That is what learning is. You suddenly understand something you've understood all your life, but in a new way.

DORIS LESSING

words used by the students were about learning in one way or another. Discovering new knowledge, determining different ways of thinking, broadening one's perspective, gaining skills for a career, and gathering the necessary expertise in a number of areas in order to be successful are all part of the larger concept of learning.

Of course, many students come to college ostensibly "to learn," but when asked for the real reason for being on campus, they answer: "My parents told me I had to," "I wanted the football scholarship," "I had nothing else to do," or "I want to be sure to get a good job." These are all valid reasons for going to college, but let's look a bit deeper.

So what exactly is learning? First of all, learning is an active, constructive process. You are asked to work with information, skills, and ideas and then to reorganize and make sense of them. Learning also depends on a rich context. This means anything learned will be more fully realized if you are not a distant observer of questions, answers, problems, and solutions, but instead are a practitioner and a problem solver. In other words, you need to be deeply involved in whatever you do in order to learn. Also, the rich context is both what you as a student bring to the learning situation and what your instructor offers.

In a university setting, learning is as diverse as the student population. Each student brings a different perspective, ability, and understanding to any learning environment. Learning is also a social process; the intellectual synergy of many minds working on a common endeavor can be powerful. In a rich learning environment, you develop your intellectual capacities, learn to articulate your own point of view, and listen to the views of others. Finally, you begin to be a responsible architect of your own knowledge and meaning.

Your journey through college will give you heavy exposure to information, knowledge, and a variety of perspectives. You will be in an environment rich in possibilities, one steeped in the past, the present, and the future. College can be an experience that moves you outside of your personal safety zone and leads you into new and uncharted spaces for discovery. Understanding how you learn will help you navigate this new territory.

Journal Entry 1

In every outthrust headland, in every curving beach, in every grain of sand there is the story of the earth.

Rachel Carson

Sketch a picture of how you view learning throughout your life. Use stick figures, symbols, or any other visual method that suits you.

When you have completed the sketches, take a few moments and make a list of at least 20 words that describe the learning experiences you have depicted visually.

Be creative!

READING

There is nothing permanent except change.

—Heraclitus

The following article by Laurent Daloz explores and contrasts the lives of two women. They both have acquired new knowledge that has transformed their lives, broadened their perspectives, and forced them to view their worlds in a new light. Read the article while keeping in mind your own new experience of entering college, and think about the role education might have in your life in the years to come.

Beyond Tribalism

Laurent A. Daloz

A central task of human development involves learning how to care for oneself in ways that increasingly incorporate the needs and concerns of others. Elementary school children learn to look after their own needs by anticipating those of their friends; Todd scratches Chris's back so Chris will scratch his. Later as Todd's capacity to extend himself matures, he learns how his friend experiences him as well, coming to view himself as part of a group and relying more on his capacity to share than to manipulate. Thus is born the culture of adolescence, a world characterized by conformity to the expectations of others, by membership in the tribe. Many people live out their lives struggling to meet the expectations of their spouses, children, or friends, finding a kind of equilibrium as loyal tribal members. But not all. For some, the world shifts again, and they lose their balance once more. Consider Lale and Susan.

Lale

A woman in her late twenties, Lale is one of a small group of people in the Southern Highlands of New Guinea known as the Kutubu, a name meaning "the people." As a girl, Lale was closely watched by her family; it would not do to have her taken without bride payment or worse, kidnapped by the enemy. When Lale came of age, she was married to a man in a neighboring village and in time became the mother of three children. Lale's husband, Beni, spends much of his time with the other men of the tribe hunting in the surrounding jungle or strengthening the village's defensive perimeter against the omnipresent danger of attack from the enemy in the North. He accepts without question his duty to join with the other men in protection of the tribe's women and children. For her part, Lale is glad to be protected. She is proud to be a Kutubu and cannot imagine any other kind of life. She accepts without question the laws and customs of her tribe, and her highest wish is to be a good wife and mother. It is a good life. To Lale, this is the way it has always been and always should be.

One day, she accompanies her friend to a regional market established by the government to foster trade and communication among the various local tribes. There she discovers women from other tribes. It is a whole new world.

Susan

Susan grew up in a small farming community in the northeastern corner of Vermont. Her parents watched her closely as a child for it would have been deeply humiliating for them had she become pregnant and been forced to marry. They were relieved when she graduated from high school and settled down to marry Armand, a young man from a neighboring village. While she raised their three children, he spent most of his time on the road driving a truck and serving his time as a member of the National Guard. Armand is a staunch patriot and is proud of the American flag on his truck he has named, "Miss Liberty." Susan shares her husband's patriotism and accepts without question his view, and echo of her father's, that America is the greatest country in the world. She is proud to be an American. She cannot understand why some people she sees on TV seem so critical and nods approvingly when her husband snorts, "if they don't like it here, they can move to Russia." This is a good life, and people should be thankful, not critical.

Then one day, going over family finances together, they come to the conclusion that Susan will need to get a job to supplement their income. Armand doesn't like the idea, but it seems they have no choice. Relieved that the children are all at school, Susan begins taking typing classes at the local community college. To meet a degree requirement, she takes a course in the Humanities where she discovers that her teacher, whom she greatly admires, does not share her husband's views. Nor do several of her classmates whom she respects. It is a whole new world.

Sustaining Ignorance

It would be a mistake, of course, to deny the differences between Lale and Susan. They live literally worlds and continents apart, in societies which, in many ways, are dramatically different. Yet the similarities are compelling. Each has encountered a new world which threatens her former balance. Let's look more closely.

Both Lale and Susan consider themselves normal people. They are well cared for, reasonably happy, and, above all, want to keep it that way. Each was carefully nurtured and protected by her family as she moved from childhood into adolescence. The delicate bridge between the first home and the second was crossed without incident, and each woman remains protected; first by her father, then by her husband. Within the circle of his arms she is safe. Their men, moreover, accept those responsibilities as given: to protect and provide for their families. Things as they are are things as they should be.

Each woman is held, as well, by her community. Each has learned right and wrong from her parents and, with little slippage, finds the same rules in her husband's home. Each takes it as her duty to pass on those same values to her children so that they, too, may be held as firmly by their community as she has been. Since they have come to see themselves as surrounded by a dangerous world, the circle of protection around their villages is doubly important, and each holds with special intensity to the beliefs with which she was reared. And although she may not express those beliefs often, when she does, it is with

a sense of the obvious: Isn't it common sense to believe as we do? Rarely does either woman reflect upon or criticize the given truths of her culture, and she views with suspicion those who do. To be critical, she believes, is, at best, the province of men, and at worst, of traitors.

But there is one problem. Because Lale's and Susan's worlds have been born of communal, given traditions rather than constructed from an individual confrontation with doubt and uncertainty, those worlds must rely on insulation from conflicting information if they are to remain stable. To sustain that tidy world of certainties, the tribe must erect a wall between itself and the outside world. Knowledge of other truths—even absurd ones, much less internally valid ones—is profoundly subversive and eats away at the tribe's security like a cancer. To maintain the stability of the tribe, a certain ignorance must be fostered.

When travelers leave home, they risk discovering a terrible secret: theirs is only one of any number of tribes, each believing its own truth to be paramount. Whether it is Lale going to market or Susan to secretarial school, the result is the same. The walls which both protected and isolated begin to crumble.

Beyond Tribal Gods

Formal education seeks more than mere indoctrination in the given values of a culture. It seeks to enable students to distance themselves from their upbringing, to see their values in a broader context. For only then can the culture remain alive to the possibility of change and develop the consequent capacity to adapt itself to an environment which is inevitably in flux. When it works, good education enables people to construct a coherent and responsive stance from complex information radiating from a rapidly shifting world. Such people are perhaps not as happy as they once were, but they probably do not view happiness as paramount. They have in some sense left the tribe and may suffer for that. Yet, in time they will make themselves at home in a larger tribe—ultimately, we hope, in a recognition of the intrinsic unity of the entire human family. The journey from one home to the next is seldom an easy one, but there is about it a kind of imperative. For some it seems a matter of life or death.

The Outward Journey

Throughout human history, maps of such growth have been handed down in the form of journey tales in which the hero leaves home in quest of some great adventure, usually symbolic of higher consciousness. Travelers in such tales invariably cross several thresholds as they move into conventional adult society. This crossing calls us to move from the security of our immediate family into the conventional adult tribe. We all recognize it as a necessary journey from a smaller to a larger home, and we call it growing up. It involves becoming normal and constitutes the chief task of adolescence. In most societies it is accomplished relatively smoothly and marked by such rituals as confirmation, bar mitzvah, and marriage.

A second crossing, departure from the tribe, is considerably less common and more dangerous. In a tribe like Lale's it is tantamount to death. One simply does not question the rules and remain an acceptable member of the tribe. And until recently, Lale would have had nowhere else to go. Although Susan's tribe will react with similar disapproval to her rebellion, she can, at least, leave her former psychological home and suffer only a ritual rather than a literal death. With luck, hard work, and good friends, she and Armand will find a way to reconstruct a new home together.

The Second Crossing

Beyond this tightly bound world lies a wider world held together not by external bonds but by the conscious choice of its membership. It is a world in which the rules, formerly invisible, are now seen and chosen. Choice and responsibility are central to entrance. But the passage into this world is difficult. It demands that the pilgrim make a conscious decision to leave home, and the password is a question: Why? With the answer to that question, the world becomes visible in a new way.

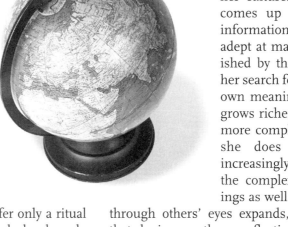

Out of the gap between old givens and new discoveries, an inner voice is born, resonates with other voices in the market or at school, and grows stronger. Over time, Susan learns that it may be more important to receive a lesson than an answer. She sees with a crisper clarity that authorities do not always agree and begins to take authority into her own heart, to listen with greater respect to the inner voice even though it may contradict that of her culture. As she repeatedly comes up against conflicting information, she grows more adept at making choices. Nourished by the new light cast by her search for a way to make her own meaning, her inner world grows richer, she acknowledges more complex feelings. And as she does this, she grows increasingly able to understand the complexity of others' feelings as well. Her capacity to see through others' eyes expands, and she discovers that she is more than a reflection in her former tribal mirror. Seeing herself as strangers do, she comes to view herself in a fresh way. As she acknowledges new inner voices, she welcomes new members to the tribe. In time, she grows to recognize that even women with whom she has no personal acquaintance might share her own pain. So for the first time, when she hears a friend declare that she has never been discriminated against, she retorts, "Just because you don't feel that way doesn't mean others don't!" Her horizon no longer stops at the edge of the village.

Journal Entry 2

All adventures, especially into new territory, are scary.

Sally Ride

To help you contemplate how changes have affected your lives, you can approach this journal writing assignment three different ways. Please choose one of the following options.

1. Change brings growth and conflict. Using the Venn diagram below, consider that the left-hand circle represents an old viewpoint or tribal view and the right-hand circle represents a new viewpoint or tribal view. The area shared between the two circles represents common elements or beliefs to both viewpoints. Little conflict occurs there. Those areas outside the intersection of the circles represent beliefs or areas where there is a possibility of conflict.

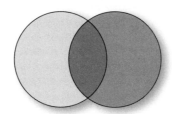

Think about a time when you were going through a change of viewpoints, and describe the situation as it relates to the Venn diagram. Write the commonly shared ideas and the conflicting ideas on your own diagram in your journal. Then write about the growth and conflict you experienced because of changing viewpoints. Be sure to describe the event that precipitated this experience of growth and change.

2. Think of a tribe (such as a team, family, or church group) you have been a part of, and think of a time when you grew, changed, and moved beyond the boundaries of that tribe. What did you gain in the process of finding this new perspective? What did you lose? Ultimately, did you experience the shift as positive or negative? What did you learn as a result of your decision to allow for change? Would you make the same decision again? Why or why not?

3. Sometimes a person has an opportunity to change, to move beyond their present tribe, and actually chooses *not* to change. Describe such a time in your own life. What was your reasoning in making the decision not to change? What might you have missed out on by not changing? What (if any) are your regrets about the choice you made? In what ways did you benefit from the decision not to change? Would you make the same decision again? Why or why not?

Below you will find a series of dots in groups of nine. Your first task is to see if you can connect all nine dots by drawing *five* contiguous (without lifting your pencil or retracing a line) lines. Try as many times as you can. Draw more groups of nine dots on another paper if necessary.

Now see if you can do the same by drawing *four* contiguous lines while still touching each of the nine dots only once.

How about *three* contiguous lines?

How about *one* line? If you can't actually do it with one, can you tell someone how to do it?

What did you find out? Let's first take a look at the solutions to these tasks.

Here are some ways you might have done this exercise:

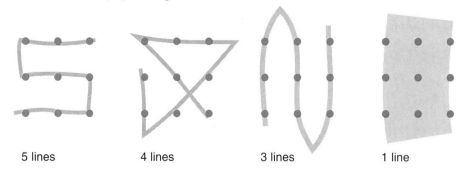

5 lines   4 lines   3 lines   1 line

Looking over your own work, answer the following questions:

1. What do you think the key is to solving any of these dot problems?

2. What implications does this have for your learning?

3. Did you find yourselves imposing a "box" around any of the nine dot groupings?

Were you surprised at how difficult this was at the beginning? Was it amazing to see how "boxed" in you were even though you thought you were pretty open-minded? We are always astounded to discover that we put parameters around our own thinking without knowing it. Keep this exercise in mind as you begin to be challenged by new ideas, ways of thinking, concepts, and information. The more open you are to change, the more fulfilling your education will be.

A closed mind is like a closed book; just a block of wood.

—Chinese Proverb

We all have an innate first reaction to change: resistance. However, it is important to overcome this resistance to change. All creative ideas are by definition new and unexpected departures from what is usual and accepted. Everything really new is far from what we know to be normal and tends to make us uncomfortable. A resistance to change blocks your ability to think critically. You need to be impartial as you analyze new information and make sense of it. If you are truly resisting any change, be it in thought or action, you can't really extend your thinking into new realms.

Most of us don't think we are that resistant and are surprised when we find ourselves reacting in ways that show we aren't so comfortable with change after all.

Find a partner to work with and follow the directions below.

Read some of the following ideas, and reach a tentative conclusion about each statement—react to it, and then observe your reaction.

- A law should be passed requiring women to retain their maiden names when they marry.
- All high school varsity sports should be eliminated, and their budgets should be used to fund intramural sports.
- Colleges should not admit any student who has been out of high school for more than three years.
- Higher tuition fees should be charged to seniors in college than to freshmen.
- Cats should not be allowed to wander in neighborhoods but should be kept in people's houses.
- We should give prizes to people who turn out to vote in general elections.

How did you react? How did your partner react? Were either of you outraged? Did you shrug your shoulders and not care? Did you have strong feelings? Spend some time talking about your individual reactions to the statements. Think about why you might have reacted as you did. Explain yourselves to each other.

Let's think about some ways you might actually be able to overcome your resistance to change. First, expect yourself to react negatively to new ideas. We all do. Expect your reaction to be especially strong if the new idea you face actually challenges a belief or value to which you are attached. Second, refuse to let this initial negative (or positive) reaction be the only way you evaluate this new idea. Force yourself to step back far enough from your first reaction to give the new idea a fair appraisal. Finally, judge the idea on the basis of your second, more critical, assessment, not just on your initial reaction. If you find that you still feel the way you did at the beginning, and have good reason to reject the new idea, then go ahead and do that. However, be honest with yourself. Judge the new idea fairly. Acknowledge that you might actually be bringing some prejudice to the idea. Then give it one last shot.

In the following excerpt from Chapter Eleven in *The Autobiography of Malcolm X,* Malcolm X describes a time he spent in prison and how he took this as an opportunity to finally understand about learning. One might even see his time as a "retreat" of sorts. After all, one definition of "retreat" is to "withdraw from what is difficult, dangerous, or disagreeable." Certainly, time in prison would qualify, yet prison is difficult, dangerous, and disagreeable at best.

After this excerpt, you will find a response written by a first-year student at the University of Hawaii. This student's strong reaction to Malcolm X should prompt you to do some critical thinking of your own.

Saved

Malcolm X

It was because of my letters that I happened to stumble upon starting to acquire some kind of a homemade education.

I became increasingly frustrated at not being able to express what I wanted to convey in letters that I wrote, especially those to Mr. Elijah Muhammad.* In the street, I had been the most articulate hustler out there—I had commanded attention when I said something. But now, trying to write simple English, I not only wasn't articulate, I wasn't even functional. How would I sound writing in slang, the way I would say it, something such as, "Look, daddy, let me pull your coat about a cat, Elijah Muhammad—"

Many who today hear me somewhere in person, or on television, or those who read something I've said, will think I went to school far beyond the eighth grade. This impression is due entirely to my prison studies.

It had really begun back in the Charlestown Prison, when Bimbi first made me feel envy of his stock of knowledge. Bimbi had always taken charge of any conversations he was in, and I had tried to emulate him. But every book I picked up had few sentences which didn't contain anywhere from one to nearly all of the words that might as well have been in Chinese. When I just skipped those words, of course, I really ended up with little idea of what the book said. So I had come to the Norfolk Prison Colony still going through only book-reading motions. Pretty soon, I would have quit even these motions, unless I had received the motivation that I did.

I saw that the best thing I could do was get hold of a dictionary—to study, to learn some words. I was lucky enough to reason also that I should try to improve my penmanship. It was sad. I couldn't even write in a straight line. It was both ideas together that moved me to request a dictionary along with some tablets and pencils from the Norfolk Prison Colony school.

I spent two days just riffling uncertainly through the dictionary's pages. I'd never realized so many words existed! I don't know which words I needed to learn. Finally, just to start some kind of action, I began copying.

In my slow, painstaking, ragged handwriting, I copied into my tablet everything printed on that first page, down to the punctuation marks.

I believe it took me a day. Then, aloud, I read back, to myself, everything I'd written on the tablet. Over and over, aloud, to myself, I read my own handwriting.

I woke up the next morning, thinking about those words—immensely proud to realize that not only had I written so much at one time, but I'd written words that I never knew were in the world. Moreover, with a little effort, I also could remember what many of these words meant. I reviewed the words whose meanings I didn't

---

* Elijah Muhammad was a leader of the Black Muslims' Temple of Islam in the 1940s, 1950s, and 1960s.

remember. Funny thing, from the dictionary first page right now, that "aardvark" springs to my mind. The dictionary had a picture of it, a long-tailed, long-eared, burrowing African mammal, which lives off termites caught by sticking out its tongue as an anteater does for ants.

I was so fascinated that I went on—I copied the dictionary's next page. And the same experience came when I studied that. With every succeeding page, I also learned of people and places and events from history. Actually the dictionary is like a miniature encyclopedia. Finally the dictionary's A section had filled a whole tablet—and I went on into the B's. That was the way I started copying what eventually became the entire dictionary. It went a lot faster after so much practice helped me to pick up handwriting speed. Between what I wrote in my tablet, and writing letters, during the rest of my time in prison I would guess I wrote a million words.

I suppose it was inevitable that as my word-base broadened, I could for the first time pick up a book and read and now begin to understand what the book was saying. Anyone who has read a great deal can imagine the new world that opened. Let me tell you something: from then until I left that prison, in every free moment I had, if I was not reading in the library, I was reading on my bunk. You couldn't have gotten me out of books with a wedge. Between Mr. Muhammad's teachings, my correspondence, my visitors—usually Ella and Reginald—and my reading of books, months passed without my even thinking about being imprisoned. In fact, up to then, I never had been so truly free in my life.

The Norfolk Prison Colony's library was in the school building. A variety of classes was taught there by instructors who came from such places as Harvard and Boston universities. The weekly debates between inmate teams were also held in the school building. You would be astonished to know how worked up convict debaters and audiences would get over subjects like "Should Babies Be Fed Milk?"

Available on the prison library's shelves were books on just about every general subject. Much of the big private collection that Parkhurst had willed to the prison was still in crates and boxes in the back of the library—thousands of old books. Some of them looked ancient: covers faded, old-time parchment-looking binding.

Parkhurst, I've mentioned, seemed to have been principally interested in history and religion. He had the money and the special interest to have a lot of books that you wouldn't have in general circulation. Any college library would have been lucky to get that collection.

As you can imagine, especially in a prison where there was heavy emphasis on rehabilitation, an inmate was smiled upon if he demonstrated an unusually intense interest in books. There was a sizable number of well-read inmates, especially the popular debaters. Some were said by many to be practically walking encyclopedias. They were almost celebrities. No university would ask any student to devour literature as I did when this new world opened to me, of being able to read and understand.

I read more in my room than in the library itself. An inmate who was known to read a lot could check out more than the permitted maximum number of books. I preferred reading in the total isolation of my own room.

When I had progressed to really serious reading, every night at about ten P.M. I would be outraged with the "lights out." It always seemed to catch me right in the middle of something engrossing.

Fortunately, right outside my door was a corridor light that cast a glow into my room. The glow was enough to read by, once my eyes adjusted to it. So when "lights out" came, I would sit on the floor where I could continue reading in that glow.

At one-hour intervals the night guards paced past every room. Each time I heard the approaching footsteps, I jumped into bed and feigned sleep. And as soon as the guard passed, I got back out of bed onto the floor area of that light-glow, where I would read for another 58 minutes—until the guard approached again. That went on until three or four every morning. Three or four hours of sleep a night was enough for me. Often in the years in the streets I had slept less than that.

The teachings of Mr. Muhammad stressed how history had been "whitened"—when white men had written history books, the black man simply had been left out. Mr. Muhammad couldn't have said anything that would have struck me much harder. I had never forgotten how when my class, me and all of those whites, had studied seventh-grade United States history back in Mason, the history of the Negro had been covered in one paragraph, and the teacher had gotten a big laugh with his joke, "Negroes' feet are so big that when they walk, they leave a hole in the ground."

This is one reason why Mr. Muhammad's teachings spread so swiftly all over the United States, among all Negroes, whether or not they became followers of Mr. Muhammad. The teachings ring true—to every Negro. You can hardly show me a black adult in America—or a white one, for that matter—who knows from the history books anything like the truth about the black man's role. In my own case, once I heard of the "glorious history of the black man," I took special pains to hunt in the library for books that would inform me on details about black history.

I can remember accurately the very first set of books that really impressed me. I have since bought that set of books and I have it at home for my children to read as they grow up. It's called Wonders of the World. It's full of pictures of archeological finds, statues that depict, usually, non-European people.

I found books like Will Durant's *Story of Civilization*. I read H. G. Wells' *Outline of History*. *Souls of Black Folk* by W. E. B. Du Bois gave me a glimpse into the black people's history before they came to this country. Carter G. Woodson's *Negro History* opened my eyes about black empires before the black slave was brought to the United States, and the early Negro struggles for freedom.

J. A. Rogers' three volumes of *Sex and Race* told about race-mixing before Christ's time; about Aesop being a black man who told fables; about Egypt's Pharaohs; about the great Coptic Christian Empires; about Ethiopia, the earth's oldest continuous black civilization, as China is the oldest continuous civilization.

Mr. Muhammad's teaching about how the white man had been created led me to *Findings in Genetics* by Gregor Mendel.* (The dictionary's G section was where I had learned what "genetics" meant.) I really studied this book by the Austrian monk. Reading it over and over, especially certain sections, helped me to understand that if you started with a black man, a white man could be produced; but starting with a white man, you never could produce a black man—because the white chromosome is recessive. And since no one disputes that there was but one Original Man, the conclusion is clear.

During the last year or so, in the *New York Times*, Arnold Toynbee used the word "bleached" in describing the white man. (His words were: "White [i.e. bleached] human beings of North European origin . . .:) Toynbee also referred to the European geographic area as only a peninsula of Asia. He said there is no such thing as Europe. And if you look at the globe, you will see for yourself that America is only an extension of Asia. (But at the same time Toynbee is among those who have helped to bleach history. He has written that Africa was the only continent that produced no history. He won't write that again. Every day now, the truth is coming to light.)

I never will forget how shocked I was when I began reading about slavery's total horror. It made such an impact upon me that it later became one of my favorite subjects when I became a minister of Mr. Muhammad's. The world's most monstrous crime, the sin and the blood on the white man's hands, are almost impossible to believe. Books like the one by Frederick Olmstead opened my eyes to the horrors suffered when the slave was landed in the United States. The European woman, Fannie Kimball, who had married a Southern white slaveowner, described how human beings were degraded. Of course I read *Uncle Tom's Cabin*. In fact, I believe that's the only novel I have ever read since I started serious reading.

Parkhurst's collection also contained some bound pamphlets of the Abolitionist Anti-Slavery Society of New England. I read descriptions of atrocities, saw those illustrations of black slave women tied up and flogged with whips; of black mothers watching their babies being dragged off, never to be seen by their mothers again; of dogs after slaves, and of the fugitive slave catchers, evil white men with whips and clubs and chains and guns. I read about the slave preacher Nat Turner, who put the fear of God into the white slavemaster. Nat Turner wasn't going around preaching pie-in-the-sky and "non-violent" freedom for the black man. There in Virginia one night in 1831, Nat and seven other slaves started out at his master's home and through the night they went from one plantation "big house" to the next, killing, until by the next morning 57 white people were dead and Nat had about 70 slaves follow him. White people, terrified for their lives, fled from

* Gregor Mendel (1822–1884), Austrian Augustinian monk, father of genetic science.

their homes, locked themselves up in public buildings, hid in the woods, and some even left the state. A small army of soldiers took two months to catch and hang Nat Turner. Somewhere I have read where Nat Turner's example is said to have inspired John Brown to invade Virginia and attack Harper's Ferry nearly thirty years later, with thirteen white men and five Negroes.

I read Herodotus, "the father of History," or, rather, I read about him. And I read the histories of various nations, which opened my eyes gradually, then wider and wider, to how the whole world's white men had indeed acted like devils, pillaging and raping and bleeding and draining the whole world's non-white people. I remember, for instance, books such as Will Durant's *The Story of Oriental Civilization,* and Mahatma Gandhi's accounts of the struggle to drive the British out of India.

Book after book showed me how the white man had brought upon the world's black, brown, red, and yellow peoples every variety of the sufferings of exploitation. I saw how since the sixteenth century, the so-called "Christian trader" white man began to ply the seas in his lust for Asian and African empires, and plunder, and power. I read, I saw, how the white man never has gone among the non-white peoples bearing the Cross in the true manner and spirit of Christ's teachings—meek, humble, and Christlike.

I perceived, as I read, how the collective white man had been actually nothing but a piratical opportunist who used Faustian machinations to make his own Christianity his initial wedge in criminal conquests. First, always "religiously," he branded "heathen" and "pagan" labels upon ancient non-white cultures and civilizations. The stage thus set, he then turned upon his non-white victims his weapons of war.

I read how, entering India—half a billion deeply religious brown people—the British white man, by 1759, through promises, trickery and manipulations, controlled much of India through Great Britain's East India Company. The parasitical British administration kept tentacling out to half of the subcontinent. In 1857, some of the desperate people of India finally mutinied—and, excepting the African slave trade, nowhere has history recorded any more unnecessary bestial and ruthless human carnage than the British suppression of the non-white Indian people.

Over 115 million African blacks—close to the 1930's populations of the United States—were murdered or enslaved during the slave trade. And I read how when the slave market was glutted, the cannibalistic white powers of Europe next carved up, as their colonies, the richest areas of the black continent. And Europe's chancelleries for the next century played a chess game of naked exploitation and power from Cape Horn to Cairo.

Ten guards and the warden couldn't have torn me out of those books. Not even Elijah Muhammad could have been more eloquent than those books were in providing indisputable proof that the collective white man had acted like a devil in virtually every contact he had with the world's collective non-white man. I listen today to the radio, and watch television, and read the headlines about the collective white man's fear and tension concerning China. When the white man professes ignorance about why the Chinese hate him so, my mind can't help flashing back to what I read, there in prison, about how the blood forebears of this same white man raped China at a time when China was trusting and helpless. Those original white "Christian traders" sent into China millions of pounds of opium. By 1839, so many of the Chinese were addicts that China's desperate government destroyed twenty thousand chests of opium. The first Opium War was promptly declared by the white man. Imagine! Declaring war upon someone who objects to being narcotized! The Chinese were severely beaten, with Chinese-invented gunpowder.

The Treaty of Nanking made China pay the British white man for the destroyed opium: forced open China's major ports to British trade; forced China to abandon Hong Kong; fixed China's import tariffs so low that cheap British articles soon flooded in, maiming China's industrial development.

After a second Opium War, the Tientsin Treaties legalized the ravaging opium trade, legalized a British-French-American control of China's customs. China tried delaying that Treaty's ratification; Peking was looted and burned.

"Kill the foreign white devils!" was the 1901 Chinese war cry in the Boxer Rebellion. Losing again, this time the Chinese were driven from Peking's choicest areas. The vicious, arrogant white man put up the famous signs, "Chinese and dogs not allowed."

Red China after World War II closed its doors to the Western white world. Massive Chinese agricultural, scientific, and industrial efforts are described in a book that *Life* magazine recently published. Some observers inside Red China have reported that the world never has known such a hate-white campaign as is now going on in this non-white country where, present birthrates continuing, in fifty more years Chinese will be half the earth's population. And it seems that some Chinese chickens will soon come home to roost, with China's recent successful nuclear tests.

Let us face reality. We can see in the United Nations a new world order being shaped, along color lines—an alliance among the non-white nations. American's U.N. Ambassador Adlai Stevenson complained not long ago that in the United Nations "a skin game" was being played. He was right. He was facing reality. A "skin game" is being played. But Ambassador Stevenson sounded like Jesse James accusing the marshal of carrying a gun. Because who in the world's history ever has played a worse "skin game" than the white man?

Mr. Muhammad, to whom I was writing daily, had no idea of what a new world had opened up to me through my efforts to document his teachings in books.

When I discovered philosophy, I tried to touch all the landmarks of philosophical development. Gradually, I read most of the old philosophers, Occidental and Oriental. The Oriental philosophers were the ones I came to prefer; finally, my impression was that most Occidental philosophy had largely been borrowed from the Oriental thinkers. Socrates, for instance, traveled in Egypt. Some sources even say that Socrates was initiated into some of the Egyptian mysteries. Obviously Socrates got some of his wisdom among the East's wise men.

I have often reflected upon the new vistas that reading opened to me. I knew right there in prison that reading had changed forever the course of my life. As I see it today, the ability to read awoke inside me some long dormant craving to be mentally alive. I certainly wasn't seeking any degree, the way a college confers a status symbol upon its students. My homemade education gave me, with every additional book that I read, a little bit more sensitivity to the deafness, dumbness, and blindness that was afflicting the black race in America. Not long ago, an English writer telephoned me from London, asking questions. One was, "What's your alma mater?" I told him, "Books." You will never catch me with a free fifteen minutes in which I'm not studying something I feel might be able to help the black man.

Yesterday I spoke in London, and both ways on the plane across the Atlantic I was studying a document about how the United Nations proposes to insure the human rights of the oppressed minorities of the world. The American black man is the world's most shameful case of minority oppression. What makes the black man think of himself as only an internal United States issue is just a catch-phrase, two words, "civil rights." How is the black man going to get "civil rights" before first he wins his human rights? If the American black man will start thinking about his human rights, and then start thinking of himself as part of one of the world's great peoples, he will see he has a case for the United Nations.

I can't think of a better case! Four hundred years of black blood and sweat invested here in America, and the white man still has the black man begging for what every immigrant fresh off the ship can take for granted the minute he walks down the gangplank.

But I'm digressing. I told the Englishman that my alma mater was books, a good library. Every time I catch a plane, I have with me a book that I want to read—and that's a lot of books these days. If I weren't out here every day battling the white man, I could spend the rest of my life reading, just satisfying my curiosity—because you can hardly mention anything I'm not curious about. I don't think anybody ever got more out of going to prison than I did. In fact, prison enabled me to study far more intensively than I would have if my life had gone differently and I had attended some college. I imagine that one of the biggest troubles with colleges is there are too many distractions, too much panty-raiding, fraternities, and boola-boola and all of that. Where else but in a prison could I have attacked my ignorance by being able to study intensely sometimes as much as fifteen hours a day?

". . . and then they all lived happily ever after. The End."

Now wasn't **that** the most uplifting and righteously nice-nice article by our good friend Malcolm X? Kind of makes you get those little goose bumps all over your skin, now, don't it? Did I not like the Malcolm article? You **bet** your . . . . .

You see, what gets to **me** is what Malcolm X forgets to include in his rhetoric, which was, unfortunately, the most important little sneaky bit of all: the reason exactly as to **why** he had suddenly found himself so gloriously spirited with the breath of education. Instead of breaking new ground on the fun aspects of becoming self-motivated, he instead finds it much more appealing to lead us all onto a different, very disheartening path of modern social thinking: that in fact, the best and most efficient way a young African-American (or, for that matter, an ANY-AMERICAN) teenager can find a meaningful education is, indeed, to simply plop his or her merry self into a dirty, dingy prison cell and find some sort of keen self-discovery there, which isn't **quite** the advertisement for the **"IF YOU WANNA BE COOL, STAY IN SCHOOL"** campaign, I can tell you . . . . .

Gee . . . Now just hold on—let's have a little minute to ourselves, there, self. What say we go and be emphatically hypocritical by backing up a wee bit and thinking **exactly** about what we've just said.

Well . . . Okay, alright, now listen. Admittedly, I can say for a fact that I know Malcolm X wasn't **really** advocating going to prison to become educated; for the most part, that was **really** all just introductory fluff and a cheapened use of artistic license. For me to have said that Malcolm X wanted blacks to go to jail is pretty preposterous, and frankly, kind of embarrassing . . .

How**ever,** The fact unfortunately **still** remains that he sent out to the near-thousands of his amiable, easily influenced followers the wrong and utterly inexcusable message: that a good education can only be achieved through solitude, and that an "organized" system of teaching (like those we sometimes see in many colleges and high schools) is almost entirely detrimental to the personal learning process. What our good Muslim preacher has mistakenly failed to realize is that a constant streak of good reading and the ever-pleasant role of "the Phantom of the Library" **doesn't** make you smart or enlighten your mind at all; there are probably many, in fact, who go out of their way to read the world like total freaks and find themselves **still** muddled by all the knowledge they have worked like sickos to attain. What Malcolm X doesn't see in his experiences is the fact that it wasn't **any** of the knowledge or **any** of the reading or **any** of the completely brutal dictionary-copying that brought him to that level of intelligence he found himself in when he wrote his autobiography, although it certainly **did** help him out at times. Rather, it was his understanding of the world that led to his enlightenment, as well as his motivation to understand exactly what was going on around him that made him such an intelligent human being; it was his newfound mental razor-sharpness and keen intuition that got him all the way to the top of that big "smart-people's ladder." What Malcolm X fails to tell his people is that it was **this** kind of thinking that was the sole reason for his intellect, and that understanding and **not** knowledge is **true** intelligence.

. . . and pretty smart, too.

—Justin Quezon

Journal Entry 3

We don't receive wisdom; we must discover it for ourselves after a journey that no one can take for us or spare us.

Marcel Proust

Look at the diagram below and consider that it illustrates the process that Malcolm X went through during his metamorphosis from illiteracy and ignorance to self-realization and becoming a community leader.

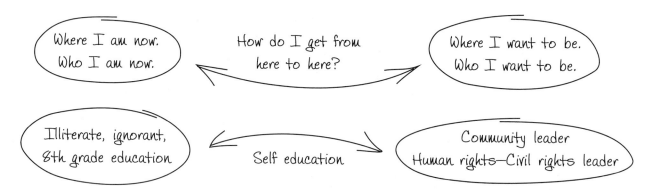

What journey is required to make a change? Draw your own diagram to illustrate a process of change. This diagram can be about someone you know or about yourself. Accompany your diagram with a paragraph explaining the change and how the diagram illustrates your points.

All students come to college for reasons of their own. Take a moment to reflect on why you decided to come to college. Remember the few reasons given at the beginning of this chapter? There are no wrong answers or reasons here. All are valid. Do the following four steps.

1. Gather into groups of three or four students. Very quickly, but with genuine thoughtfulness, make a list of your reasons for getting a college education. Use all reasons given by everyone in the group.

2. As a group, reflect on the following questions and come up with a list of 10 statements that describe the purpose of a college education.
   - What will your college education do for you?
   - Why should you continue to study at the college level?
   - How do you think you will be affected or changed at the end of your college years?

3. Share your list with the other groups, and discuss at length the similarities and differences among the lists.

4. Read the following article by A. Bartlett Giamatti, and reflect on what he says about the value of a liberal education.

A human being should be able to change a diaper, plan an invasion, butcher a hog, conn a ship, design a building, write a sonnet, balance accounts, build a wall, set a bone, comfort the dying, take orders, give orders, cooperate, act alone, solve equations, analyze a new problem, pitch manure, program a computer, cook a tasty meal, fight efficiently, die gallantly. Specialization is for insects.

—Robert Heinlein

The following article by A. Bartlett Giamatti, a former president of Yale University as well as a one-time Major League Baseball commissioner, is an address to freshmen as they begin their first year in college. Giamatti suggests that students must alter their attitudes toward studying in order to get the most out of a liberal education. As you read this article, pay particular attention to the ideas he espouses. Think about what he says in relation to the general education you are about to approach. Before you read the Giamatti article, read the Robert Heinlein quote above and take a minute to reflect on its meaning.

The Earthly Use of a Liberal Education

A. Bartlett Giamatti

The summer before college is the time when in a thousand different circumstances mythology dresses up as epistemology. Parents, older siblings and friends, former teachers, coaches, and employers, dimly but vividly remembering how it was, propound with certainty how they know the way it might, or should or could, or will be.

By and large, the versions of your life to come are well meant. All summer long, however, you have simply wanted to get on with it. There, of course, is the rub. Despite all you have heard and read, no one can tell you what it is you are now so desirous of getting on with. Nor can anyone tell you what it, whatever it is, will be like. You wonder, Will everyone else know? Will he or she be more sure, less insecure, less new? Will I ever get to know anyone? Will I be able to do it? Whatever it is.

I will tell you, in a moment, what I think it is. I cannot tell you with certainty what it will be like; no one can. Each of us experiences college differently. I can assure you that soon your normal anxieties will recede and a genuine excitement will begin, a rousing motion of the spirit unlike anything you have experienced before. And that will mark the beginning of it, the grand adventure that you now undertake, never alone but on your own, the voyage of exploration in freedom that is the development of your own mind. Generations have preceded you in this splendid opening out of the self as you use the mind to explore the mind, and, if the human race is rational, generations will come after you. But each of you will experience your education uniquely—charting and ordering and dwelling in the land of your own intellect and sensibility, discovering powers you had only dreamed of and mysteries you had not imagined and reaches you had not thought that thought could reach. There will be pain and some considerable loneliness at times, and not all the terrain will be green and refreshing. There will be awesome wastes and depths as well as heights. The adventure of discovery is, however, thrilling because you will sharpen and focus your powers of analysis, of creativity, of rationality, of feeling—of thinking with your whole being. If at Yale you can experience the joy that the acquisition and creation of knowledge for its own sake brings, the adventure will last your whole life and you will have discovered the distinction between living as a full human being and merely existing.

If there is a single term to describe the education that can spark a lifelong love of learning, it is the term liberal education. A liberal education has nothing to do with those political designer labels liberal and conservative that some so lovingly stitch on to every idea they pull off, or put on, the rack. A liberal education is not one that seeks to implant the precepts of a specific religious or political orthodoxy. Nor is it an education intending to prepare for immediate immersion in a profession. That kind of professional education is pursued at Yale at the graduate level in eleven graduate and professional schools. Such training ought to have in it a liberal temper; that is, technical or professional study ought to be animated by a love of learning, but such training is necessarily and properly pointed to the demands and proficiency requirements of a career or profession. Such is not the tendency of an education, or of the educational process, in Yale College.

In Yale College, education is "liberal" in Cardinal Newman's sense of the word. As he says, in the fifth discourse of *The Idea of the University*,

> . . . that alone is liberal knowledge which stands on its own pretensions, which is independent of sequel, expects no complement, refuses to be informed (as it is called) by any end, or absorbed in any art, in order duly to present itself to our contemplation. The most ordinary pursuits have this specific character, if they are self-sufficient and complete; the highest lose it, when they minister to something beyond them.

As Newman emphasizes, a liberal education is not defined by the content or by the subject matter of a course of study. It is a common error, for instance, to equate a liberal education with the so-called liberal arts of studia humanitatis.* To study the liberal arts or the humanities is not necessarily to acquire a liberal education unless one studies these and allied subjects in a spirit that, as Newman has it, seeks no immediate sequel, that is independent of a profession's advantage. If you pursue the study of anything not for the intrinsic rewards of exercising and developing the power of the mind but because you press toward a professional goal, then you are pursuing not a liberal education but rather something else.

A liberal education is defined by the attitude of the mind toward the knowledge the mind explores and creates. Such education occurs when you pursue knowledge because you are motivated to experience and absorb what comes of thinking—

thinking about the traditions of our common human heritage in all its forms, thinking about new patterns or designs in what the world proffers today—whether in philosophic texts or financial markets or chemical combinations—thinking in order to create new knowledge that others will then explore. A liberal education at Yale College embraces physics as well as French, lasers as well as literature, social science, and physical and biological sciences as well as the arts and humanities. A liberal education rests on the supposition that our humanity is enriched by the pursuit of learning for its own sake; it is dedicated to the proposition that growth in thought, and in the power to think, increases the pleasure, breadth, and value of life.

"That is very touching," I will be told, "that is all very well, but how does someone make a living with this joy of learning and pleasure in the pursuit of learning? What if the earthly use of all this kind of education later on, in the practical, real world?" These are not trivial questions, though the presuppositions behind them puzzle me somewhat. I am puzzled, for instance, by the unexamined assumption that the "real world" is always thought to lie outside or beyond the realm of education. I am puzzled by the confident assumption that only in certain parts of daily life do people make "real" decisions and so "real" acts lead to "real" consequences. I am puzzled by those who think that ideas do not have reality or that knowledge is irrelevant to the workings of daily life.

To invert Plato and to believe that ideas are unreal and that their pursuit has no power for practical or useful good is to shrink reality and define ignorance. To speak directly to the questions posed by the skeptic of the idea of a liberal education, I can say only this: ideas and their pursuit define our humanity and make us human. Ideas, embodied in data and values, beliefs, principles, and original insights, must be pursued because they are valuable in themselves and because they are the stuff of life. There is nothing more necessary to the full, free, and decent life of a person or of a people or of the human race than to free the mind by passionately and rationally exercising the mind's power to inquire freely. There can be no more practical education, in my opinion, than one that launches you on the course of fulfilling your human capacities to reason and to imagine freely and that hones your abilities to express the results of

* See "A City of Green Thoughts."

your thinking in speech and in writing with logic, clarity, and grace.

While such an education may be deemed impractical by those wedded to the notion that nothing in life is more important than one's career, nevertheless I welcome you to a liberal education's rigorous and demanding pleasures. Fear not, you will not be impeded from making a living because you have learned to think for yourself and because you take pleasure in the operation of the mind and in the pursuit of new ideas. And you will need to make a living. The world will not provide you with sustenance or employment. You will have to work for it. I am instead speaking of another dimension of your lives, the dimension of your spirit that will last longer than a job, that will outlast a profession, that will represent by the end of your time on earth the sum of your human significance. That is the dimension represented by the mind unfettered, "freely ranging onley within the Zodiack of his owne wit," as the old poet said. There is no greater power a human being can develop for the individual's or for the public's good.

And I believe that the good, for individuals and for communities, is the end to which education must tend. I affirm Newman's vision that a liberal education is one seeking no sequel or complement. I take him to be writing of the motive or tendency of the mind operating initially within the educational process. But I believe there is also a larger tendency or motive, which is animated by the pursuit of ideas for their own sake. I believe that the pleasure in the pursuit of knowledge joins and is finally at one with our general human desire for a life elevated by dignity, decency, and moral progress. That larger hope does not come later; it exists inextricably intertwined with a liberal education. The joy of intellectual pursuit and the pursuit of the good and decent life are no more separable than on a fair spring day the sweet breeze is separable from the sunlight.

In the common pursuit of ideas for themselves and of the larger or common good, the freedom that the individual mind wishes for itself, it also seeks for others. How could it be otherwise? In the pursuit of knowledge leading to the good, you cannot wish for others less than you wish for yourself. Thus, in the pursuit of freedom, the individual finds it necessary to order or to limit the surge to freedom so that others in the community are not denied the very condition each of us seeks. A liberal education desires to foster a freedom of the mind that will also contribute, in its measure, to the freedom of others.

We learn, therefore, that there is no true freedom without order; we learn that there are limits to our freedom, limits we learn to choose freely in order not to undermine what we seek. After all, if there were, on the one hand, no restraints at all, only anarchy of intellect and chaos of community would result. On the other hand, if all were restraint, and release of inquiry and thought were stifled, only a death of the spirit and a denial of any freedom could result. There must be an interplay of restraint and release, of order and freedom, in our individual lives and in our life together. Without such interplay within each of us, there can be no good life for any of us. If there is no striving for the good life for all of us, however, there cannot be a good life for any one of us. We must learn how freedom depends for its existence upon freely chosen (because rationally understood) forms of order.

At Yale College, you will find both the spur for freedom of inquiry and civility's curbing rein. One could, I suppose, locate these conditions in the classroom and in the residential colleges; one could posit that in the classroom the release of the mind is encouraged and in the residential colleges the limits to civil behavior are learned. That view is oversimplified, for in both contexts, as well as on playing fields, in community service, in extracurricular activities, in services of worship, in social events, the interplay of freedom and order obtains. In all these contexts, as in each one of us, the surge of freedom and the restraint that compounds freedom's joy and significance occur all the time.

The ideal of this community is therefore composed of intellectual and ethical portions, the freedom of the mind and the freedom to express the results of the mind's inquiry disciplined by the imperative to respect the rights and responsibilities of others. It is a community open to new ideas, to disagreement, to debate, to criticism, to the clash of opinions and convictions, to solitary investigation, to originality, but is it not tolerant of, and will not tolerate, the denial of the dignity and freedoms of others. It will not tolerate theft of another's intellectual product. It will not tolerate denials of another's freedom of expression. It will not tolerate sexist or racist or other acts or expressions of bigotry based on prejudices about ethnic or religious backgrounds or about personal sexual preference or private philosophic or political beliefs. It will not tolerate these denials, because the freedom we possess to foster free inquiry and the greater good is too precious. What I have stated are matters of moral conviction. They are also matters of University policy. The policies that reflect those convictions are designed to protect an environment where individual rights are respected because responsibilities are shared. They are designed to create a community where freedom exists because order is sustained by the moral courage to affirm the good by all members of the community.

I have told you what I think it is, the "it" I guessed you might be concerned with upon your arrival. It is a quest to become the best in all that is meant by being human. This quest has been going on in this College for a long time, in the old New England city by the water. In 1701 Yale made a promise to itself and a pact with America, to contribute to the increase of scholarship, service, and spiritual enlightenment. You now assume part of the obligation of that promise. And you will be essential to maintaining the faith of that pact. As you deepen in the commitment to ideals and in the excellence I know you possess, this community will continue to shape itself in intellectual and ethical ways that are faithful to our ancient roots and in ways that are ever new.

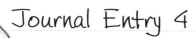

Journal Entry 4

Heard These Before?

"love of learning"

"developing the power of the mind"

"attitude of the mind toward knowledge"

"humanity is enriched by the pursuit of learning for its own sake"

"growth in thought"

"power to think increases the pleasure, value of life"

"pursuit of new ideas"

"pursuit of ideas for their own sake"

"pursuit of knowledge"

"joy of intellectual pursuit"

"pursuit of a good and decent life"

"pursuit of freedom for self and others"

"liberal education fosters freedom of mind"

"freedom of inquiry"

"pursuit of being the best human you can be"

These are a list of phrases that were part of the freshmen address given by A. Bartlett Giamatti in the previous article and that you probably have heard from parents, teachers, and others. They were used to describe the purpose of a liberal education. What do you think of these ideas and concepts? Do you agree with Giamatti and what he says about the purpose of a liberal education? How do these ideas compare with your own reflection on the purpose of an education at the college level?

Responding to the questions above, choose one of the following three options for your travel log.

1. Create a song (borrow the tune from another song) using as many of the phrases as possible.

2. Develop an original rap using as many of the phrases as possible.

3. Write a poem or a short essay using as many phrases as possible.

CASH IN ON EDUCATION

Bob Silk

Vice President, Sales and Marketing, Fatline Corporation

Today I drive a $75,000 Porsche 911 sports car, live in a $700,000 house, am a vice president of an Internet startup, and am planning my retirement at age 55. This is a stark contrast to the college student who could barely pay his tuition, had four different majors, and did not have a clue what the future would hold. Now, as I look back over my 23-year career in sales, sales management, business development, and indirect channels, as well as starting a company, I see a few things that I think are part of the recipe for all successful people.

Finish What You Start

I probably look at a new resume every day. Although I think that the knowledge learned in a college education could be gathered in other ways, the mere act of completing college says a lot about a potential candidate. College is the first great test in life since it is almost always your choice, and finishing or not is typically not controlled by your parents. Therefore, since I normally have multiple choices for any open position I am hiring, I always go with the person who has shown that he can finish what he starts and has a college degree.

Be Yourself

My first job out of college was as a salesperson, a position that I felt was below my stature as a newly mined college graduate. What I learned was that fitting myself into the stereotyped salesperson was a mistake both because it was not satisfying and, more importantly, because it didn't work. The best people in any profession mold the job, if possible, to fit their personality. It took a long time for me to figure this out, but the rewards both personally and financially were well worth the effort.

Learn How to Communicate

Whether you are engineer, artist, or biologist, your chances of being successful are severely limited if you don't learn how to express yourself in ways that people can understand. Although these skills come naturally to some, they can be learned and are critical for career advancement. Take any opportunity to build your listening skills, learn to make good eye contact, and create goals for every encounter with another person.

In summary, cashing in on your education is great if you can keep a few simple ideas in mind. First, consider college your first and probably most important personal test. Commit to crossing the finish line to show yourself and the world that you are a person who can get the job done no matter what obstacles get in your way. Second, don't think that you have to be a conformist in order to succeed. The best people in any profession mold any job to fit their personality. This allows them to stand out as well as to enjoy what they are doing. Finally, learn the essentials of communication, since they are lessons that are essential to achieving success and moving forward in almost any profession. Although these tools are not traditionally taught in your normal curriculum, go out of your way to gain them. The reward will serve you in all aspects of your life. Good luck.

Your Story

CHAPTER TWO

Objectives

- to understand the concept of story-telling

- to learn how to give oral and visual pre-sentations

- to write sketches of your own life

- to engage in self-reflection and self-evaluation

"We build our trust by talking,
Of our faith in you and me, . . ."

33

SNAPSHOT

SNAPSHOT

SNAPSHOT

SNAPSHOT

SNAPSHOT

SNAPSHOT

SNAPSHOT

By the grace of God I had a mamma that wouldn't let me turn out just any type of way. Mamma. The word mamma needs to be clarified because I have a mamma, not a mother, but a mamma. A mamma differs from a mother in that a mother can have two kids, a low income job, bills due, no food in the fridg, and Christmas right around the corner with only $20 in her pocket, and then have a breakdown. A mamma, on the other hand, could have the exact same circumstances and somehow the bills would be paid, nobody went hungry, and there would be presents under the Christmas tree in the morning—and a mamma wouldn't even break a sweat. That's the kind of mamma I had and I thank God every night that she didn't give up on me, but stayed on my behind. Because if she didn't, I don't know where I would be.

—*Thomas Graham*

TRAVEL ESSENTIAL

Information Literacy and Personal Narratives

There are many "official" definitions of information literacy for students. These definitions include such skills as the ability to know when information is needed, the ability to find information sources, and an awareness of how to evaluate information to ensure that it is accurate, relevant, and persuasive.

However, the essential ability is that you can integrate information from any source into the story you are telling. Your story can be as simple as relating an experience you had to a friend or as formal as a class paper about an assigned topic.

These examples are personal in the sense that you are telling them. These stories are coming from your particular view of the world and the information available. All use of information comes from and is a part of your personal narrative, the story of your life. You decide what information to use and how to use it. The mechanics of searching a database, talking to someone who knows something you want to know, watching a television program, or searching a website are used to gain something you have decided you want or need. You decide what you will use and, more important, what meaning it will have.

The key question for determining if you are information literate is: Can I use information in a way that enhances my own personal narrative, my story of being in the world and experiencing it?

Information literacy is personal. You must have a personal definition of how information influences your understanding of yourself. What is the nature of knowing something for you? Some people must experience something first-hand. Others emphasize what peers, parents, teachers, or other authority figures say or write. Some individuals trust their eyes more than their ears or need to compare different interpretations of something before they decide what they consider important.

Furthermore, information is interpreted through personal prisms of values, cultural perspective, and patterns of belief. Our religion, culture, society, gender, and age form patterns we use to gather, use, and evaluate information. They determine when we look for, where we look for, and how we evaluate information.

What patterns are important to you, and when should you question them? Knowing when to adjust your personal patterns to enhance the story you are telling makes you information literate.

READING

The following two readings begin your journey into storytelling. Both are snapshots of people's lives, told in very different styles but capturing a particular perspective on life. As you read, think about some of your own "stories," because you will be asked to share them later in this chapter.

An Eighth Grader's Prayer

Jolyn Marie Yamashita

If I'm real quiet
maybe they'll forget
stop asking me to do their homework
stop calling me a "brain"
it's not that I'm smart
it's not easy for them?
why not?

Tired being tough
got treated like a leper for
that one
decked Jerome in 4th grade
called me a "Jap slap"
he's more Japanese than me
felt real good to hit him too
thanks for your help Dad

Tried ignoring them
only got teased more for
that one
turned my back in 5th grade
gave them the other cheek
so to speak
they tried to see how much I could take
thanks for your help Mom

Tried hiding out in the library
only got called "bookworm" for
that one
read half the library in 6th grade
Little House on the Prairie series
Nancy Drew mysteries, The Hobbit
A Wrinkle in Time, the Narnia books
thanks for your help, Ms. June

Tried showing off
only got hated for
that one
became teacher's pet in 7th grade
Mr. Lau, Mr. Poliahu,
Ms. Kanemitsu, Mr. Park,
Mrs. Martin, Mrs. Fujii
thanks for all your help

What shall I try this year
only to get hated for
it
be myself in 8th grade
that's what I'll do
but who am I?
I hate being 13
boy do I need help . . .

Joolz

Wendy Chapkis

"Punks are rejecting their class position but you have to be there before you can reject it."

I was nineteen when I married a man who became a Satan's Slave. During the time I was with him, I looked pretty normal. Bikers don't like outrageous looking girls—at all. They do like "nice-looking" girls, though. And they prefer it if you have long hair. It fits with the heavy metal image.

You aren't to wear too much make-up or anything like that, and you wear jeans or trousers because you are on the bike so much. Though some girls did wear miniskirts which I always thought pretty stupid under the circumstances. The men clearly liked very girly girls. Oh, and they preferred blondes!

I never paid too terribly much attention to how I was supposed to look. I wore my hair short. It was more comfortable under the helmet. And I used to walk around in boy's clothes all the time. It was a bit of a problem for my husband in the club. But eventually they accepted me because they decided I was artistic and if I was an artist I was allowed to be eccentric. In general, the women were expected to be very domestic.

The club is a close tribal community. Because my background had been so insecure, I found it very reassuring in the beginning. But after five years, I left. It had become too restrictive.

Even before I left my husband, I already had become interested in the punk image. I had already dyed my hair pink—something which didn't go well in the club.

To dye your hair this color, you've got to first bleach it absolutely white, to strip it right down to the roots. I've had it this way for four years now. Pink was an easy first choice; it was a fashionable color, if you remember. Shocking pink and fluorescent green, those were the colors first associated with punk. Nowadays, I have it colored a bright scarlet, Fire Red.

Even when I was a child I wanted colored hair. I remember wanting waist-length green hair because there was this puppet in a children's show on television, a mermaid who never spoke but was extremely beautiful and had long green hair.

I've always tended toward fantasy, the fantastic. In fact my image may have more to do with fantasy than punk in the pure sense. Punk started off anti-fashion. So you set out to make yourself look as anti-pretty as possible. But I've always been too insecure to do it properly. I worry too much about what I actually look like.

My mother is very beautiful—feminine, small and pretty in the magazine style. I take after my father who is big. When I was a child, my mother was very disappointed in me and was always trying to make me more presentable. Other people's mothers used to shout at them for wearing make-up; my mother used to shout at me for not wearing any.

When I was an adolescent, I suffered very badly from acne. I was also overweight. So I was sort of a tall, fat, spotty teenager. I had good teeth though. My mother used to tell me "you have good teeth; smile, it's your best feature."

Having been a hideous adolescent, I've always been too insecure to intentionally make myself more hideous. I tend to sort of go to the "glam" side of punk rather than the anarchy end. I always wanted a Mohican, but I never quite had the nerve to shave my head. I did have very, very, short hair at one point, and I looked like a dog. And being big as well I was mistaken for a boy all the time. There are lots of things I wish I had the nerve to do with myself, but I just can't.

It's relative, of course. I suppose the way I look appears pretty outrageous to other people. Something like having a pierced nose I don't even think about anymore. But a lot of people seem to find it shocking.

My tattoos draw a lot of attention too. I got tattooed for the first time when I was about nineteen. I had one on my wrist and another around my ankles. I thought they were alright at the time—a sort of bracelet of flowers. But I only recently met a really good tattooist and have had new tattoos done over the old ones. These are in the Celtic style and are much better and much more expensive. Tattoos and tattooing fascinate me.

There are moments, though, when you get tired of it all. Everybody who looks this different feels that way sometimes, even if they don't admit it. There are mornings when I wake up and know I have to go down to the shops and wish that I looked like a perfectly ordinary person. But they are not often enough for me to want to change anything.

Not too long ago, for a giggle, I borrowed a plain brown wig off a friend and put it on. It looked pretty convincing. I didn't put on much make-up and went to a gig that way. People who have known me for months and months didn't recognize me.

It was tremendous. But after a while, I didn't find it tremendous at all. I found it extremely unpleasant. I actually entered a state of panic. I was so relieved to take the wig off and be myself again.

I felt I had lost my whole personality. My whole statement was gone and I really hated it.

The tattoos are the big thing actually. The scarlet hair you can just cut off if you get tired of it. But when you take the step of having big tattoos so close to the hands, you really make a permanent statement, especially as a woman.

I always wear long skirts and I always wear black. I don't wear jeans anymore because I wore them for so long when I was biking that I just got sick of them. They feel constricting to me. Same with underwear.

Despite all the black and the tattoos and the skull rings, some of my stage costumes, made of lycra and sequins, are extremely glam. I love feather boas and fans. But always with studs; say a studded belt at the waist. It is the combination that appeals to me. To be too completely glam would be tiresome. I like to confuse the eye.

The most important statement I am making through what I look like is one of strength. I have a strong personality and want to indicate that straight away. Especially in the business I am in, it is important to have a strong image. Not just from the point of selling your records, but more importantly so that from the moment you walk into a venue you are noticed by the sound crew, the security men, everyone. They've got to know right away you are not someone to be messed with. This is particularly true for a woman. The rock business is totally sexist. If you are not a strong person, they will walk all over you.

Of course sometimes the way I look frightens people I have no reason to want to impress with my strength. I was taking a train recently that was absolutely full—people were standing in the corridors—and there was an empty seat next to me but nobody would sit in it. People will often stare, but they don't want to get too close and only rarely will they try to make contact.

Sometimes it seems that people feel that if you look "odd" it is a license for them to abuse you or threaten you; it's as if the normal rules of politeness in society don't apply anymore. You've given up straight looks, therefore you've given up any right to be treated with respect.

A lot of people, particularly middle class people, look at punk and think it is a working class thing. But actually there are few working class

punk rockers. Only children of the middle class can afford to look ragged. It *is* a class statement, but not in the way people tend to assume. Punks are rejecting their class position, but you have to be there before you can reject it. And I am not saying that rejecting everything that's expected of you is easy.

It is, in fact, very difficult to actually put yourself outside of society; to appear so different that you are beyond the normal relationships most women have. I don't blame girls who are secretaries during the day and backcomb their hair a bit at night to come to the clubs. For those girls, punk is just fashion.

In a way, I am jealous of them because, in the end, they can become normal. They can submerge themselves in the great stream of weddings and tumble dryers. But I also think that, somewhere inside them, they're disappointed. They know they have experienced a failure of nerve.

I have my hair done by a woman named Lorraine. She works in a very small salon in the suburbs. Every time I go in there, I see this row of ladies with The Perm under the dryers just having had The Cut—which ever one it is at the time. I once asked Lorraine "don't you ever get tremendously sick of doing this?" And she said "If another woman comes in who wants that Perm I'll scream and go mad!" But of course she'd then go and start rolling up the next woman's hair . . .

The clients watch her working on me and they are fascinated. They'll come over and feel my hair and ask questions. It must be tremendously tempting for them to say "the hell with it; make mine scarlet too!"

"Dress as Success: Joolz" from *Beauty Secrets: Women and the Politics of Appearance* by Wendy Chapkis. Boston: South End Press. Copyright ©1986 by Wendy Chapkis. Reprinted by permission.

Journal Entry 5

Knowing others is intelligence; knowing yourself is true wisdom.
Mastering others is strength; mastering yourself is true power.

Lao-Tzu

Choose one of the following three for your journal. If you are feeling ambitious, do more than one!

I. *From private pleas to public requests.* Want to do something about that person you were born as or have come to be? Got inferior parts? Unbelievable shortcomings? Write a letter of explanation for why you want to make some exchanges; present a case for exchange and customer satisfaction. The letter is to be enclosed in an addressed envelope, which you will apply to the blank space on top of your travel log.

Simply begin by writing an imaginative request to someone. Explain your problem/complaint/imperfection and what you want to have done about it. Begin with a real request, but do have fun along the way. This can be in the form of a prayer, a ballad, a diary entry, a letter of complaint to a parent, a "To Whom It May Concern" or "Dear Sirs," a work order, or a proposal. Be creative!

2. *Mirror mirror on the wall.* Draw a large frame in the blank area. Imagine that this frame surrounds a mirror. Draw a picture of yourself in this mirror. Then write which of your "you's" you have drawn. The private you? The public you? Write a reflection on the "reflection" you have chosen to frame in the mirror. "There's me and then again there's ME!!!"

3. *A cloning plan.* Develop a plan for creating your own clone, but make this one better than you think you are. Which genes would you keep? Which would you eliminate? Explain.

The Plan: This is a group activity in which you are to present a short narrative about a "slice of life." This means that you will be presenting a scene to the rest of the class about some small part of life that reveals real people in real situations. What "slice" you choose is up to your group. You will want to pick a situation that will show character and relationship. Think of the most ordinary of situations: a conversation over a cup of coffee, a talk at a football game, a discussion with your sister after a funeral, a conference with a teacher, a chat in the locker room.

Working as a Team: The responsibility for creating a moment in life belongs to each of you. You must each take on a role and deal with one another in a real-life fashion. This means paying close attention to each other's words, watching the body language, and generally keeping up with the tone of the scene.

_____

_____

_____

_____

How to Do This: In scripting your scene, keep in mind that spontaneity can be wonderful. You can have cues, but sometimes the best scenes will be when you are genuinely reacting to the other people in your group yet still staying within the parameters you have set for the scene. Giving one another the space to reveal characters as the scenes unfold is what will unveil surprises and truths about how we live our lives.

_____

_____

_____

_____

The Rules: Keep your scene simple and real. Give each person in the group a clear character with which to work. Work together even though the scene might be unpredictable. Reveal your own character as the scene unfolds. The goal is to show as much about a character within the confines of a specific situation as you can. Good luck!

_____

_____

_____

_____

READING

Two additional autobiographical sketches will introduce you to more ways of telling a story. "One Liar's Beginning" marks one person's memory of when he learned that lying could be a useful tool. Pay special attention to how this author feels about this lesson later in life. Did he learn anything?

In "Black Men and Public Space," you will find yourself face-to-face with one man's understanding of the effect his skin color has on the world around him. Is his story realistic? Listen to how he feels about what happened and how it may have affected his life.

One Liar's Beginnings

Brady Udall

Before all else, let me make my confession: I am a liar. For me, admitting to being a liar is just about the most difficult confession I could make; as a rule, liars don't like to admit to anything. But I'm trying to figure out how I came to be this way—what influences, what decisions at what forked roads have led me to be the devious soul I am today. And as any clergyman worth a nickel can tell you, before you can discover the truth about yourself, first you must confess.

I can't say I remember the first lie I ever told. It's been so long, and there have been so many lies in between. But I can only believe that my first steps, first day of school, first kiss—all those many firsts we love to get so nostalgic about—none of them was in any way as momentous as that first lie I ever told.

It's a dusty summer day. I am three years old, and in the Udall household there is going to be hell to pay; some fool has gone and eaten all the cinnamon red-hots my mother was going to use to decorate cupcakes for a funeral luncheon.

Down in the basement, I am bumping the back of my head against the cushion of the couch. This peculiar habit, *head-bouncing* we called it in our house, was something I liked to do whenever I was nervous or bored. I was most satisfied with the world when I could sit on that couch and bounce my head against the back cushion—you know, really get up a good rhythm, maybe a little Woody Woodpecker on the TV—and not have anyone bother me about it. Along with worrying that their son might be retarded on some level, my parents also became concerned about the living room couch—all this manic head-bouncing of mine was wearing

a considerable divot in the middle cushion (my preferred section) right down to the foam. So my father, after trying all he could think of to get me to desist, finally threw up his hands and went to the town dump and came back with a prehistoric shaggy brown couch that smelled like coconut suntan oil. He put it down in the basement, out of sight of friends and neighbors, and I was allowed to head-bounce away to my heart's content.

So there I am down on the couch, really going at it, while my mother stomps around up above. She is looking for the red-hots thief, and she is furious. My mother is beautiful, ever-smiling and refined, but when she is angry she could strike fear in to the heart of a werewolf.

As for me, I am thoroughly terrified, though not too terrified to enjoy the last of the red-hots. I put them in my mouth and keep them there until they turn into a warm, red syrup that I roll around on my tongue.

My mother is yelling out all the kids' names: *Travis! Symonie! Brady! Cord!* But none of us is dumb enough to answer. Finally, she stomps down the steps and sees me there on my couch, bobbing back and forth like the peg on a metronome, trying not to look her way, hoping that if I can keep my eyes off her long enough she just might disappear.

"Brady, did you eat those red-hots?" She asks, her mouth set hard. I begin to bounce harder.

"Hmmm?" I say.

"Did you eat them?"

I imagine for a second what my punishment will be—maybe spending the rest of the afternoon cooped up in my room, maybe being forced to watch while the rest of the family hogs down the leftover cupcakes after dinner—or maybe she will have mercy on me and opt for a simple swat on the butt with a spatula.

"Did you eat them?"

I don't really think about it, don't even know where it comes from—I look my mother straight in the eye, say it loud and clear as you please: "No."

She doesn't press me, just takes my answer for what it is. Why would she suspect anything from me, a baby who's never lied before, innocent as can be, a sweet little angel who doesn't know any better than to spend all his free time banging his head against the back cushion of a couch from the dump.

"All right," she says, smiling just a little now. She can't help herself—I am that innocent and cute. "Why don't you come upstairs and have a cupcake?"

Right then I stop bouncing altogether. It feels as if there is light blooming in my head, filling me up, giving me a sensation I've never had before, a feeling of potency and possibility and dominion. With a word as simple as "no" I can make things different altogether; no, it wasn't me who ate those red-hots; no, it's not me who deserves a swat on the butt or no cartoons for the rest of the afternoon. What I deserve is a cupcake.

It's a wonderful epiphany: with a lie I can change reality; with a lie I can change the world.

From *Personals: Dreams and Nightmares from the Lives of 20 Young Writers*, edited by Thomas Beller. Boston: Houghton Mifflin Co. Copyright ©1998 by Brady Udall. Reprinted by permission of Brady Udall and the Watkins/Loomis Agency.

Black Men and Public Space

Brent Staples

My first victim was a woman—white, well dressed, probably in her late twenties. I came upon her late one evening on a deserted street in Hyde Park, a relatively affluent neighborhood in an otherwise mean, impoverished section of Chicago. As I swung onto the avenue behind her, there seemed to be a discreet, uninflammatory distance between us. Not so. She cast back a worried glance. To her, the youngish black man—a broad six feet two inches with a beard and billowing hair, both hands shoved into the pockets of a bulky military jacket—seemed menacingly close. After a few more quick glimpses, she picked up her pace and was soon running in earnest. Within seconds she disappeared into a cross street.

That was more than a decade ago. I was twenty-two years old, a graduate student newly arrived at the University of Chicago. It was in the echo of that terrified woman's footfalls that I first began to know the unwieldy inheritance I'd come into—the ability to alter public space in ugly ways. It was clear that she thought herself the quarry of a mugger, a rapist, or worse. Suffering a bout of insomnia, however, I was stalking sleep, not defenseless wayfarers. As a softy who is scarcely able to take a knife to a raw chicken—let alone hold one to a person's throat—I was surprised, embarrassed, and dismayed all at once. Her flight made me feel like an accomplice in tyranny. It also made it clear that I was indistinguishable from the muggers who occasionally seeped into the area from the surrounding ghetto. That first

encounter, and those that followed, signified that a vast, unnerving gulf lay between nighttime pedestrians—particularly women—and me. And I soon gathered that being perceived as dangerous is a hazard in itself. I only needed to turn a corner into a dicey situation, or crowd some frightened, armed person in a foyer somewhere, or make an errant move after being pulled over by a policeman. Where fear and weapons meet—and they often do in urban America—there is always the possibility of death.

In that first year, my first away from my hometown, I was to become thoroughly familiar with the language of fear. At dark, shadowy intersections, I could cross in front of a car stopped at a traffic light and elicit the *thunk, thunk, thunk, thunk* of the driver—black, white, male, or female—hammering down the door locks. On less traveled streets after dark, I grew accustomed to but never comfortable with people crossing to the other side of the street rather than pass me. Then there were the standard unpleasantries with policemen, doormen, bouncers, cabdrivers, and others whose business it is to screen out troublesome individuals *before* there is any nastiness.

I moved to New York nearly two years ago and I have remained an avid night walker. In central Manhattan, the near-constant crowd cover minimizes tense one-on-one street encounters. Elsewhere—in SoHo, for example, where sidewalks are narrow and tightly spaced buildings shut out the sky—things can get very taut indeed.

After dark, on the warrenlike streets of Brooklyn where I live, I often see women who fear the worst from me. They seem to have set their faces on neutral, and with their purse straps strung across their chests bandolier-style, they forge ahead as though bracing themselves against being tackled. I understand, of course, that the danger they perceive is not a hallucination. Women are particularly vulnerable to street violence, and young black males are drastically overrepresented against the kind of alienation that comes of being ever the suspect, a fearsome entity with whom pedestrians avoid making eye contact.

It is not altogether clear to me how I reached the ripe old age of twenty-two without being conscious of the lethality nighttime pedestrians attributed to me. Perhaps it was because in Chester, Pennsylvania, the small, angry industrial town where I came of age in the 1960s, I was scarcely noticeable against a backdrop of gang warfare, street knifings, and murders. I grew up one of the good boys, had perhaps a half-dozen fistfights. In retrospect, my shyness of combat has clear sources.

As a boy, I saw countless tough guys locked away; I have since buried several, too. They were babies, really—a teenage cousin, a brother of twenty-two, a childhood friend in his mid-twenties—all to doubt the virtues of intimidation early on. I chose, perhaps unconsciously, to remain a shadow—timid, but a survivor.

The fearsomeness mistakenly attributed to me in public places often has a perilous flavor. The most frightening of these confusions occurred in the late 1970s and early 1980s, when I worked as a journalist in Chicago. One day, rushing into the office of a magazine I was writing for with a deadline story in hand, I was mistaken for a burglar. The office manager called security and, with an ad hoc posse, I had no way of proving who I was. I could only move briskly toward the company of someone who knew me.

Another time I was on assignment for a local paper and killing time before an interview. I entered a jewelry store on the city's affluent Near North Side. The proprietor excused herself and returned with an enormous red Doberman pinscher straining at the end of a leash. She stood, the dog extended toward me, silent to my questions, her eyes bulging nearly out of her head. I took a cursory look around, nodded, and bade her good night.

Relatively speaking, however, I never fared as badly as another black male journalist. He went to nearby Waukegan, Illinois, a couple of summers ago to work on a story about a murderer who was born there. Mistaking the reporter for the killer, police officers hauled him from his car at gunpoint and but for his press credentials would probably have tried to book him. Such episodes are not uncommon. Black men trade tales like this all the time.

Over the years, I learned to smother the rage I felt at so often being taken for a criminal. Not to do so would surely have led to madness. I now take precautions to make myself less threatening. I move about with care, particularly late in the evening. I give a wide berth to nervous people on subway platforms during the wee hours, particularly when I have exchanged business clothes for jeans. If I happen to be entering a building behind some people who appear skittish, I may walk by, letting them clear the lobby before I return, so as not to seem to be following them. I have been calm and extremely congenial on those rare occasions when I've been pulled over by the police.

And on late-evening constitutionals I employ what has proved to be an excellent tension-reducing measure: I whistle melodies from Beethoven and Vivaldi and the more popular classical composers. Even steely New Yorkers hunching toward nighttime destinations seem to relax, and occasionally they even join in the tune. Virtually everybody seems to sense that a mugger wouldn't be warbling bright, sunny selections from Vivaldi's *Four Seasons*. It is my equivalent of the cowbell that hikers wear when they know they are in bear country.

Journal Entry 6

All my life, I always wanted to be somebody. Now I see that I should have been more specific.

Jane Wagner/Lily Tomlin

Is there some realization about yourself that you have come to that if shared would make interesting material? Like the young black journalist or the now fully matured "liar" whose reflections you have just read, what interesting observation about you or your life experience do you have to share with a stranger?

In this journal entry, carefully craft text that is rich in detail and true to your own voice and personality and that creates an interesting self-portrait of some part of your life.

As a way of beginning, use the blank space below as though it were a wall and draw some doodles or graffiti that relate to what you are about to write. For both the drawing and the writing, use an easy stream of consciousness—a free-flowing technique that should allow you to be creative.

WRITING

Personal Sketch

You have just read a number of short autobiographical sketches in which you heard particular individuals' voices sharing small bits of their stories with you. The individual voices of these storytellers add a special realness to their tale.

For this writing assignment, think back over your life from this moment (the present) to some other moment in the past. Find your "voice" and the personality that goes with it (or borrow a voice and style from one of the authors you have just read), and share a bit of yourself with the reader. While your personal life story is already a long and fascinating one, limit this particular reflection to two pages.

Guidelines: While your reflection will be just a small part of your life's experience, your story should have:

- a catchy beginning
- a solid body
- an ending that leaves the reader satisfied that something special has been learned through the sharing

Add details, feelings, depth, and examples. Let the reader see and feel what you are describing. Evoke visual images in your reader, and help the reader picture what you are describing. Use your senses when you write:

- Sound: someone's voice
- Taste: your grandmother's fried chicken
- Touch: hugging your cat
- Sight: the dilapidated doghouse in the corner of your backyard
- Smell: wet grass

Stepping Stones
DEVELOPING YOUR PERSONAL STORY

Topic

Who are you? How did you get to be the person you have become? Where have you been? Where are you going? You have experienced your life as a long succession of individual moments. These moments have been influenced by people you have encountered and the times in which you live. Imagine your personal success of moments (your life events) in the form of a stone pathway that you have walked.

In this assignment, you will share a bit of your personal story (narrative). This will be good practice for the more complex and involved writing assignment at the end of this chapter. This activity involves both an oral and a visual presentation based on the idea that your life is a path of stepping stones.

Oral Presentation

You can't cover your entire life in a five-minute oral presentation, but by using the "stepping stone" graphic below, you should be able to choose and describe the most remarkable or important influences along your path. This will help you give shape and form to your oral presentation. Do the following:

- Create note cards or an outline to help you organize your oral presentation.
- Plan and execute a five-minute presentation.
- Accompany the presentation with an overhead reproduction of the pathway visual.

Visual Presentation

As you create your visual, use these stepping stones to represent significant events and personal influences over the course of your life. **The stepping stones in this pathway can be designed to:**

- Point out significant moments in your life
- Illuminate family members who have most influenced who you are and where you are today
- Introduce peers or acquaintances who have had significant influence on your life
- Illustrate public/popular figures who have influenced your thinking in some important way
- Target specific dates or special years that are associated with significant periods in your life
- Portray particular words that represent influential concepts/ideas that you have come to believe in and live by (such as values, attitudes, perspectives, learning styles, and multiple intelligences)
- Indicate specific place-names important in your history or personal development
- What other stepping stones can you picture as part of your life's path?

Here is an example of what your stepping stone graphic could look like. The graphic can be used vertically or horizontally; it's your choice. You can completely fill all of the stones or only do some of them.

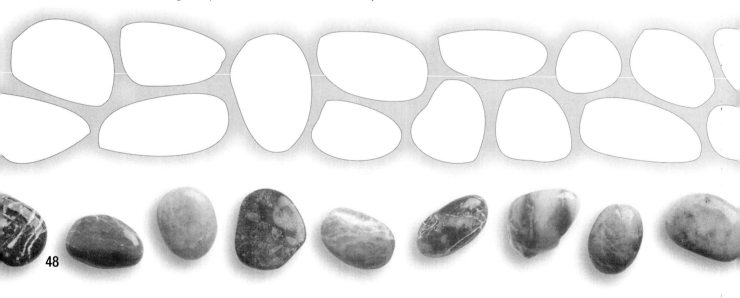

You might think of the smaller stones as representative of small influences or occasions in your life and the others as reflective of the larger ones. This is also your choice. Just remember, whatever you decide to put into your stepping stone graphic should be an illustration of whatever you are actually going to say during your presentation. Use the visual as an aid to your oral presentation.

For special tips on oral and visual presentations and how to do them easily and well, read the next few pages.

EFFECTIVE VISUAL PRESENTATIONS

When you are doing a presentation that includes a visual component, you should pay attention to three elements: design, method, and function.

Design includes such elements as size, shape, color, scale, and contrast. These elements should be familiar to you from your art classes. They relate to the message you wish to convey in your presentation.

Method is how you present your ideas. Will it be better to show your ideas by drawing a picture (or cutting one out of a magazine or using clip art) of, for example, a person, a tree, or a logo? Or would it be more powerful to depict your memory of something through a range of color or through shapes? This would be the difference between presenting your idea *literally* or *abstractly*. Having decided on these, you might then consider the *juxtaposition* of colors or shapes or pictures. The decisions you make about any of this will alter the impact of your presentation. You may decide to introduce your ideas symbolically, and perhaps a picture of a pond surrounded by tall trees would be the best way to present the concept of a calm person.

The *function* is the purpose of the visual part of your presentation. Are you telling a story? Communicating a message? Creating movement for the audience to follow? Summarizing an idea? Motivating people to buy an idea? Supporting and confirming what you are telling your audience? Knowing the function of the visual element will make your decisions about design and method more meaningful.

EFFECTIVE ORAL PRESENTATIONS

When you are giving an oral presentation, you should pay special attention to voice, body, and attitude. If you take the following tips into consideration, you should do a fine job of conveying your ideas to your audience.

Voice is more than the sum of your own voice making noise. You need to pay attention to *inflection,* which is the change in pitch or loudness of your voice. You can deliberately use inflection to make a point, to get people's attention, or to make it very obvious that what you are saying *right now* is important. You can also change the volume of your voice. Speak softly and people will think you are shy or unwilling to share your ideas. Speak too **LOUDLY** and people will think you are shouting at them. You need to control your volume to fit the audience.

Some people have a tendency to rush through their presentations. This means they speed up their speech, and the audience has a difficult time following along. Take care to control the speed at which you give a presentation so that everyone can listen comfortably. Also, to add to the comfort of the listener, it is always nice to carry a conversational tone in a presentation—much the way I am talking with you now, almost as though we are in the same room and I am telling you about voice.

Body includes such components as stance, gesture, and eye contact—overall body language. How do you stand when you are giving a presentation? Do you move around and fidget? Do you look down at the ground or just at your note cards? Are you chewing gum or sticking your hands in and out of your pockets nervously? Obviously, you don't want to do any of these things. You want to make eye contact as often as possible. Stand in a comfortable manner, but don't fidget. And use your hands sparingly as gestures to make certain points.

Attitude is everything. Your enthusiasm for your presentation will prime the audience. If you are bored by your own words, the audience will be yawning. If you are jazzed by what you have to offer, they will sit up in their seats and listen intently. Also, be interested in your audience. Let them know that you are excited to share your ideas with them because they are worth your effort.

WRITING

Your Life

I am a part of all that I have met.

—Alfred Lord Tennyson

It can be interesting to take the time and find out what we already know, what experiences we have already had, and how we seem to have created a persona without planning it. Writing your own autobiography gives you an opportunity to document an account of your days and to analyze how you might have come to this point in your life, why you think the way you do, and what might have contributed to your values and perspectives. Once you have taken the time to pore over your own life, you will understand that the people around you all have equally rich pasts that have created their worldviews.

Assignment

Tell the story of your life by describing the numerous communities to which you have belonged. In this way, you will provide a context for each part you write. Examples of communities are your family, sports teams, church, neighborhood, ethnic group, dance class, the state in which you lived, Boy Scouts or Girl Scouts, and any other large or small community in which you had some role.

Hints for Descriptive Writing

Help the reader see and feel what you are describing by evoking visual images. For instance, if you are talking about the first house you lived in, say something about the age of the house and its color, texture, and style—let the reader picture it. In other words, add concrete details. Say "hot chocolate" rather than just "drink," or name a relative instead of saying "my aunt," or talk about a "dried crumpled corsage," rather than just a "corsage."

Use your senses when you write. Talk about someone's voice, the taste of a special meal, the feel of petting your dog or hugging your cat, the sight of your father digging for worms, and the smell of the pine tree on Christmas eve. Use specifics rather than generalities. Talk about your car as a "rusty old car with towels for seats."

Tell how you feel. Illustrate your emotions by giving examples throughout your autobiography. Re-create an emotion by talking about how you actually felt. Make the reader "feel" with you. Add stories within your story. Expand a memory. Humor is always appropriate and helpful. Remember, everyone's life has funny, sad, difficult, and challenging times. Let your autobiography ebb and flow just as life does.

When you end your autobiography, don't conclude just with "and so I graduated from high school." Summarize what you have accomplished and what you have learned. Or, if you have discovered an overriding theme in your life, talk about it. Perhaps you can talk about your own philosophy of life or make a tribute to friends and family for bringing you to this point in your life.

Possible Data to Include

You might wish to break your life into time periods. Sometimes, it is easier to think of it that way. For example:

Early Years

- Facts surrounding your birth—where, when
- Any memories of those first few years

Elementary School Years

- Economic condition of your family
- Illnesses, accidents
- Where did you live?
- Did you have pets?
- Religious training
- School, teachers, friends

Junior and High School Years

- Classes, hobbies, activities
- Honors and awards
- Driving a car
- Special friends
- Sporting events
- First date
- Fads that were part of your life
- Clothes you wore
- Trouble? Pranks?

Turning Points

Of course, there are other ways to organize your autobiography. Perhaps you might like to look at your life by talking about the turning points in your life. What are turning points? Everything moves along in your life rather smoothly and then all of a sudden something happens that changes the direction of your life. For instance, you move to a new home, city, or state; you meet someone or make a team; or someone important dies, your parents divorce, or some other tragedy occurs.

A turning point is anything dramatic that has a clear impact, positive or negative, on your life. When you write about turning points, include:

- A summary of life before the turning point
- Events as they lead up to the change
- What actually happens
- How it affected your life

1. What do you do in your free time?
2. What was the most memorable moment in your life?
3. What qualities do you look for in people?
4. If someone looked into your trash, what would they find?
5. What did your parents believe when they raised you?
6. What in your life do you most value and why?
7. Describe your ideal mate.
8. What do you enjoy doing most?
9. What makes you different from everyone else?
10. How do you plan to live your life to the fullest?
11. What are your religious beliefs?
12. What are your goals in life?
13. Who are your favorite music groups?
14. Have you been labeled in your life?
15. What is the most embarrassing moment in your life?
16. Where do you see yourself in 10 years?
17. What do you treasure most?
18. Who were your role models?
19. What do you like best about yourself?
20. What is the closest you have come to dying?
21. Has your life made a difference to anyone?
22. What is the most important piece of information you have had in your lifetime?
23. What event has influenced your lifestyle?
24. Describe the worst day of your life.
25. What is the one word that describes you best?
26. What is your relationship with your parents?
27. What do you like about yourself?
28. If you could fulfill your wildest fantasy, what would it be?
29. What is your greatest accomplishment to date?
30. If you had three wishes, what would they be?

More Questions about You

Western philosophy virtually began with Socrates' advice: "Know thyself." Self-knowledge is important because so many of the obstacles to clear and open-minded thinking are found not in the exterior problems we face but within ourselves. Look at the questions below, and decide which of them might help you write a more solid and in-depth autobiography.

1. Am I quiet or talkative?
2. Optimistic? Pessimistic?
3. Hardworking? Lazy?

4. Fearful? Brave?

5. Serious? Easygoing?

6. Modest? Proud?

7. Competitive?

8. Nervous? At ease with strangers?

9. How trustworthy am I?

10. Am I jealous of anyone?

11. Do I resent certain types of people?

12. Do I ever use people?

13. How intelligent am I?

14. Do I work well under pressure?

15. Do I enjoy causing trouble?

16. Am I loyal to my friends?

17. Do I criticize others?

18. How many roles do I play with other people?

19. Do I keep my promises?

20. How reasonable are my plans for the future?

Adding the answers to some of these questions to your autobiography will help you create something of substance.

Prompts

Think about the following list of prompts to help you engage more memories about your life.

1. The magic song for me that summer was . . .

2. I'll never forget that meal . . .

3. My favorite time of day was . . .

4. I remember being scared . . .

5. Someday she would be sorry because . . .

6. I felt stupid that day . . .

7. Today it seems silly, but that day it was the most humiliating event of my life when . . .

8. . . . believed in me from the very beginning.

9. I wore it because . . .

10. My first tie was unbelievably . . .

11. I earned my money . . .

12. I couldn't stand that cousin because . . .

13. My favorite movies are . . .

14. I was shocked by . . .

15. He was impossible to please . . .

16. I wasn't guilty, but . . .

17. At the time, I thought I couldn't lose . . .

18. My best friend in second grade didn't . . .

19. It hurt worse than . . .

20. All the other kids had . . .

21. A relative I wish I resembled had . . .

22. My most embarrassing habit was . . .

23. It began when we . . .

24. That sickness made me . . .

25. I did it to show her that I could . . .

26. I never told him/her that . . .

27. I let it get out of hand, so . . .

28. I should have agreed to . . .

29. I wish I hadn't been so concerned . . .

30. No one else showed up, therefore I . . .

31. She had more than her share and . . .

32. I forgot . . .

33. I had too much pride to . . .

34. I convinced him to change his mind and . . .

35. We started out as friends, but . . .

36. I worked my way around . . .

37. When I have a hangover I . . .

38. I am confident, but . . .

39. I hated it when she . . .

40. I admired him because . . .

41. That person changed my life when . . .

42. The locker room smelled like . . .

43. I loved that city because . . .

44. My bedroom was full of . . .

45. No one told me to wear long pants, so . . .

46. Even the dishes were dirty, and . . .

47. She always took the largest piece and . . .

48. He never did his share, so . . .

49. I could never give up that . . .

50. The food tasted funny that day when . . .

CASH IN ON EDUCATION

Heather Hiatt
J. P. Morgan Securities

I graduated from the University of Michigan in 1993, but it still feels like just yesterday. I am convinced this is because I am constantly reminded of how educational those four years were—but not education in just the academic sense. I believe letter grades fall short in measuring the true success of a college graduate; a complete education is composed equally of both academic learning and the intangible feat of learning about life. It's this type of education that opens the doors of opportunity and gives graduates the resources to make sound choices throughout the rest of their lives.

I grew up in Hawaii, and attending college so far away from home was my first stab at independence. Despite my nervousness and fear, I relished the fact that daily choices were mine to make. I decided what and when to study, what and when to eat, when to sleep and when to come home at night. While I basked in my successes, I also had no one to blame when I made mistakes. Independence could have become overwhelming, but I learned to set incremental goals in all facets of my life; my primary goal was to do well academically.

There was no way around having a solid work ethic. While it was important for me to work hard, I also knew I had to work smart. A key component to college is having choices, and I wanted to be in control of my studying. Since I believed socializing was an integral part of a well-balanced college life, I wanted to maximize my free time. I tried not to procrastinate, so that I could decide when to put down the books and just relax. When my friends and I weren't studying, we enjoyed one another's company and the social scene Ann Arbor had to offer. We traveled on spring breaks together, went to restaurants and parties, and learned about people and the world outside the shelter of our parents' homes. Unbeknownst to me, these types of experiences were preparing me for a life after college—a life in the working world.

Despite the fact that I graduated with a degree in communications, I currently work as a bond salesperson for J. P. Morgan Securities in San Francisco. I started in an entry-level job at J. P. Morgan when I first moved to San Francisco and never expected to pursue this career path. My employers, however, knew I was a college graduate and began to give me responsibilities that normal entry-level employees did not get. With a college degree, I was taken seriously and given on-the-job training and the opportunity to climb the proverbial corporate ladder to test out a profession I have grown to love. The skill to learn quickly coupled with my ability to adapt to new situations helped me excel at a job I didn't even know existed while in college. Because I had always felt in control of my learning process, I also knew I was in control of my destiny. Even if I had hit a dead end at J. P. Morgan, I had learned to be resilient enough to keep searching for something I could master.

I have cashed in on my college education over and over again. I have not only bounced back from several misguided career turns, but my life has been enriched by the college experiences I had and the close friends I made during those four years. Our collective learning process is ongoing, eight years later; we are constantly expanding our knowledge at work and still lean on one another for advice and support while learning life's innumerable lessons. After all, being able to cash in on your college education does not necessarily mean achieving financial success. Rather, it means having a life rich with opportunities, friendships, and the wisdom and ability to choose your own path in life.

CHAPTER THREE

Styles and Intelligences

Objectives

- to learn about learning styles

- to understand multiple intelligences

- to discover how you learn

"We reach our dreams by dreaming,
Even when we lose our way, . . ."

SNAPSHOT

SNAPSHOT

SNAPSHOT

SNAPSHOT

SNAPSHOT

SNAPSHOT

SNAPSHOT

I learned that a project is just as much group contribution as it is individual. A group wouldn't be a group it if weren't for the individuals. Every individual contributes to the group. They have their ideas, their talent, their creativity, their knowledge. A group with one less person may be a group that is missing an individual with the talent that their group requires.

—*Wendy Orita*

The beauty of life is that each person is unique. No two people are exactly alike, although sometimes we may appear this way. Therefore each individual has a set of values which he or she follows throughout life. . . . Reasons for *why* these values are important facets in our lives represent who we are as individuals.

—*First-year student*

Information Literacy and Learning Styles

Many of us want information to be unambiguous. We are busy, and there is too much information to digest. "Just tell me what I need to know," we say. We like the idea of a world that is clear-cut: true or false, right or wrong, relevant or irrelevant. The popularity of political and cultural talk show programs is in part because these programs create an arena for "experts" to state what is true in a simple way so that other "experts" can disagree with their "truth" or "right" version of something. This dualistic thinking seems to make life easier.

However, a central element of our world is that information is perceived by human beings and created by human beings. We have habitual patterns for perceiving the world around us and communicating our perceptions to others. These patterns are called *learning styles* or *intelligences.*

Being information literate is being aware that we prefer our information in certain forms and presented in certain ways. We have preferences for format and content beyond whatever data might be presented. For instance, some of us like a rousing public speaker who persuades us with emotion and colorful language. Others of us like our information with pictures and moving images. And there are some of us who respond to the written word, relishing effective vocabulary, sentence structure, and the ability to take in the information at our own speed.

You may be someone for whom a picture is worth a thousand words or who listens for an hour and still can't understand what a speaker is talking about. Each of us perceives both the world and the relevance of information in different ways.

If we don't think about our individual learning styles, we will be attracted only to information in forms and with content that matches our style. We will miss out on information that can be equally significant but doesn't obviously "suit" us.

To be information literate is to stretch your style toward information that matches your information need. Start with the type of information you like, but search also for information that is suitable for your understanding.

THE IMPORTANCE OF STYLE

Your learning "style" is an indication of how you acquire knowledge. Individuals process and absorb information differently. This means that each of you will also approach tasks in various ways. Think about it. When you have something new

We don't see things as they are. We see them as we are.

ANAIS NIN

to learn, what is your approach? If you take a moment to ponder this, you will find that you have developed a pattern of behavior that works for you. This pattern is probably your dominant learning style.

Think of times when you have said to yourself, "That was *not* my kind of exam," or "I hate long lectures," or "I'm not happy in a small class," or "I can't believe she wants me to memorize this!" The purpose of examining your learning style is to see when it is helpful and when it is not. People learn differently—you can call it a preference if you wish. But whatever your "preferred" way of learning, you will find yourself in situations where your "style" just doesn't fit that of the instructor. What do you do then?

The following learning style inventory will help you determine more about your style. Later, you can explore ways to accommodate your learning style to those of your teachers.

Name:

School:

Grade or Year: *Date:*

Counselor/Teacher/Examiner:

To gain a better understanding of yourself as a learner you need to evaluate the way you prefer to learn. We all should develop a style that will enhance our learning potential. The following evaluation is a short, quick way of assessing your learning style.

This is not a timed test. Try to do as much as you can by yourself. You surely may, however, ask for assistance when and where you feel you need it. Answer each question as honestly as you can. There are thirty-two questions.

When you are finished, transfer each number to its proper place on the last page. Then, total each of the four columns on that page. You will then see very quickly what your best method of learning is, i.e., whether you are a **visual**, **auditory**, **tactile**, or **kinesthetic** learner. By this we mean, whether you as an individual learn best through seeing things, hearing them, through the sense of touch, or through actually performing the task.

For example:

- If you are a visual learner, that is, if you have a high visual score, then by all means be sure you *see* all study materials. Use charts, maps, filmstrips, notes, and flashcards. Practice visualizing or picturing spelling words, for example, in your head. Use brightly colored markers to highlight your reading assignments. Write out everything for frequent and quick visual review.

- If you are an auditory learner, that is, if you have a high auditory score, then be sure to use tapes. Sit in the lecture hall or classroom where you can hear lectures clearly. Tape your class or lecture notes so that you can review them frequently. After you have read something, summarize it on tape. Verbally review spelling words and lectures with a friend.

- If you are a tactile learner, that is, if you have a high tactile score, you might trace words, for example, as you are saying them. Facts that must be learned should be written several times. Keep a supply of scratch paper just for this purpose. Taking and keeping lecture notes will be very important.

- If you are a kinesthetic learner, that is, if you have a high kinesthetic score, it means you need to involve your body in the process of learning. Take a walk and study your notes on flashcards at the same time. It is easier for you to memorize school work if you involve some movement in your memory task.

If several of your scores are within 4 or 5 points of each other, it means that you can use any of those senses for learning tasks. *When you are in a hurry, use your best learning styles. When you have extra time, improve your weak sensory areas.* Discuss the results of this test with your teacher or counselor. You will develop through conversation other helpful ways to study more efficiently. Good luck in your efforts to identify and use a more effective study pattern.

Circle the appropriate letter after each statement.

	Often	Sometimes	Rarely
1. Can remember more about a subject through listening than reading.	O	S	R
2. I follow written directions better than oral directions.	O	S	R
3. Once shown a new physical movement, I perform it quickly with few errors.	O	S	R
4. I bear down extremely hard with a pen or pencil when writing.	O	S	R
5. I require explanations of diagrams, graphs, or visual directions.	O	S	R
6. I enjoy working with tools.	O	S	R
7. I am skillful with and enjoy developing and making graphs and charts.	O	S	R
8. I can tell if sounds match when presented with pairs of sounds.	O	S	R
9. I can watch someone do a dance step and easily copy it myself.	O	S	R
10. I can understand and follow directions on maps.	O	S	R
11. I do better at academic subjects by listening to lectures and tapes.	O	S	R
12. I frequently play with coins or keys in my pocket.	O	S	R
13. I enjoy perfecting a movement in a sport or in dancing.	O	S	R
14. I can better understand a news article by reading about it in the paper than by listening to the radio.	O	S	R
15. I chew gum, smoke, or snack during studies.	O	S	R
16. I feel the best way to remember is to picture it in my head.	O	S	R
17. I enjoy activities that make me aware of my body's movement.	O	S	R
18. I would rather listen to a good lecture or speech than read the same material in a textbook.	O	S	R
19. I consider myself an athletic person.	O	S	R
20. I grip objects in my hands during learning.	O	S	R
21. I would prefer listening to the news on the radio rather than reading about it in the newspaper.	O	S	R
22. I like to obtain information on an interesting subject by reading relevant materials.	O	S	R
23. I am highly aware of sensations and feelings in my hips and shoulders after learning a new movement or exercise.	O	S	R
24. I follow oral directions better than written ones.	O	S	R
25. It would be easy for me to memorize something if I could just use body movements at the same time.	O	S	R
26. I like to write things down or take notes for visual review.	O	S	R

27. I remember best when writing things down several times.   (O)   (S)   (R)

28. I learn to spell better by repeating the letters out loud than by writing the word on paper.   (O)   (S)   (R)

29. I frequently have the ability to visualize body movements to perform a task, e.g., correction of a golf swing, batting stance, dance position, etc.   (O)   (S)   (R)

30. I could learn spelling well by tracing over the letters.   (O)   (S)   (R)

31. I feel comfortable touching, hugging, shaking hands, etc.   (O)   (S)   (R)

32. I am good at working and solving jigsaw puzzles and mazes.   (O)   (S)   (R)

Scoring Procedures

OFTEN = 5 points, SOMETIMES = 3 points, RARELY = 1 point

Place the point value on the line next to its corresponding item number. Next, add the points to obtain the preference scores under each heading.

VISUAL		AUDITORY		TACTILE		KINESTHETIC	
No.	Points	No.	Points	No.	Points	No.	Points
2.	_____	1.	_____	4.	_____	3.	_____
7.	_____	5.	_____	6.	_____	9.	_____
10.	_____	8.	_____	12.	_____	13.	_____
14.	_____	11.	_____	15.	_____	17.	_____
16.	_____	18.	_____	20.	_____	19.	_____
22.	_____	21.	_____	27.	_____	23.	_____
26.	_____	24.	_____	30.	_____	25.	_____
32.	_____	28.	_____	31.	_____	29.	_____
VPS _____		APS _____		TPS _____		KPS _____	

VPS = Visual Preference Score
APS = Auditory Preference Score
TPS = Tactile Preference Score
KPS = Kinesthetic Preference Score

How to Use This Information

This form is to be used in conjunction with other diagnostic tools to help you determine some of the ways you are best able to learn. Discuss your scores with someone who is qualified to interpret them in order to make the best use of the time and effort you have invested.

WRITING

How I Learn

I'm not smart, but I like to observe. Millions saw the apple fall, but Newton was the one who asked why.

—Bernard Mannes Baruch

Pick one of the following two choices for your paper. Each addresses the issue of how you learn. Place your emphasis on clarity, thoughtfulness, and imagination.

    1. **Open Letter.** Write a letter to *two* teachers you had. First, write to the best or most favorite; second, write to your least favorite one. In these letters, talk about what went right and what went wrong in your classes. Talk about what happened that made you tune out and what might have happened when you tuned in and found yourself loving to learn. Tell these teachers how you learned best and what you wish had gone on in class to have been able to maximize your learning.

    2. **Self-Analysis.** Write this paper in the third person, but about yourself. Come up with a new category about yourself as a learner. Be creative—do not use the categories given you in the previous learning styles inventory. Here is an example:

> I remember this student in high school; her name was Sarah and she always sat right smack in the back of the class. You might have thought she wasn't paying attention; however, whenever the teacher asked a question, her hand was always up, and she was most often correct with her answers. The trouble was, the teacher didn't call on her much. She was quiet and always seen reading a book. Most people thought . . . etc.

Eventually you can come up with a premise for the kind of learner this person (you) might be. Invent a title or name for the learning style.

Locate a map that shows the Mississippi River and all the states that border it. Locate St. Louis, Missouri, and New Orleans, Louisiana. This is the part of the Great River Road that Mark Twain spent four years learning and navigating and about which you will read in your next reading.

In a small group, trace the length of the river and see how much of it you can understand.

What are your thoughts as you look at that stretch of the Mississippi? Try to comprehend the almost incomprehensible complexity of navigating a steamboat that 1,200-mile distance, as described in your next reading.

In your group, do or answer the following:

1. Make a list of forms of transportation that have evolved since the last half of the 1800s.

2. Are there any that require complex learning?

3. What kinds of skills does one need to use current forms of transportation? What kinds of learning are involved?

Mark Twain (AKA Samuel Clemens, 1835–1910) was a skilled author, humorist, and commentator on life in America during the last half of the 19th century. He grew up in Hannibal, Missouri, one of many small towns along the Mississippi River. He spent four years of his life piloting a steamboat along the "Great River Road," as the Mississippi was called.

The following is Chapter 8 of his book *Life on the Mississippi*. In this chapter, Twain touches upon multiple facets of learning. He talks about "perplexing lessons" and says:

It was plain that I had got to learn the shape of the river in all the different ways that could be thought of,—upside down, wrong end first, inside out, fore-and-aft, and 'thort-ships'—and then know what to do on gray nights when it hadn't any shape at all.

Think about this particular quote while reading this chapter, and then consider what it might mean to your own concept of learning, especially as it relates to learning styles.

Perplexing Lessons

Mark Twain

At the end of what seemed a tedious while, I had managed to pack my head full of islands, towns, bars, "points," and bends; and a curiously inanimate mass of lumber it was, too. However, inasmuch as I could shut my eyes and reel off a good long string of these names without leaving out more than ten miles of river in every fifty, I began to feel that I could take a boat down to New Orleans if I could make her skip those little gaps. But of course my complacency could hardly get start enough to lift my nose a trifle into the air, before Mr. Bixby would think of something to fetch it down again. One day he turned on me suddenly with this settler: —

"What is the shape of Walnut Bend?"

He might as well have asked me my grandmother's opinion of protoplasm. I reflected respectfully, and then said I didn't know it had any particular shape. My gunpowdery chief went off with a bang, of course, and then went on loading and firing until he was out of adjectives.

I had learned long ago that he only carried just so many rounds of ammunition, and was sure to subside into a very placable and even remorseful old smooth-bore as soon as they were all gone. That word "old" is merely affectionate; he was not more than thirty-four. I waited. By and by he said, —

"My boy, you've got to know the *shape* of the river perfectly. It is all there is left to steer by on a very dark night. Everything else is blotted out and gone. But mind you, it hasn't the same shape in the night that it has in the day-time."

"How on earth am I ever going to learn it, then?"

"How do you follow a hall at home in the dark? Because you know the shape of it. You can't see it."

"Do you mean to say that I've got to know all the million trifling variations of shape in the banks of this interminable river as well as I know the shape of the front hall at home?"

"On my honor, you've got to know them *better* than any man ever did know the shapes of the halls in his own house."

"I wish I was dead!"

"Now I don't want to discourage you, but" —

"Well, pile it on me; I might as well have it now as another time."

"You see, this has got to be learned; there isn't any getting around it. A clear starlight night throws such heavy shadows that if you didn't know the shape of a shore perfectly you would claw away from every bunch of timber, because you would take the black shadow of it for a solid cape; and you see you would be getting scared to death every fifteen minutes by the watch. You would be fifty yards from shore all the time when you ought to be within fifty feet of it. You can't see a snag in one of those shadows, but you know exactly where it is, and the shape of the river tells you when you are coming to it.

Then there's your pitch-dark night; the river is a very different shape on a pitch-dark night from what it is on a starlight night. All shores seem to be straight lines, then, and mighty dim ones, too; and you'd *run* them for straight lines only you know better. You boldly drive your boat right into what seems to be a solid, straight wall (you knowing very well that in reality there is a curve there), and that wall falls back and makes way for you. Then there's your gray mist. You take a night when there's one of these grisly, drizzly, gray mists, and then there isn't *any* particular shape to a shore. A gray mist would tangle the head of the oldest man that ever lived. Well, then, different kinds of *moonlight* change the shape of the river in different ways. You see" —

"Oh, don't say any more, please! Have I got to learn the shape of the river according to all these five hundred thousand different ways? If I tried to carry all that cargo in my head it would make me stoop-shouldered."

"No! you only learn *the* shape of the river; and you learn it with such absolute certainty that you can always steer by the shape that's *in your head*, and never mind the one that's before your eyes."

"Very well, I'll try it; but after I have learned it can I depend on it? Will it keep the same form and not go fooling around?"

Before Mr. Bixby could answer, Mr. W— came in to take the watch, and he said, —

"Bixby, you'll have to look out for President's Island and all that country clear away up above the Old Hen and Chickens. The banks are caving and the shape of the shores changing like everything. Why, you wouldn't know the point above 40. You can go up inside the old sycamore snag, now."*

So that question was answered. Here were leagues of shore changing shape. My spirits were down in the mud again. Two things seemed pretty apparent to me. One was, that in order to be a pilot a man had got to learn more than any one man ought to be allowed to know; and the other was, that he must learn it all over again in a different way every twenty-four hours.

That night we had the watch until twelve. Now it was an ancient river custom for the two pilots to chat a bit when the watch changed. While the relieving pilot put on his gloves and lit his cigar, his partner, the retiring pilot, would say something like this: —

"I judge the upper bar is making down a little at Hale's Point; had quarter twain with the lower lead and mark twain** with the other."

"Yes, I thought it was making down a little, last trip. Meet any boats?"

"Met one abreast the head of 21, but she was away over hugging the bar, and I couldn't make her out entirely. I took her for the 'Sunny South'—hadn't any skylights forward of the chimneys."

And so on. And as the relieving pilot took the wheel his partner would mention that we were in such-and-such a bend, and say we were abreast of such-and-such a man's wood-yard or plantation. This courtesy; I supposed it was *necessity*. But Mr. W— came on watch full twelve minutes late on this particular night,—a tremendous breach of etiquette; in fact, it is the unpardonable sin among pilots. So Mr. Bixby gave him no greeting whatever, but simply surrendered the wheel and marched out of the pilot-house without a word. I was appalled; it was a villainous night for blackness, we were in a particularly wide and blind part of the river, where there was no shape or substance to anything, and it seemed incredible that Mr. Bixby should have left that poor fellow to kill the boat trying to find out where he was. But I resolved that I would stand by him any way. He should find that he was not wholly friendless. So I stood around, and waited to be asked where we were. But Mr. W— plunged on serenely through the solid firmament of black cats that stood for an atmosphere, and never opened his mouth. Here is a proud devil, thought I; here is a limb of Satan that would rather send us all to destruction than put himself under obligations to me, because I am not yet one of the salt of the earth and privileged to snub captains and lord it over everything dead and alive in a steamboat. I presently climbed up on the bench; I did not think it was safe to go to sleep while this lunatic was on watch.

However, I must have gone to sleep in the course of time, because the next thing I was aware of was the fact that day was breaking, Mr. W— gone, and Mr. Bixby at the wheel again. So it was four o'clock and all well—but me: I felt like a skinful of dry bones and all of them trying to ache at once.

Mr. Bixby asked me what I had stayed up there for. I confessed that it was to do Mr. W— a benevolence,—tell him where he was. It took five minutes for the entire preposterousness of the thing to filter into Mr. Bixby's system, and then I judge it filled him nearly up to the chin; because he paid me a compliment—and not much of a one either. He said,—

"Well, taking you by-and-large, you do seem to be more different kinds of an ass than any creature

---

* It may not be necessary, but still it can do no harm to explain that "inside" means between the snag and the shore.—M. T.

** Two fathoms. Quarter twain is 2 1/4 fathoms, 13 1/2 feet. Mark three is three fathoms.

I ever saw before. What did you suppose he wanted to know for?"

I said I thought it might be a convenience to him.

"Convenience! D-nation! Didn't I tell you that a man's got to know the river in the night the same as he'd know his own front hall?"

"Well, I can follow the front hall in the dark if I know it *is* the front hall; but suppose you set me down in the middle of it in the dark and not tell me which hall it is; how am *I* to know?"

"Well, you've *got* to, on the river!"

"All right. Then I'm glad I never said anything to Mr. W—"

"I should say so. Why, he'd have slammed you through the window and utterly ruined a hundred dollars' worth of window-sash and stuff."

I was glad this damage had been saved, for it would have made me unpopular with the owners. They always hated anybody who had the name of being careless, and injuring things.

I went to work now to learn the shape of the river; and of all the eluding and ungraspable objects that ever I tried to get mind or hands on, that was the chief. I would fasten my eyes upon a sharp, wooded point that projected far into the river some miles ahead of me, and go to laboriously photographing its shape upon my brain; and just as I was beginning to succeed to my satisfaction, we would draw up toward it and the exasperating thing would begin to melt away and fold back into the bank! If there had been a conspicuous dead tree standing upon the very point of the cape, I would find that tree inconspicuously merged into the general forest, and occupying the middle of a straight shore, when I got abreast of it! No prominent hill would stick to its shape long enough for me to make up my mind what its form really was, but it was as dissolving and changeful as if it had been a mountain of butter in the hottest corner of the tropics. Nothing ever had the same shape when I was coming down-stream that it had borne when I went up. I mentioned these little difficulties to Mr. Bixby. He said,—

"That's the very main virtue of the thing. If the shapes didn't change every three seconds they wouldn't be of any use. Take this place where we are now, for instance. As long as that hill over yonder is only one hill, I can boom right along the way I'm going; but the moment it splits at the top and forms a V, I know I've got to scratch to starboard in a hurry, or I'll bang this boat's brains out against a rock; and then the moment one of the prongs of the V swings behind the other, I've got to waltz to larboard again, or I'll have a misunderstanding with a snag that would snatch the keelson out of this steamboat as neatly as if it were a sliver in your hand. If that hill didn't change its shape on bad nights there would be an awful steamboat graveyard around here inside of a year."

It was plain that I had got to learn the shape of the river in all the different ways that could be thought of,—upside down, wrong end first, inside out, fore-and-aft, and "thort-ships,"—and then know what to do on gray nights when it hadn't any shape at all. So I set about it. In the course of time I began to get the best of this knotty lesson, and my self-complacency moved to the front once more. Mr. Bixby was all fixed, and ready to start it to the rear again. He opened on me after this fashion: —

"How much water did we have in the middle crossing at Hole-in-the-Wall, trip before last?"

I considered this an outrage. I said: —

"Every trip, down and up, the leadsmen are singing through that tangled place for three quarters of an hour on a stretch. How do you reckon I can remember such a mess as that?"

"My boy, you've got to remember it. You've got to remember the exact spot and the exact marks the boat lay in when we had the shoalest water, in every one of the five hundred shoal places between St. Louis and New Orleans; and you mustn't get the shoal soundings and marks of one trip mixed up with the shoal soundings and marks of another, either, for they're not often twice alike. You must keep them separate."

When I came to myself again, I said, —

"When I get so that I can do that, I'll be able to raise the dead, and then I won't have to pilot a steamboat to make a living. I want to retire from this business. I want a slush-bucket and a brush; I'm only fit for a roustabout. I haven't got brains enough to be a pilot; and if I had I wouldn't have strength enough to carry them around, unless I went on crutches."

"Now drop that! When I say I'll learn* a man the river, I mean it. And you can depend on it, I'll learn him or kill him."

* "Teach" is not in the river vocabulary.

Journal Entry 7

I hear and I forget. I see and I remember. I do and I understand.

Confucius

In a paragraph each, respond to the following two sets of questions.

I. What kind of learning skills did Mark Twain have to demonstrate to be successful as he learned to pilot a steamboat along the Mississippi? List the characteristics that enabled him to be a successful student and steamboat pilot. In contemporary times, given these same learning skills and styles, what career might he have enjoyed preparing for?

2. What forms of contemporary job training can you think of where the learner is faced with the "learn or die" form of teaching that was indicated in the Twain reading? Create a list of careers that people train for in which, as students in training, the learner is required to recall incredible numbers of details to keep from harming themselves or others.

After doing the previous exercises, respond to the following:

Most of life's lessons are benign. But active learning can be dangerous, and practicing what one has learned can be hazardous. Reflect on this as it has related to your life and your family's life.

MULTIPLE INTELLIGENCES

You are often considered intelligent if you have high grades or do well on tests in school. Unfortunately, the standard IQ tests measure how intelligent a person is based on math and English. What about drawing? Singing? Playing a sport? Relationship skills? None of these is taken into consideration. Therefore, many areas that a person may excel in, or have a natural ability in, are totally ignored.

Though a mother gives birth to nine sons, all nine will be different.

CHINESE PROVERB

However, you know that each individual is unique and has different features, personalities, talents, gifts, and abilities. Not all of these are in the areas of math and language. So the new question should really be, *"How* are you smart?"—not "How smart are you?"

Howard Gardner is a professor of education and a codirector of Project Zero at the Harvard Graduate School of Education. He is most known for his theory of multiple intelligences (MI). This theory originally stated that there are at least seven different ways of learning and that, therefore, there are seven intelligences—verbal-linguistic, logical-mathematical, visual-spatial, bodily-kinesthetic, musical-rhythmic, interpersonal, and intrapersonal—that match up with these various ways of learning. He has most recently added an eighth intelligence, the naturalist, to the list. Gardner's theories have had wide-ranging effects on educational philosophy as teachers struggle to understand the major differences in ability among their students. The way Gardner separated the intelligences helped to explain the strengths and weaknesses found within the learning environment.

For you, a new college student, learning a little about these intelligences will add to your understanding of how you learn, what strengths you can rely on, and where you might need to compensate.

The eight intelligences that Gardner has identified are as follows:

1. **Verbal-Linguistic.** The ability to use language to solve problems, describe events, develop arguments, and be expressive. This intelligence involves understanding the order and meaning of words. A person with a high linguistic intelligence likes to write and tell jokes and stories; has a good memory for names, places, and dates; spells well; and uses language well to communicate.

> Books are very important to me.
> I enjoy Scrabble and Boggle and anagrams.
> I can hear words in my head before I speak them.

2. **Logical-Mathematical.** The ability to use numbers to problem solve, to apply mathematics in daily life, and to be sensitive to patterns, symmetry, and logic. This is often referred to as *scientific thinking* because it deals with inductive and deductive reasoning. This kind of person enjoys using technology, often plays chess or other strategy games, and spends time working out logic puzzles.

> I can easily compute numbers in my head.
> Math and science are my favorite subjects.
> I enjoy brainteasers.

3. **Visual-Spatial.** The ability to perceive and represent the world accurately in line, shape, form, and space. This relies on the sense of sight and the ability to create internal mental images and pictures. A spatially intelligent individual is involved in artistic activities, easily reads maps and charts and diagrams, can draw accurate representations of people or things, and can rearrange a room perfectly.

> I often see visual images when I close my eyes.
> I can generally find my way around a new place.
> I like to draw or doodle.

4. **Bodily-Kinesthetic.** The ability to use the body and physical movement. This ability involves a keen mind and body awareness and excellent control of voluntary movements. This kind of person does well in competitive sports, is often seen fidgeting or twitching while sitting in a chair, and works skillfully with projects involving fine motor movements.

> I would describe myself as well coordinated.
> I love physical activity.
> I need to touch things to learn.

5. **Musical-Rhythmic.** The ability to understand musical technique and to respond emotionally to music. This involves a recognition of tonal patterns, a sensitivity to rhythms and beats, and an appreciation for the structure of music. This type of person can usually play a musical instrument, remember the melodies of songs, and sing to themselves.

> I have a nice singing voice.
> I play with a band.
> I can easily keep time to a piece of music.

6. **Interpersonal.** The ability to organize people and communicate well. This involves the ability to notice and make distinctions among individuals and a sensitivity to others' moods, temperaments, motivations, and feelings. This type of person has a lot of friends, is extremely social, and is involved in many activities.

> I have at least three close friends.
> People come to me for advice.
> I feel comfortable in a crowd.

7. **Intrapersonal.** The ability to assess one's own strengths and talents and the capacity to examine one's own feelings and an awareness of spiritual realities. This intelligence allows deep concentration and metacognition. This type of person reacts with strong personal opinions, appears to be living in her own world, and likes to be alone pursuing her own interests.

> I spend time meditating and like being alone.
> I am independent minded.
> I keep some things totally to myself.

8. **Naturalist.** The ability to recognize and classify flora, fauna, cultural artifacts, and so forth. This involves the ability to readily notice characteristics and patterns and to sense appropriate categories as well as the capacity to group

items and the desire to collect items from nature. Although one would naturally assume that this intelligence is manifested in natural settings, Gardner speculates that in today's world, you would recognize this intelligence in people who can recognize, sort, and organize such things as baseball cards, cars, or shoes.

I enjoy rocks, plants, and animals.

I collect and trade sports cards.

I understand the links in nature.

As you can see, there are ways you can be intelligent that are far removed from just math and language skills. So where do you fit into all of this? Do you know which of these is your obvious strength? Do you have an area that is especially weak? None of us has only one intelligence. We are complex beings and have a sprinkling of several intelligences—stronger in some, weaker in others. Enjoy finding out more about your own intelligences.

INTELLIGENCE(S)   3.3

This experience will help you discover the strengths among your peers. The activity is based on the premise that each of you has a special gift, your intelligence(s). Each of the items below is linked to one of the eight intelligences you have learned about. Take this sheet and find people who can actually *do* these things (only one person per task). If they can, pencil in their names in the lines preceding each task.

Find someone who can:

_____ Whistle a few notes from the "Star Spangled Banner"

_____ Stand on one foot with closed eyes for at least five seconds

_____ Draw a picture that shows how a machine works

_____ Tell you the details of a dream he or she had recently

_____ Explain the logic behind this numerical sequence: 43, 37, 32, 28, 25

_____ Honestly say he or she is relaxed and comfortable relating to other people during this activity

_____ Happily spend a weekend outdoors rather than go to clubs and movies with friends

_____ Recite at least six lines from a popular song

Later, see if you can link the eight intelligences to the particular tasks completed. Have fun.

WRITING

Prescription for Learning

Are you really sure that a floor can't also be a ceiling?

—M. C. Escher

You have learned about two ways to look at yourself—learning styles and multiple intelligences. Thoughtful analysis of these two ways of assessing the way you think and do things should give you a better understanding of your needs as a learner as well as help you identify the most successful ways for you to approach learning situations.

Imagine that you are a doctor whose specialty is working with college students. For many of your patients, life in academia consists of an ongoing series of nagging frustrations, recurring cases of the "hohums," and a sense that something needs to be "fixed." A student comes to you complaining of major problems in the academic areas of her life. As usual, you administer two tests—the learning style inventory and the multiple intelligence assessment.

In a two-page paper, summarize the student's background and basic complaints and then write *two* prescriptions for academic change.

1. A prescription for the student to facilitate her learning
2. A prescription for the faculty members who work with this student

The key to this assignment is that the prescriptions you make should be based on the tests *you* recently took. Pretend that you are both the doctor and the patient. You are analyzing your personal learning style and intelligence and prescribing a creative prescription for both yourself and your faculty over the course of your academic lives together.

CASH IN ON EDUCATION

Bruce B. Ibbetson

1980 and 1984 Olympic rowing teams

An undergraduate degree will rarely, by itself, provide the final skills and knowledge necessary to be successful in life. What it will do is provide the crucial foundation from which to build your life. The college experience equips a person with the ability and confidence to keep learning! It, in fact, trains you how to learn. It provides you the tools to investigate, question, and find solutions to problems you can't even dream about yet. Can you be successful without college? Certainly. Does success come more easily with college? Absolutely.

Winning an Olympic silver medal and having a great wife, two fantastic teenage girls, a million-dollar house, and a partnership in a successful commercial real estate investment company are not the result of a B.S. in biology from UC Irvine. These things are, however, the direct result of learning how to learn. Since I am, in most cases, a slow learner, I can emphatically state with confidence that without my college experience, my rate of gaining success would very nearly equal a slow boat to nowhere.

CHAPTER FOUR

Values and Perspectives

Objectives

- to discover what you value
- to understand different perspectives
- to grasp the effects of gender, race, and culture

"On our journey, now and then,
Till we find our way again,
Down the road we make today."

SNAPSHOT

SNAPSHOT

SNAPSHOT

SNAPSHOT

SNAPSHOT

SNAPSHOT

For all of you who thought you knew . . .

I am what I am; this is me. And you can try as hard as you want and you can believe what you *think* you see, but you will never really understand who I am just by looking at me. Am I just another face in the crowd? Or am I just another Japanese girl that everyone looks at with their stereotypes?

Innocent, shy, stuck-up, boring, smart, Japanese girl; these are the titles I was born into before I was even given a chance to earn them. Is that what you really see, or is that what you want to see? I guess I understand why you look at me this way. My Japanese mother brought me up to be humble and diligent, and it is in my nature to be a little shy around people I don't know. People often think Japanese girls like myself look like snobs because we are so reticent and we stick together. So because I am shy, I somehow end up being labeled as a snob that none of those people want to deal with? And they call *us* stuck-up?!

People shouldn't allow themselves to be so ignorant as to critique others with stereotypes before they get to know the person. People who stereotype me have an expectation of how I should be. *Oh . . . , look at the rich Japanese girl. Spoiled, stuck-up brat. She thinks she's so smart. She probably has her whole life set for her. She just has it so easy.*

So, what would you say if you found out these things were untrue? What would you think if I told you I came from a middle-class family with barely enough money to send one child to college, let alone three? What if I told you I wasn't an exceptional student, but just among the average struggling to get a B? What would you say if I told you I don't know what I want to do with my life and just thinking about my future scares me? I have no advantages over any-one else just because I am Japanese.

I am what I am. I am not a stereotype. I am me. If you look past everything you heard and everything you assumed when you first looked at me, you will find a real person. You will find someone as human, as American, and as real as yourself. I have my issues and I am often judged as you are often judged.

So go on thinking what you want to think about me because, no matter what, I'll always be here just being me. I am what I am. I am American. I am a Japanese-American, and I am a part of your world, too.

—First-year student

Information Literacy and Values, Perspectives, and Methodology

Viewing the world dualistically (good–bad, right–wrong, true–false) camouflages the richness of the world in which we live. How often have we heard someone say, "Well, that's one way to look at it"? Values, perspectives, and methodology are about point of view. These things create the context by which we find, use, understand, and evaluate information. Very few of us are "blank slates" about anything. We have opinions about almost everything. These opinions are created from values.

Values are ethical or moral principles that we think are important. Our values are most easily defined by what we think is right or wrong. We make definitions for such things as integrity, honesty, goodness, evil, and so forth. Often, when we disagree with information we use, our disagreement is partly based on a mismatch between that information, the values stated or implied in that information, and our own values. We might choose to not use some information because we don't agree with the values we perceive in that information.

Perspective is the way we apply our values to the world around us. It is the context for our understanding. When we decide something is good or bad (a value judgment), how we made that judgment is perspective. What factors did we consider? What data did we use? How did we get that data? How did we interpret that data?

Methodology is the element of scholarship that states how an author's perspective was achieved. When researchers say that they think there is a relationship between two factors and that they will determine if that relationship is true or false by doing a survey, they are beginning a process of making obvious their point of view. The interpretation of the survey results will tell you what they think, why they think it, and on what basis they are thinking it.

Information is influenced by its author's values and perspective. A common criticism of research is that it is "biased." *Bias* means that the author's values and perspective were not connected well to the data being used or the topic being researched. Bias can be avoided by researchers being aware of their own values and different perspectives.

Most topics have a history of being discussed, which is called "discourse." Researchers often use the discourse on their topic to support, reject, or show that they are aware of different perspectives.

To be information literate is to be able to identify what values and perspectives you are using when finding and using information. Is there information you should find that reflects different values and perspectives? Does the information you find use a methodology that you can identify so you can better understand the author's values and perspectives?

VALUES AND PERSPECTIVES

No matter what topic, subject, or issue is being discussed, people come to think what they think based on many variables. These can include their family dynamics, ethnic background, place on a socioeconomic scale, religious influences, gender, geography, political disposition, life experiences, and so forth. These variables, in one way or another, guide everyone's values and perspectives.

Learning about other ways of looking at life, and reading about or discussing multiple points of view, will unquestionably be some of the most important facets of your educational experience in college. Therefore, as you learn new

To become open to multiple layers of vision is to be both practical and empathic.

MARY CATHERINE BATESON

things, make sure that you are not agreeing with a statement just because it agrees with your own point of view, sounds good, or has been said by someone who is considered an expert. Obviously, when you hear something that fits your own view of things, it is easy simply to agree. Or, when you read something in a text or hear an authority on a subject say something, it is equally as comfortable to agree with this new viewpoint.

Instead of doing either of these—holding your own views as infallible or blindly taking a new point of view from an "expert," begin to question new information. When reading a text, listening to a lecture, or participating in a class group discussion, ask yourself these questions: What is this person trying to say? What kind of variables in this person's life might have an effect on his way of thinking? Does this person have his facts straight? Is he arguing from evidence or just from assumptions? Do his ideas balance or is his argument based on a one-sided view of an issue?

Throughout this chapter, you will be introduced to various ways of looking at the world. You will also be involved in some activities to help you focus on your own values and perspectives in relation to your peers. Keep in mind that the way we think and what we know are ever changing. In fact, an exciting aspect of learning is being able to understand the "other"—someone else's point of view, perception, or "take" on the world—and then compare that to our own. From this, you find the meaning of information, the beginning of knowledge.

1. Divide into groups. Read the "Alligator River" story

2. After reading the story, each individual is to rank the five characters—Abigail, Gregory, Sluggo, Ivan, and Sinbad—in order of *most* to *least* likable.

_____

_____

_____

_____

_____

3. Share the individual ranking within your group.

4. Take about 15 minutes to come up with a group ranking. This time can be spent attempting to change one another's minds about the ranking of the characters.

5. After the ranking is completed, the whole class should have a discussion about the reasons behind the ranking. How did individual values and perspectives modify each ranking?

_____

_____

_____

_____

_____

Alligator River

Once upon a time there was a woman named Abigail, who was in love with a man named Gregory. Gregory lived on the shore of a river. Abigail lived on the opposite shore of the river. The river that separated the two lovers was teeming with man-eating alligators. Abigail wanted to cross the river to be with Gregory. Unfortunately, the bridge had been washed out. So she went to ask Sinbad, a river boat captain, to take her across. He said he would be glad to if she would consent to go to bed with him preceding the voyage. She promptly refused and went to a friend named Ivan to explain her plight. Ivan did not want to be involved at all in the situation. Abigail felt her only alternative was to accept Sinbad's terms. Sinbad fulfilled his promise to Abigail and delivered her into the arms of Gregory.

When she told Gregory about her amorous escapade in order to cross the river, Gregory cast her aside with disdain. Heartsick and dejected, Abigail turned to Sluggo with her tale of woe. Sluggo, feeling compassion for Abigail, sought out Gregory and beat him brutally. Abigail was overjoyed at the sight of Gregory getting his due. As the sun sets on the horizon, we hear Abigail laughing at Gregory.

Journal Entry 8

In Activity 4.1, you were asked to rank the story's characters first as an individual and then as a group. Group ranking was facilitated by persuading individual members to compromise their original opinions in order to reach consensus.

In your journal, write on one or more of the following prompts:

1. What happened as your group went through the process of coming to an agreement? Reflect on your reaction to this process.

2. Were you most often a *persuader* or a *compromiser* in the decision-making process? How did you feel about your work in the group? In what ways is being *willing to compromise* a good trait? In what ways is it a negative trait? What were some of the most effective methods of persuading group members? What were some of the least effective? What traits are need to be a persuader? A compromiser?

3. List some common activities that require the compromise of individual opinion to achieve group goals.

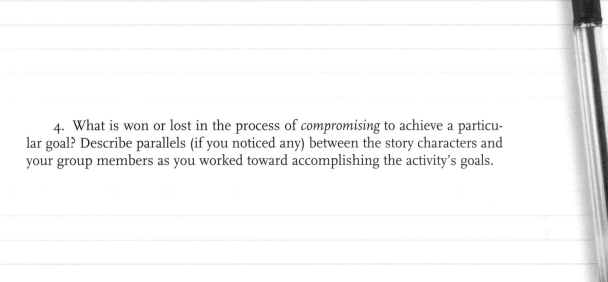

4. What is won or lost in the process of *compromising* to achieve a particular goal? Describe parallels (if you noticed any) between the story characters and your group members as you worked toward accomplishing the activity's goals.

Much of what we value or think has been taught to us by others—our families, schools, church groups, peers. Values commit us to action; we act on what we believe. In other words, what we value guides our decisions and behaviors. However, do you actually know for a fact what you value? Can you articulate your own values easily? Can you prioritize them? Take the time to put the following items in rank order according to your own value system (for example, your top priority would be number 1 and so forth).

_____ having fun

_____ time alone

_____ love

_____ service

_____ family

_____ environment

_____ friends

_____ honesty

_____ integrity

_____ health

_____ safety

_____ peace

_____ religion

_____ money

_____ work

_____ politics

_____ parties

_____ kindness

_____ fairness

_____ laughter

September 11, 2001—Student Writing

The following is a journal entry written a day after the terrorists took down the World Trade Center in New York City, hit a portion of the Pentagon in Washington, D.C., and crashed a plane of passengers in Pennsylvania. After reading this first-year student's response, you will be asked to do a group activity to discover what values you believe were behind the actions of the terrorists.

9-11-01

Ryan Kalei Tsuji

After an event like the one that has just occurred, I begin to wonder if all the little petty things in life are really worth it. We often take life for granted and forget that every day that we have is a blessing in itself. Personally, it's hard to imagine all those people who have lost someone close to them due to these unthinkable acts. I feel that I should appreciate my time with those close to me and really express my love and gratitude that I have for them. I remember thinking just a few days ago about the things I didn't have here with me in college like my car, computer, and other materialistic things that reminded me of home. I was upset because even though these things belonged to me, they weren't here. However, now looking back, I really don't care about the things I do not have, but rather am grateful that I have a life I can appreciate. In life today, we often measure success by the things we own and the way that others perceive us. Instead, it is important that we be grateful every day to have the ability to live another day and spend it with those we love. It's sad to say that an event like this needs to take place in order for me to think that way.

As for the future, I think that the entire world was forever changed yesterday. Nothing will ever be the same, and no longer will people have the mentality that they once did. In a way I do believe that this could be the beginning of the end. Who knows what will happen and how we will react? Will others try to "copy" these events? I just hope that I will be able to raise my children in a world not consumed in fear. I hope that we come together not only as a country, but also as an entire race of humanity, striving to put an end to these times of war and hate.

Get together in small groups, and look over the list of the individual values you checked. Add other things that you value which were not on the list so that you have a long list with which to work.

Now, take some time individually to think about the value system that guided the actions of the terrorists on September 11, 2001 (or any other terrorist action that has occurred in history). Make a list, individually, of the values you think might have been on a terrorist list.

Write your list of terrorist values below:

_____

_____

_____

_____

_____

_____

_____

_____

_____

_____

_____

_____

_____

_____

Now, get back together in your group and compare your individual lists of terrorist values. As a group, see how many of the ones you have chosen match values you first put on your own composite list (that list of values that you as a group decided were most important).

Do you see any of the same values on both lists? Can the same value be construed differently? Can different actions evolve from the same values? Discuss in class.

Journal Entry 9

What is life? It is the flash of a firefly in the night. It is the breath of a buffalo in the wintertime. It is the little shadow which runs across the grass and loses itself in the sunset.

Crowfoot, Blackfoot warrior and orator

People have had many different responses to what occurred on September 11, 2001. Some were angry. Others were frightened. Most everyone was outraged. And, of course, all were very sorry for those directly involved in the attacks.

Spend a few moments thinking back on your own reaction to these events. Draw or write something that captures the essence of your reaction when you heard the news. Then think about how you feel about it now. Have you changed your attitude at all? Why or why not?

WRITING

Want Ads

Before reading the article entitled "The Just-Right Wife," reflect for a moment on what qualities you desire in your chosen life partner.

Men

1. Write an imaginary newspaper want ad and in 25 words or less describe the qualities you would like in an applicant for the position of your partner-to-be.

2. Write a second newspaper want ad—the one that your father might conceivably have written years ago.

3. Write a few sentences on the differences you see between the two ads.

4. Create a checklist of 10 skills or qualities that could be used in a job description.

Women

1. Write an imaginary newspaper want ad in 25 words or less that you would *hope to find* in the newspaper describing the qualities and characteristics that you as a female perceive to be the "just right wife."

2. Write a second ad—the one you would write to describe the applicant for the position of your "just right husband."

3. Create a list of 10 skills or qualities that *you* feel would qualify you as a candidate for the position of the "just right wife."

Share these lists and ads in groups and discuss.

READING

Male and Female Perceptions

Ellen Goodman is very adept at pinpointing the nuances of our lives. In the following article, "The Just-Right Wife," she compares two cultures and, in her usual humorous manner, points out the conflicting viewpoints we have regarding the role of women in our society. She happens to be making a comparison between American and Moslem men and their preferences for wives; however, her article has much wider implications. What might they be?

The Just-Right Wife

Ellen Goodman

The upper-middle-class men of Arabia are looking for just the right kind of wife. Arabia's merchant class, reports the Associated Press, finds the women of Libya too backward, and the women of Lebanon too forward, and have therefore gone shopping for brides in Egypt.

Egyptian women are being married off at the rate of thirty a day—an astonishing increase, according to the Egyptian marriage bureau. It doesn't know whether to be pleased or alarmed at the popularity of its women. According to one recent Saudi Arabian groom, the Egyptian women are "just right."

"The Egyptian woman is the happy medium," says Aly Abdul el-Korrary of his bride, Wafaa Ibrahiv (the happy medium herself was not questioned). "She is not too inhibited as they are in conservative Moslem societies, and not too liberal like many Lebanese."

Is this beginning to sound familiar? Well, the upper-middle-class, middle-aged, merchant-professional-class man of America also wants a "happy medium" wife. He is confused. He, too, has a problem and he would like us to be more understanding.

If it is no longer chic for a sheik to marry a veiled woman, it is somehow no longer "modern" for a successful member of the liberal establishment to be married to what he used to call a "housewife" and what he now hears called a "household drudge."

As his father once wanted a wife who had at least started college, now he would like a wife who has a mind, and even a job, of her own. The younger men in his office these days wear their wives' occupations on their sleeves. He thinks he, too, would like a wife—especially for social occasions—whose status would be his status symbol. A lady lawyer would be nice.

These men, you understand, now say (at least in private to younger working women in their office) that they are bored with women who "don't do anything." No matter how much some of them conspired in keeping them at home Back Then, many are now saying, in the best Moslem style, "I divorce thee." They are replacing them with more up-to-date models. A Ph.D. candidate would be nice.

The upper-middle-class, middle-aged man of today wants a wife who won't make him feel guilty. He doesn't want to worry if she's happy. He doesn't want to hear her complain about her dusty American history degree. He doesn't want to know if she's crying at the psychiatrist's office. He most definitely doesn't want to be blamed. He wants her to fulfill herself already! He doesn't mean that maliciously.

On the other hand, Lord knows, he doesn't want a wife who is too forward. The Saudi Arabian merchant believes that the Egyptian woman adapts more easily to his moods and needs.

The American merchant also wants a woman who adapts herself to his moods and needs—his need for an independent woman and a traditional wife.

He doesn't want to live with a "household drudge," but it would be nice to have an orderly home and well-scrubbed children. Certainly he wouldn't want a wife who got high on folding socks—he is not a Neanderthal—but it would be nice if she arranged for these things to get done. Without talking about marriage contracts.

He wants a wife who agreed that "marriage is a matter of give and take, not a business deal and 50-50 chores." It would help if she had just enough conflict herself (for not being her mother) to feel more than half the guilt for a full ashtray.

Of course, he sincerely would like her to be involved in her own work and life. But on the other hand, he doesn't want it to siphon away her energy for him. He needs to be taken care of, nurtured. He would like her to enjoy her job, but be ready to move for his, if necessary (after, of course, a long discussion in which he feels awful about asking and she ends up comforting him and packing).

He wants a wife who is a sexually responsive and satisfied woman, and he would even be pleased if she initiated sex with him. Sometimes. Not too often, however, because then he would get anxious.

He is confused, but he does, in all sincerity (status symbols aside), want a happy marriage to a happy wife. A happy medium. He is not sure exactly what he means, but he, too, would like a wife who is "just right."

The difference is that when the upper-middle-class, middle-aged man of Arabia wants his wife he goes out and buys one. His American "brother" can only offer himself as the prize.

READING

Differences are not only due to one's being male or female. Our varied perspectives are derived from our family background, race, ethnicity, religious views, and so much more. In Jesus Colon's story, you will find a concisely written synopsis of an event that was extremely significant to his life. As you read through the essay think about all of the things he is writing about: racism . . . prejudice . . . what else?

Little Things Are Big

Jesus Colon

It was very late at night on the eve of Memorial Day. She came into the subway at the 34th Street Pennsylvania Station. I am still trying to remember how she managed to push herself in with a baby on her right arm, a valise in her left hand and two children, a boy and gal about three and five years old, trailing after her. She was a nice looking white lady in her early twenties.

At Nevins Street, Brooklyn, we saw her preparing to get off at the next station—Atlantic Avenue—which happened to be the place where I too had to get off. Just as it was a problem for her to get on, it was going to a problem for her to get off the subway with two small children to be taken care of, a baby on her right arm and a medium sized valise in her left hand.

And there I was, also preparing to get off at Atlantic Avenue, with no bundles to take care of—not even the customary book under my arm without which I feel that I am not completely dressed.

As the train was entering the Atlantic Avenue station, some white man stood up from his seat and helped her out, placing the children on the long, deserted platform. There were only two adult persons on the long platform some time after midnight on the eve of last Memorial Day.

I could perceive the steep, long concrete stairs going down to the Long Island Railroad or into the street. Should I offer my help as the American white man did at the subway door placing the two children outside the subway car? Should I take care of the girl and the boy, take them by their hands until they reached the end of the steep long concrete stairs of the Atlantic Avenue station?

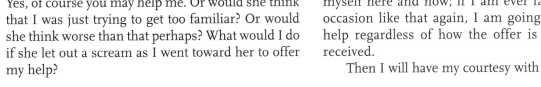

Courtesy is a characteristic of the Puerto Rican. And here I was—a Puerto Rican—hours past midnight, a valise, two white children and a white lady with a baby on her arm palpably needing somebody to help her at least until she descended the long concrete stairs.

But how could I, a Negro and a Puerto Rican, approach this white lady who very likely might have preconceived prejudices against Negroes and everybody with foreign accents, in a deserted subway station very late at night?

What would she say? What would be the first reaction of this white American woman, perhaps coming from a small town, with a valise, two children and a baby on her right arm? Would she say: Yes, of course you may help me. Or would she think that I was just trying to get too familiar? Or would she think worse than that perhaps? What would I do if she let out a scream as I went toward her to offer my help?

Was I misjudging her? So many slanders are written every day in the daily press against the Negroes and Puerto Ricans. I hesitated for a long, long minute. The ancestral manners that the most illiterate Puerto Rican passes on from father to son were struggling inside me. Here was I, way past midnight, face to face with a situation that could very well explode into an outburst of prejudices and chauvinistic conditioning of the "divide and rule" policy of present day society.

It was a long minute. I passed on by her as if I saw nothing. As if I was insensitive to her need. Like a rude animal walking on two legs, I just moved on half running by the long subway platform leaving the children and the valise and her with the baby on her arm. I took the steps of the long concrete stairs in twos until I reached the street above and the cold air slapped my warm face.

This is what racism and prejudice and chauvinism and official artificial divisions can do to people and to a nation!

Perhaps the lady was not prejudiced after all. Or not prejudiced enough to scream at the coming of a Negro toward her at a solitary subway station a few hours past midnight.

If you were not that prejudiced, I failed you, dear lady. I know that there is a chance in a million that you will read these lines. I am willing to take that millionth chance. If you were not that prejudiced, I failed you, lady. I failed you, children. I failed myself to myself.

I buried my courtesy early on Memorial Day morning. But here is a promise that I make to myself here and now; if I am ever faced with an occasion like that again, I am going to offer my help regardless of how the offer is going to be received.

Then I will have my courtesy with me again.

Journal Entry 10

Responses to situations often are based on experience. Jesus Colon had no way of knowing how the young mother would react to his offer to help—thus, his dilemma. Try to respond in two different ways. Imagine that you are the young mother, and write a short note to the young Puerto Rican man. Did he do the right thing to let you struggle that night, or had you hoped he would offer the help you needed? What insight can you share with him in a short note?

Second, try to put yourself in the place of the young Puerto Rican man. Do you think his reaction to the situation was warranted? If so, why? Write a note to the young mother explaining the reasons for your actions. Tell her what she could have done to have your encounter end differently.

The National Anthem

Oh, say, can you see, by the dawn's early light,

What so proudly we hailed at the twilight's last gleaming?

Whose broad stripes and bright stars, thro' the perilous fight

O'er the ramparts we watched, were so gallantly streaming?

And the rockets' red glare, the bombs bursting in air,

Gave proof through the night that our flag was still there.

Oh, say, does that star-spangled banner yet wave

O'er the land of the free and the home of the brave?

On the shore dimly seen, thro' the mists of the deep,

Where the foe's haughty host in dread silence reposes,

What is that which the breeze, o'er the towering steep,

As it fitfully blows, half conceals, half discloses?

Now it catches the gleam of the morning's first beam,

In full glory reflected, now shines on the stream:

'Tis the star-spangled banner; oh, long may it wave

O'er the land of the free and the home of the brave.

And where is that band who so vauntingly swore

That the havoc of war and the battle's confusion

A home and a country should leave us no more?

Their blood has wash'd out their foul footsteps' pollution.

No refuge could save the hireling and slave

From the terror of flight or the gloom of the grave,

And the star-spangled banner in triumph doth wave

O'er the land of the free and the home of the brave.

Oh, thus be it ever when free men shall stand,

Between their loved homes and the war's desolation;

Blest with vict'ry and peace, may the heav'n-rescued land

Praise the Power that has made and preserved us a nation!

Then conquer we must, when our cause it is just,

And this be our motto: "In God is our trust!"

And the star-spangled banner in triumph shall wave

O'er the land of the free and the home of the brave!

Did you know the words to the national anthem? Even the words to the first verse? It is amazing how many people really don't remember the actual words or why they might have been written in the first place. The next section of this chapter focuses on differences of opinion about being "American." Listen carefully to the voices you hear.

The next article, "I Forgot the Words to the National Anthem," explores both political discrimination (due to international politics related to Iranian revolution at the time) and xenophobia (unreasonable fear or hatred of foreigners or strangers).

James Seilsopour, an American by birth but only recently emigrated from Iran with his family to seek political asylum in his country of birth, lived his high school years excluded from the typical American teenager's life because of political discrimination and xenophobia. He loved apple pie, fast cars, and beautiful American movie stars but came to understand that he could not participate fully in the life of the typical American teenager. He existed outside the circle of the general community's acceptance.

I Forgot the Words to the National Anthem

James Seilsopour

The bumper sticker read, "Piss on Iran."

To me, a fourteen-year-old living in Teheran, the Iranian revolution was nothing more than an inconvenience. Although the riots were just around the corner, although the tanks lined the streets, although a stray bullet went through my sister's bedroom window, I was upset because I could not ride at the Royal Stable as often as I used to. In the summer of 1979 my family—father, mother, brothers, sister, aunt, and two cousins—were forced into exile. We came to Norco, California.

In Iran, I was an American citizen and considered myself an American, even though my father was Iranian. I loved baseball and apple pie and knew the words to the "Star-Spangled Banner." That summer before high school, I was like any other kid my age; I listened to rock 'n roll, liked fast cars, and thought Farrah Fawcett was a fox. Excited about going to high school, I was looking forward to football games and school dances. But I learned that it was not meant to be. I was not like other kids, and it was a long, painful road I traveled as I found this out.

The American embassy in Iran was seized the fall I started high school. I did not realize my life would be affected until I read that bumper sticker in the high school parking lot that read, "Piss on Iran." At that moment I knew there would be no football games or school dances. For me, Norco High consisted of the goat ropers, the dopers, the jocks, the brains, and one quiet Iranian.

I was sitting in my photography class after the hostages were taken. The photography teacher was fond of showing travel films. On this particular day, he decided to show a film about Iran, knowing full well that my father was Iranian and that I grew up in Iran. During the movie, this teacher encouraged the students to make comments. Around the room, I could hear "Drop the bomb" and "Deport the mothers." Those words hurt. I felt dirty, guilty. However, I managed to laugh and assure the students I realized they were just joking. I went home that afternoon and cried. I have long since forgiven those students, but I have not and can never forgive that teacher. Paranoia set in. From then on, every whisper was about me: "You see that lousy son of a bitch? He's Iranian." When I was not looking, I could feel their pointing fingers in my back like arrows. Because I was absent one day, the next day I brought a note to the attendance office. The secretary read the note, then looked at me. "So you're Jim Seilsopour?" I couldn't answer.

As I walked away, I thought I heard her whisper to her co-worker, "You see that lousy son of a bitch? He's Iranian." I missed thirty-five days of school that year.

My problems were small compared to those of my parents. In Teheran, my mother had been a lady of society. We had a palatial house and a maid. Belonging to the women's club, she collected clothes for the poor and arranged Christmas parties for the young American kids. She and my father dined with high government officials. But back in the States, when my father could not find a job, she had to work at a fast-food restaurant. She was the proverbial pillar of strength. My mother worked seventy hours a week for two years. I never heard her complain. I could see the toll the entire situation was taking on her. One day my mother and I went grocery shopping at Stater Brothers Market. After an hour of carefully picking our food, we proceeded to the cashier. The cashier was friendly and began a conversation with my mother. They spoke briefly of the weather as my mother wrote the check. The cashier looked at the check and casually asked, "What kind of name is that?" My mother said, "Italian." We exchanged glances for just a second. I could see the pain in her eyes. She offered no excuses; I asked for none.

Because of my father's birthplace, he was unable to obtain a job. A naturalized American citizen with a master's degree in aircraft maintenance engineering from the Northrop Institute of Technology, he had never been out of work in his life. My father had worked for Bell Helicopter International, Flying Tigers, and McDonnell Douglas. Suddenly, a man who literally was at the top of his field was unemployable. There is one incident that haunts me even today. My mother had gone to work, and all the kids had gone to school except me. I was in the bathroom washing my face. The door was open, and I could see my father's reflection in the mirror. For no particular reason I watched him. He was glancing at a newspaper. He carefully folded the paper and set it aside. For several long moments he stared blankly into space. With a resigned sigh, he got up, went into the kitchen, and began doing the dishes. On that day, I know I watched a part of my father die.

My father did get a job. However, he was forced to leave the country. He is a quality control inspector for Saudi Arabian Airlines in Jeddah, Saudi Arabia. My mother works only forty hours a week now. My family has survived, financially and emotionally. I am not bitter, but the memories are. I have not recovered totally; I can never do that.

And no, I have never been to a high school football game or dance. The strike really turned me off to baseball. I have been on a diet for the last year, so I don't eat apple pie much anymore. And I have forgotten the words to the national anthem.

Journal Entry 11

Sometimes I feel discriminated against, but it does not make me angry. It merely astonishes me. How can they deny themselves the pleasure of my company? It's beyond me.

Zora Neale Hurston

Have you ever had the experience of the "outsider," the newcomer, the different one? Have you ever been excluded from a community by insiders? Have you ever experienced political, racial, sexual, religious, or another form of discrimination and had to endure being barred from the "good life" that others were experiencing at that moment? Share the story of your being different and excluded. Add a graphic representing how you felt.

READING

The following two short essays address identity. They were both written by first-year students in response to the question Who are you?

I am an American. I am not confused nor conceited. I was born in one country, with only one body, how can I be more? From the outermost layer of my skin, to the deepest crevice of my soul, my labeling be American. There were people before me, my family, those responsible for my life. They were from other countries. They are not me, nor am I them, so why should I be labeled by their origin. Men have traveled since the beginning of time, and supposedly, life began in one place. Should I call myself every name that has ever been thrown upon a particular section of land? I won't I, being me and responsible for me, will call myself what I am, and that is American. I am related in many ways, to what some may refer to as German, Hawaiian, Italian, American Indian, and many others. Why should I have to be so many individuals, when I see only one body belonging to me? Upon American soil I was born, so an American I will die. I am no traitor; to my past, nor myself; American blood will be what sustains my existence, for now and for always. Simple fact.

Garrett Dearing

I am American. I am Hawaiian. I am Chinese. I am what I am. I am considered to be lazy by the white mainlanders. But who are they to criticize when I am like them, an American. I am the Big Island girl, Waimanalo tita and Kailua chick. Pake eyes and pake hair with brown skin and pigeon language. Because I am not like you or others, people categorize me as Mexican or Indian. I am what I am. I am Hawaiian-Chinese.

Hey! Menehunes look at her, she is in college! I am a real and true Hawaiian and I am in college. Supposed to be lazy eh? Then why am I in college? Hawaiians are hard workers, but more so with hands. Haoles work hard but only with their mouth. I am looked upon as dumb and as the lower class of our society. However, I am just like all of you unless you are not American. Yes, I am what I am. I am Hawaiian-Chinese.

I may be different in ways that I live my life. I eat raw fish, poi, kalua pig, laulau, and yes—even spam. Sometimes when I talk Haoles don't understand. I have broken English and Hawaiian slang. Although I look Chinese, my culture is Hawaiian, and I live in the U. S. I am what I am. I am Hawaiian, Chinese, and a U. S. American.

Shalia Kamakele

Journal Entry 12

Humankind has not woven the web of life. We are but one thread within it. Whatever we do to the web, we do to ourselves. All things are bound together. All things connect.

Chief Seattle

After reading the writing of Garrett Dearing and Shalia Kamakele, think about your own notion of this place we call America and your place in it. Have you ever given it much thought? Try your hand at writing a freeform poem or essay describing your reaction to the two essays. Then write about your own definition of being an American, or a particular race, ethnicity, religion, or other distinction you feel.

CASH IN ON EDUCATION

Looking Backward . . . Four Decades Later

David Earl Kaleoikaika Cooper
President and CEO, Hana Engineering, Inc.

It was a beautiful day in Hawaii, just your typical day, on September 8, 1959. I was wedged in between two eager-looking college freshmen in the sixth row on our first day on campus and in our first class of the morning—nearly 1,000 students for World Civilization 101. I was in awe, and maybe a little scared, as I glanced up the slopes to row 110, which then seemed like the great Mauna Kea Mountain. No question that I felt I should have been outdoors or at least playing volleyball on the beach.

Shortly a rather pleasant looking professor walked on to the raised platform, and without his raising a finger, the mass fell silent. But I was ready, pencil out, and prepared to write furiously and just as fast as he could lecture. Curiously, he walked the length of the platform and back staring at us. I was hoping he would see that I was prepared—just pump it out. History, that is.

Then he spoke.

As I look back to that morning, my very first day at a university and my very first class as a freshman, the professor's words continue to ring out to me. The moment jolted me, it created a significant psychological event that was to be repeated only seldom in my lifetime, and it caused me to make a choice between looking forward, to the future and whatever it may bring, or contenting myself with wishing I could have been or would have done just if . . .

Now, nine years from having said farewell to the U. S. Army as a general officer after 30 years of service and launching a successful national nonprofit organization, starting two thriving businesses, and serving on boards and committees that support our communities, I still take time to remember in more tranquil settings, perhaps, that day of September 8, 1959.

"Look around you, to the person directly to your front, the person to your back, the person to your left, and the person to your right. At the end of your first semester in this university, only two of you will be back for World Civilization 102; at the end of your freshman year, perhaps a third of you will go on to graduate in four years."

That was it—short, straightforward, no frills, no long philosophical defense, no presentation of statistical analyses, and no questions taken. Just, here it is— education is hard work, it demands sacrifice, it does not tolerate short-term goals, it requires a lifelong commitment, and once begun, it changes your world.

No one had ever said this to me or to my friends—no counselor, no teacher, no mentor, no advisor.

I had worked all summer, starting the very next day after graduation from high school, at $1.20 an hour for 12 to 14 hours a day just to make enough money for my first year of college. Even slept on the sidewalk because I could not get a ride home. And on my very first day in my very first class, I was looking at failure. I had a choice to make.

The university years tend to be the best years of your life simply because they are exciting, challenging, filled with new ideas and concepts, stressful, and fun; they give you a small glimpse into who you are and where you could go; and they provide you with life's experiences as memorable events. They give you a lot of tools for your tool kit in your journey to be all you dream, achieve all you believe, and make a difference with your life.

Taking the first step for me happened that September 8, and I haven't looked back.

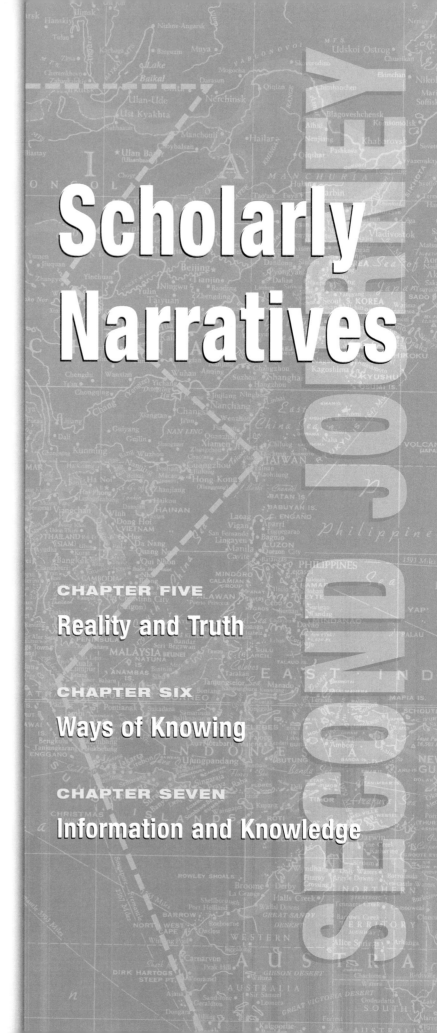

Scholarly Narratives

SECOND JOURNEY

SOUVENIR

The Restaurant Story

I learned early in my career that the personal narrative is crucial to making the move into understanding the scholarly.

In one of my first years teaching in a learning community, I invited members of the community to become mentors to my students. These people agreed to meet with up to three students monthly— for lunch, breakfast, a chat, job shadowing, or other appropriate activities. When my students first met their mentors, I came along to introduce them. After that, they were on their own. One such meeting was held at a fancy steak house. I joined three students (one female and two male) and an airline president for lunch. There was a lively discussion among the male students and the president, who had also been a pilot. The female student was silent and gently picked at her blackened ahi salad. The guys asked her, "Hey, have you ever been off the island?" She responded "No." "Oh," they said, "well, how about on a boogie board?" "Yes," she replied. "Oh, and what about a canoe?" "Yes," she said, "I've been on a canoe." "Oh, OK, so you've been off the island!"

I grinned inside at this banter but was also sorry she had never had the opportunity to travel away from her island home. Soon after

Introduction to the Second Journey

Just as personal narratives are stories that inform your lives, scholarly narratives are stories that enlighten you. There are distinct reasons that institutions of higher education require you to sample a wide variety of scholarly information. Outlining some of these reasons here should help you move into the realm of scholarly narratives with a better notion of why you should do so.

Your college curriculum is grounded in solid educational philosophy. The general core of courses that you are required to take are a reflection of this philosophy. Certain skills and competencies will be crucial to your ability to transfer your education to the marketplace and to your life. You learn these by delving into the diversity of courses within a liberal arts curriculum. Some of the more important skills you need to develop are:

- **Communication (written, oral, visual).** This includes organizing your thoughts, conducting research (whether serious academic or just planning a vacation), articulating your ideas to others, and defending a position you might take. This skill allows you to define, list, name, explain, and describe. Courses that help can be found in composition, communications, literature, and speech. Of course, you can learn these skills in many other classes.

- **Argumentation.** You need to learn to think critically, understand the impact of ideas from around the world, formulate problems clearly, and find hidden assumptions and values. Often you learn these in political science, philosophy, history, and economics courses.

- **Analytical skills.** Problem solving, logical thinking, and understanding how to use statistics are emphasized in literature, philosophy, mathematics, and science courses. Using this skill allows you to differentiate, compare, analyze, plan, design, and create as well as critique, evaluate, assess, and judge information.

- **Multicultural understanding.** Being flexible and adaptable, relating well with others, and setting aside your biases and prejudices can be learned in anthropology, psychology, sociology, and other social science courses.

- **Historical perspective.** It is important to learn about the past in order to understand the future, to appreciate cultural diversity, to understand social issues and movements, and to be able to predict historical trends. These skills are often learned in history, literature, and social science classes.

- **Aesthetic appreciation.** Understanding the visual representation of ideas and the sensitivities of peoples around the world through music, art, and general humanities is an important aspect of a liberal education.

this conversation, the airline president turned to the young lady and told her he would indeed make certain that she could leave the island and finally fly somewhere. She was surprised, and I was completely delighted. I almost patted myself on the back for being such an excellent teacher and bringing these people together. What an opportunity she was going to have!

As we left the restaurant, the young woman came over to me. She tugged at my jacket sleeve and said, "Dr. Watts! Dr. Watts! That's the first time I've ever been in a restaurant!"

I was silent. She followed with a statement about having driven through a fast-food place a few times with her family. I was still silent. I was remembering her looking at the menu, ordering something that she didn't understand or enjoy, being quiet during the two-hour lunch, listening but not participating. I was ashamed and embarrassed at having visions of flying her to Paris and yet not attending to the fact that she was at that very moment experiencing something new. Just being in that restaurant was moving outside her comfort zone.

This began my commitment to ensuring that students would have the opportunity to bring their stories to me before I introduced them to the stories of scholars. I hope you have all had the opportunity to do so and are now prepared to move forward into new realms.

- **Scientific inquiry.** Taking courses in mathematics and the sciences helps you acquire problem-solving skills and learn to think logically.

So how does any of this transfer to the marketplace? Imagine how useful the following skills would be in any kind of employment opportunity you face:

- Knowing how to write reports
- Feeling confident about making presentations
- Readily responding to issues
- Thinking on your feet
- Evaluating business plans
- Analyzing marketing trends
- Presenting and evaluating study results
- Imagining new possibilities
- Interacting with diverse colleagues
- Knowing the customs of other cultures
- Dealing with public relations
- Understanding employee benefits
- Proposing solutions to problems
- Knowing how to supervise others
- Quantifying and synthesizing information

The next three chapters tackle the concept of knowledge and provide you with strategies for understanding how you know what you know and how to be critical of new information you encounter. This journey begins by asking you to evaluate reality and then offers you a number of strategies to understand how you know what you know. After you are familiar with "ways of knowing," you will encounter a discussion about the differences between information and knowledge. This is in final preparation for your learning to understand scholarship—what it is, how it is created, how you interact with it, and how you learn from it.

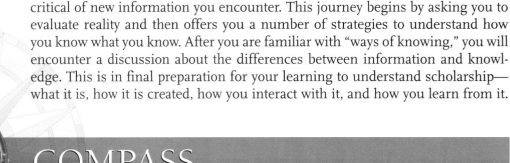

COMPASS

There are a lot of things you don't know about yourself until you give back to people who need things more than you.

The first few chapters of this text spent a lot of time helping you learn about yourself. What are your stories? How do you learn? Why do you think about the world the way you do? The readings, writing, and activities were geared to help you explore your own place in the world.

While you are doing this, it can be very useful to connect your experiences to those of others, not necessarily just your immediate family and friends. By encountering and comparing other versions of experience—other people's realities and the truths they see for themselves—you will see that perspectives and values are dependent on context.

Consider your time in some service learning project as a privilege. This kind of learning allows you to enter, if only peripherally, another person's reality, and with this privilege you will be able to reach into a diversity of visions and ways of looking at the world.

Reality is not an absolute. Yours is different from that of the person sitting next to you. What better way to begin to understand how the differing realities—and subsequently, the truths—come to be than by spending some time, albeit borrowed, in others' worlds. You derive insight from putting experiences—yours and others—together and allowing an integration to occur.

CHAPTER FIVE

Reality and Truth

Objectives

- to comprehend the notion of reality

- to understand how you might know something is real

- to discover the notion of virtual reality

"It doesn't matter where you start, It only matters that you do, . . ."

Imagine seeing all the atrocities of the world and hearing the sounds of all the things that have gone wrong in a generation. Then, once you have a good idea of the negative aspects, imagine seeing all the good in the world, with clouds, hopes, dreams, and pleasant music to accompany it all. An exhibit on Generation X done by college students, teachers, and third graders left me with a feeling of hopeful reality.

When I first entered the exhibit, the atmosphere was dark and chaotic. There were people all over the place, a multitude of pictures on the walls, and signs in the way of my walking—I was looking for a way out! . . . The visual images really got your attention. A few times I had to do a double take on what I saw. Body art and body love were what I saw; it was very interesting. The audio portion of the exhibit was unbelievable! This was the sound booth, in which everything came to life. It really helped to enhance the images I saw.

The exhibit not only was entertaining but was educational and, most importantly, had a message. That message was that individuals should not X (cross out) a generation without looking at both sides clearly. This message can be related to many things.

—Melody Cole

Information Literacy, Reality, and Truth

"Reality is what you agree with me about." Not exactly. Often reality seems to be what most people agree is "real." However, most people once agreed that the world was flat. As long as most people or "important" people agreed with that statement, the reality was defined as a flat one, at least as far as the planet was concerned. Let's take a look at the concepts of "subjective," "objective," and "evidence."

Subjective means that our personal experience, values, and perspectives are the primary ways that we connect to the world. For example, let's say you are part of a family that loves you, cares about you, and is important to your positive outlook on life. *Objective* means that we are using the experiences, values, and perspectives of others along with our own to connect to the world. Your family is an example of how a family should be, and they tell you that family is why you are so happy. *Evidence* is the way we show that we are using the experiences, values, and perspectives of others. Your friends point out to you the many things your family does to show they love you—your parents tell you they

love you at least once a day, and your teachers tell your parents that you are always eager to learn new things.

Being subjective does not necessarily mean that something is not real, nor does being objective mean that something is real. Evidence doesn't inevitably mean that something is real. Evidence can be biased because of how it was created or used. To be information literate is to apply the concepts of subjective, objective, and evidence to our selection, use, and evaluation of information.

When we read a website or view a television program, can we recognize that a particular set of values and perspectives is being used? Are we able to identify when evidence is being used? Can we determine that the evidence being used shows a relevant connection between values, perspectives, and conclusions? Are enough different values and perspectives being presented so that the conclusions can be considered objective? When we create information, are we being clear about how we are applying the concepts of subjectivity, objectivity, and evidence? By doing so, we are closer to creating and using "real" information.

Journal Entry 13

Fact is an illusion, because every fact is part of a story and is riddled with imagination. Imagination is real because every perception of the world around us is absolutely colored by the narrative or image-filled lens through which we perceive. We are all poets and artists as we live our daily lives, whether or not we recognize this role and whether or not we believe it.

Thomas Moore

In our dreams we are aware of sights, sounds, and sensations. We seemingly "see" colors, "hear" music, "smell" fragrances, and "taste" food. We are aware of our bodies, think about things, and feel emotions, such as fear, happiness, anger, and love. In our dreams we experience people, speaking and interacting with them in other ways. Our dreams seem very real to us, and sometimes after we wake up it takes a while to understand that we were only dreaming. Everything we "sensed" was only a creation of the mind.

Read the quote above, and think about what it means to "believe what you see" rather than "see what you believe." Write on your understanding of this concept. Include an example from your own life that supports your ideas about reality.

READING

The son of a wealthy and noble family, Plato (427–347 B.C.) was preparing for a career in politics when the trial and eventual execution of Socrates (399 B.C.) changed the course of his life. He abandoned his political career and turned to philosophy, opening a school on the outskirts of Athens dedicated to the Socratic search for wisdom. Plato's school, then known as the Academy, was the first university in Western history and operated from 387 B.C. until A.D. 529, when it was closed by Justinian.

Unlike his mentor Socrates, Plato was both a writer and a teacher. His writings are in the form of dialogues, with Socrates as the principal speaker. In the "Allegory of the Cave," Plato describes symbolically the predicament in which mankind finds itself and proposes a way of salvation. The allegory presents, in brief form, most of Plato's major philosophical assumptions: his belief that the world revealed by our senses is not the real world but only a poor copy of it and that the real world can only be apprehended intellectually; his idea that knowledge cannot be transferred from teacher to student, but rather that education consists in directing student's minds toward what is real and important and allowing them to comprehend it for themselves; his faith that the universe ultimately is good; and his conviction that enlightened individuals have an obligation to the rest of society and that a good society must be one in which the truly wise (the Philosopher-King) are the rulers.

The "Allegory of the Cave" can be found in Book VII of Plato's best-known work, *The Republic,* a lengthy dialogue on the nature of justice. Often regarded as a utopian blueprint, *The Republic* is dedicated toward a discussion of the education required of a Philosopher-King.

The following selection is taken from the Benjamin Jowett translation (Vintage, 1991, pp. 253–261). As you read the allegory, try to make a mental picture of the cave Plato describes. Better yet, draw a picture of it and refer to it as you read the selection. In many ways, understanding Plato's "Allegory of the Cave" will make your foray into the world of philosophical thought much less burdensome.

Plato, "Allegory of the Cave"

[Socrates] And now let me show in a figure how far our nature is enlightened or unenlightened: —Behold! Human beings living in a underground cave, which has a mouth open towards the light and reaching all along the cave; here they have been from their childhood, and have their legs and necks chained so that they cannot move, and can only see before them, being prevented by the chains from turning round their heads. Above and behind them a fire is blazing at a distance, and between the fire and the prisoners there is a raised way; and you will see, if you look, a low wall built along the way, like the screen which marionette players have in front of them, over which they show the puppets.

[Glaucon] I see.

[Socrates] And do you see men passing along the wall carrying all sorts of vessels, and statues and figures of animals made of wood and stone and various materials, which appear over the wall? Some of them are talking, others silent.

[Glaucon] You have shown me a strange image, and they are strange prisoners.

[Socrates] Like ourselves, I replied; and they see only their own shadows, or the shadows of one another, which the fire throws on the opposite wall of the cave?

[Glaucon] True; how could they see anything but the shadows if they were never allowed to move their heads?

[Socrates] And of the objects which are being carried in like manner they would only see the shadows?

[Glaucon] Yes.

[Socrates] And if they were able to converse with one another, would they not suppose that they were naming what was actually before them?

[Glaucon] Very true.

[Socrates] And suppose further that the prison had an echo which came from the other side, would they not be sure to fancy when one of the passersby spoke that the voice which they heard came from the passing shadow?

[Glaucon] No question.

[Socrates] To them, the truth would be literally nothing but the shadows of the images.

[Glaucon] That is certain.

[Socrates] And now look again, and see what will naturally follow if the prisoners are released and disabused of their error. At first, when any of them is liberated and compelled suddenly to stand up and turn his neck round and walk and look towards the light, he will suffer sharp pains; the glare will distress him, and he will be unable to see the realities of which in his former state he had seen the shadows; and then conceive some one saying to him, that what he saw before was an illusion, but that now, when he is approaching nearer to being and his eye is turned towards more real existence, he has a clearer vision,—what will be his reply? And you may further imagine that his instructor is pointing to the objects as they pass and requiring him to name them,—will he not be perplexed? Will he not fancy that the shadows which he formerly saw are truer than the objects which are now shown to him?

[Glaucon] Far truer.

[Socrates] And if he is compelled to look straight at the light, will he not have a pain in his eyes which will make him turn away to take in the objects of vision which he can see, and which he will conceive to be in reality clearer than the things which are now being shown to him?

[Glaucon] True.

[Socrates] And suppose once more, that he is reluctantly dragged up a steep and rugged ascent, and held fast until he's forced into the presence of the sun himself, is he not likely to be pained and irritated? When he approaches the light his eyes will be dazzled, and he will not be able to see anything at all of what are now called realities.

[Glaucon] Not all in a moment.

[Socrates] He will require to grow accustomed to the sight of the upper world. And first he will see the shadows best, next the reflections of men and other objects in the water, and then the objects themselves; then he will gaze upon the light of the moon and the stars and the spangled heaven; and he will see the sky and the stars by night better than the sun or the light of the sun by day?

[Glaucon] Certainly.

[Socrates] Last of all he will be able to see the sun, and not mere reflections of him in the water, but he will see him in his own proper place, and not in another; and he will contemplate him as he is.

[Glaucon] Certainly.

[Socrates] He will then proceed to argue that this is he who gives the season and the years, and is the guardian of all that is in the visible world, and in a certain way the cause of all things which he and his fellows have been accustomed to behold?

[Glaucon] Clearly, he would first see the sun and then reason about him.

[Socrates] And when he remembered his old habitation, and the wisdom of the cave and his fellow-prisoners, do you not suppose that he would felicitate himself on the change, and pity them?

[Glaucon] Certainly, he would.

[Socrates] And if they were in the habit of conferring honors among themselves on those who were quickest to observe the passing shadows and to remark which of them went before, and which followed after, and which were together; and who were therefore best able to draw conclusions as to the future, do you think that he would care for such honors and glories, or envy the possessors of them? Would he not say with Homer, Better to be the poor servant of a poor master, and to endure anything, rather than think as they do and live after their manner?

[Glaucon] Yes, I think that he would rather suffer anything than entertain these false notions and live in this miserable manner.

[Socrates] Imagine once more, such an one coming suddenly out of the sun to be replaced in his old situation; would he not be certain to have his eyes full of darkness?

[Glaucon] To be sure.

[Socrates] And if there were a contest, and he had to compete in measuring the shadows with the prisoners who had never moved out of the cave, while his sight was still weak, and before his eyes had become steady (and the time which would be needed to acquire this new habit of sight might be very considerable) would he not be ridiculous? Men would say of him that up he went and down he came without his eyes; and that it was better not even to think of ascending; and if any one tried to loose another and lead him up to the light, let them only catch the offender, and they would put him to death.

[Glaucon] No question.

[Socrates] This entire allegory you may now append, dear Glaucon, to the previous argument; the prison-house is the world of sight, the light of the fire is the sun, and you will not misapprehend me if you interpret the journey upwards to be the ascent of the soul into the intellectual world according to my poor belief, which, at your desire, I have expressed whether rightly or wrongly God knows. But, whether true or false, my opinion is that in the world of knowledge the idea of good appears last of all, and is seen only with an effort; and, when seen, is also inferred to be the universal author of all things beautiful and right, parent of light and of the lord of light in this visible world, and the immediate source of reason and truth in the intellectual; and that this is the power upon which he who would act rationally, either in public or private life must have his eye fixed.

[Glaucon] I agree, as far as I am able to understand you.

[Socrates] Moreover, you must not wonder that those who attain to this beatific vision are unwilling to descend to human affairs; for their souls are ever hastening into the upper world where they desire to dwell; which desire of theirs is very natural, if our allegory may be trusted.

[Glaucon] Yes, very natural.

[Socrates] And is there anything surprising in one who passes from divine contemplations to the evil state of man, misbehaving himself in a ridiculous manner; if, while his eyes are blinking and before he has become accustomed to the surrounding darkness, he is compelled to fight in courts of law, or in other places, about the images or the shadows of images of justice, and is endeavoring to meet the conceptions of those who have never yet seen absolute justice?

[Glaucon] Anything but surprising.

[Socrates] Any one who has common sense will remember that the bewilderments of the eyes are of two kinds, and arise from two causes, either from coming out of the light or from going into the light, which is true of the mind's eye quite as much as of the bodily eye; and he who remembers this when he sees any one whose vision is perplexed and weak, will not be too ready to laugh; he will first ask whether that soul of man has come out of the brighter light, and is unable to see because unaccustomed to the dark, or having turned from darkness to the day is dazzled by excess of light. And he will count the one happy in his condition and state of being, and he will pity the other; or, if he have a mind to laugh at the soul which comes from below into the light, there will be more reason in this than in the laugh which greets him who returns from above out of the light into the cave.

[Glaucon] That is a very just distinction.

[Socrates] But then, if I am right, certain professors of education must be wrong when they say that they can put a knowledge into the soul which was not there before, like sight into blind eyes.

[Glaucon] They undoubtedly say this.

[Socrates] Whereas, our argument shows that the power and capacity of learning exists in the soul already; and that just as the eye was unable to turn from darkness to light without the whole body, so too the instrument of knowledge can only by the movement of the whole soul be turned from the world of becoming into that of being, and learn by degrees to endure the sight of being, and of the brightest and best of being, or in other words, of the good.

[Glaucon] Very true.

[Socrates] And must there not be some art which will effect conversion in the easiest and quickest manner; not implanting the faculty of sight, for that exists already, but has been turned in the wrong direction, and is looking away from the truth?

[Glaucon] Yes, such an art may be presumed.

[Socrates] And whereas the other so-called virtues of the soul seem to be akin to bodily qualities, for even when they are not originally innate they can be implanted later by habit and exercise, the virtue of wisdom more than anything else contains a divine element which always remains, and by this conversion is rendered useful and profitable; or, on the other hand, hurtful and useless. Did you never observe the narrow intelligence flashing from the keen eye of a clever rogue—how eager he is, how clearly his paltry soul sees the way to his end; he is the reverse of blind, but his keen eyesight is forced into the service of evil, and he is mischievous in proportion to his cleverness.

[Glaucon] Very true.

[Socrates] But what if there had been a circumcision of such natures in the days of their youth; and they had been severed from those sensual pleasures, such as eating and drinking, which, like leaden weights, were attached to them at their birth, and which drag them down and turn the vision of their souls upon the things that are below—if, I say, they had been released from these impediments and turned in the opposite direction, the very same faculty in them would have seen the truth as keenly as they see what their eyes are turned to now.

[Glaucon] Very likely.

[Socrates] Yes, I said; and there is another thing which is likely, or rather a necessary inference from what has preceded, that neither the uneducated and uninformed of the truth, nor yet those who never make an end of their education, will be able ministers of State; not the former, because they have no single aim of duty which is the rule of all their actions, private as well as public; nor the latter, because they will not act at all except upon compulsion, fancying that they are already dwelling apart in the islands of the blest.

[Glaucon] Very true.

[Socrates] Then the business of us who are the founders of the State will be to compel the best minds to attain that knowledge which we have already shown to be the greatest of all—they must continue to ascend until they arrive at the good; but when they have ascended and seen enough we must not allow them to do as they do now.

[Glaucon] What do you mean?

[Socrates] I mean that they remain in the upper world: but this must not be allowed; they must be made to descend again among the prisoners in the cave, and partake of their labors and honors, whether they are worth having or not.

[Glaucon] But is not this unjust? Ought we to give them a worse life, when they might have a better?

[Socrates] You have again forgotten, my friend, the intention of the legislator, who did not aim at making any one class in the State happy above the rest; the happiness was to be in the whole State, and he held the citizens together by persuasion and necessity, making them benefactors of the State, and therefore benefactors of one another; to this end he created them, not to please themselves, but to be his instruments in binding up the State.

[Glaucon] True, I had forgotten.

[Socrates] Observe, Glaucon, that there will be no injustice in compelling our philosophers to have a care and providence of others; we shall explain to them that in other States, men of their class are not obliged to share in the toils of politics: and this is reasonable, for they grow up at their own sweet will, and the government would rather not have them. Being self-taught, they cannot be expected to show any gratitude for a culture which they have never received. But we have brought you into the world to be rulers of the hive, kings of yourselves and of the other citizens, and have educated you far better and more perfectly than they have been educated, and you are better able to share in the double duty. Wherefore each of you, when his turn comes, must go down to the general underground abode, and get the habit of seeing in the dark. When you have acquired the habit, you will see ten thousand times better than the inhabitants of the cave, and you will know what the several images are, and what they represent, because you have seen the beautiful and just and good in their truth. And thus our State which is also yours will be a reality, and not a dream only, and will be administered in a spirit unlike that of other States, in which men fight with one another about shadows only and are distracted in the struggle for power, which in their eyes is a great good. Whereas the truth is that the State in which the rulers are most reluctant to govern is always the best and most quietly governed, and the State in which they are most eager, the worst.

[Glaucon] Quite true.

[Socrates] And will our pupils, when they hear this, refuse to take their turn at the toils of State, when they are allowed to spend the greater part of their time with one another in the heavenly light?

[Glaucon] Impossible, for they are just men, and the commands which we impose upon them are just; there can be no doubt that every one of them will take office as a stern necessity, and not after the fashion of our present rulers of State.

[Socrates] Yes, my friend, and there lies the point. You must contrive for your future rulers another and a better life than that of a ruler, and then you may have a well-ordered State; for only in the State which offers this, will they rule who are truly rich, not in silver and gold, but in virtue and wisdom, which are the true blessings of life. Whereas if they go to the administration of public affairs, poor and hungering after their own private advantage, thinking that hence they are to snatch the chief good, order there can never be; for they will be fighting about office, and the civil and domestic broils which thus arise will be the ruin of the rulers themselves and of the whole State.

[Glaucon] Most true.

[Socrates] And the only life which looks down upon the life of political ambition is that of true philosophy. Do you know of any other?

[Glaucon] Indeed, I do not.

[Socrates] And those who govern ought not to be lovers of the task? For, if they are, there will be rival lovers, and they will fight.

[Glaucon] No question.

[Socrates] Who then are those whom we shall compel to be guardians? Surely they will be the men who are wisest about affairs of State, and by whom the State is best administered, and who at the same time have other honors and another and a better life than that of politics?

[Glaucon] They are the men, and I will choose them.

[Socrates] And now shall we consider in what way such guardians will be produced, and how they are to be brought from darkness to light,—as some are said to have ascended from the world below to the gods?

[Glaucon] By all means.

[Socrates] The process is not the turning over of an oyster-shell, but the turning round of a soul passing from a day which is little better than night to the true day of being, that is, the ascent from below, which we affirm to be true philosophy?

[Glaucon] Quite so.

Journal Entry 14

The man who has no imagination has no wings.

Muhammad Ali

The allegory can be confusing. Take a few moments and draw a picture of what you think the inside of the cave looked like. Where were the prisoners? Where was the fire? The wall? Who carried objects? Where were they in relation to the prisoners?

Once you have figured out the "map" of this allegory, reflect on what you think the significance of this story might be.

READING

Reality Television

Most of you are familiar with the "reality TV" genre of television programming. There have been many discussions about how "real" shows like *Survivor* or even game shows might be. Is there some kind of conspiracy to make you think everything you are watching is real? Is there something in human nature that wants to believe? Read the following article, and reflect on your own responses to television programming—be it a game show, a reality TV show, or just the news.

Unreal TV

Mary Kaye Ritz

Is it real, or is it "reality TV"? Reality TV, a genre born of the "Real World"/"Survivor"/"Big Brother" phenomenon and father to numerous offspring the viewing public will encounter in the fall, raises many questions for thinkers as well as for the often naive players in the game.

Some of those questions are process-oriented, such as: Can networks adequately police the genre?

"We're all playing with fire," Fox chairman Sandy Grushow was quoted as saying after the "Who Wants to Marry a Multimillionaire?" debacle and other backlash.

Some questions are anthropological, such as: What does reality TV say about today's society?

Tom Brislin, chairman of UH Manoa school of communications, likens reality TV to a car wreck.

"You feel guilty for gawking, but you can't turn away from it," he said. "In some ways, it shows the innate drama of the human spirit. You put a group of people together and the human drama will emerge, albeit through editing."

The professor relayed how, at a conference 11 days ago, a group of 11 Ph.D.s huddled around the TV screen in a hotel room, chanting "Rudy! Rudy!" and heckling the television as Colleen was voted off the "Survivor" island.

While it does provide a common experience for many, Brislin opines that the advent of reality TV also shows how disconnected our society has become.

"Initially, the mass media brought us together: Everybody knew what Groucho said on TV," said Brislin. "We were bound together because we watched the same things.

"Now that we have so many channels, we're spending more time with the medium, but less in a social way. We're using it more to peer into life than to share life and comment on it."

Brislin pointed out that with these multitudes of channels, scholars have predicted that one day, everyone will have the Me Channel.

To fill that kind of demand, "we turn the cameras on ourselves," he said.

More questions arise, falling to players both on and off the field. Questions such as: How do the habitues of these mini-dramas manage to live in the reality-TV fishbowl for an extended length of time? How true to life is what we see; is there behind-the-scenes manipulation of the players, or the film? And on a human scale, what's the effect on family and friends, who perhaps didn't sign up for gag orders and other hassles many reality-show contracts require?

Take Iolani graduate Ikaika Kaho'ano, who signed up for the ABC–Bunim Murray production "Making the Band," in which a group of young performers competed for positions in O-Town, a new boy band being groomed by Lou Pearlman, the Orlando-based impresario behind 'N Sync and the Backstreet Boys.

Kaho'ano, 22, who quit the production in February, was prohibited by contract from talking about his decision until Aug. 4, when his choice was revealed on the air. That meant keeping his jaws clamped shut for six months, even as the show continued and folks who ran into him here were asking, "Hey, bro, whattup?"

With the clarity of time and distance, Kaho'ano is resigned about the experience these days.

"I know reality TV is not really reality," said Kaho'ano, though he recalls with resentment the lack of privacy during shooting, with surveillance both visible (10 cameras in hallways alone) and hidden in the house occupied by the eight finalists who were the focus of most of the show's season. "We were excommunicated from the rest of the world: no newspaper, one computer, one telephone. Even in the bathrooms, they had microphones. The whole house was bugged."

He likened the experience to being in prison, and knew that it was just as hard on some of the camera operators, who had to film those heart-wrenching calls home to his girlfriend, Malia Yamamoto.

"It was a very oppressive situation," said the singer, who now is forming a new band with other exiles from the TV show. "It was their job to tape our stuff, but I could see on the cameramen's faces it was hurting them to film me. I made it hard for them because I have so much heart."

Brislin predicted that Kaho'ano won't be the last to find the O-Town–type experience disruptive. "When you lose that sense of privacy, you do lose some integrity," he said. "You can see it's an abnormal situation."

So what possessed the UH student, deep into pre-med studies, to sign on for such a thing?

It certainly wasn't for the money: The band members received only living expenses and a house in which to live.

Performing is in the family; his dad is a well-known radio announcer; he and his brother Kamuela had put out a CD, "Fruit From the Tree: 'Ano." There was the chance for national exposure.

But, he says now: "I didn't know what to expect. I went into the whole thing blind."

Then, at the end of the wild ride, he faced six months of seclusion. People would ask, "What's going on?" and "Weren't you on that show?" He couldn't answer.

"Slipping my jaws, they could've come after me with a lawsuit," he said by phone from the East Coast, where he's working on his new band. "It was a hard thing for me to do. I like to talk, I'm very truthful. It was hard for me to not to say anything."

Countering arguments about how "real" reality TV might be, Pearlman described it simply as "no scripts . . . real circumstances."

Then he launched into a mind-bending, hair-splitting declamation on the word "real."

Nothing that occurs outside real time can really be defined as reality, Pearlman said. "It can't be as real as when you're looking at them," he said. "How can you see something on television (and think it was real)? If it was real (it) wouldn't be on TV. It is reality, because there are no scripts. But if you want it real, don't watch television."

Pearlman said he understands how difficult the process can be for someone who signed on as an innocent in the way of the media.

"I think it is a tough thing, because . . . you have the people in front of the camera who at the beginning know they're on TV," he said. "And then they forget the cameras are running. You definitely will forget the cameras are there after a while."

The producer said he isn't too worried about how he comes off: "If the TV captures it, they capture it. . . . Nobody ate any rat steaks. We didn't make them do that."

However, Kaho'ano counters that Pearlman did try to distort reality offscreen, by trying to convince the would-be bandmember to break up with his girlfriend on camera. Having a girlfriend wasn't the image they wanted for the handsome star; they wanted fans to believe he was available.

That concerns Brislin. "The thing that bothers me the most is the manipulation," he said.

In the case of "Survivor," he pointed out, the group is on a quest designed to be hyper-competitive because only one person can survive to win the cash prize. But if a true group of survivors was stranded on an island, they would cooperate to perpetuate the species.

"Normally, you can sit people down and work out solutions," he said. "It's rather a case of 'Let's heighten the drama.' . . . I worried a little more (about shows such as 'making the Band') because (the participants) were young. For 'Survivor,' they went into it with their eyes wide open, to grab a piece of fame."

The peripheral players, such as Ikaika's girlfriend, a 21-year-old UH dance student, and his father, KORL radio deejay Kimo Kaho'ano, knew that between February and August, time marched on for the O-Town wannabe-turned-didn't-wannabe.

They saw Kaho'ano struggle with the decision to leave, and they saw him weigh his options afterward: Go back to school? Take a job at Manoa Summer Fun (which he did for a short period)? Sign on with other "making the Band" exiles who were putting together their own four-man band, called LMNT ("Element")?

After some soul-searching, Kaho'ano did opt for the latter, but he still intends someday to become a doctor and to marry his fiancée.

Some good has come of Kaho'ano's experience. A highlight was appearing on the Rosie O'Donnell talk show. O'Donnell, who pretended to have a crush on a young man whose name she could never quite pronounce, pestered him on-air to tell her if he was going to make the show.

"I told her off-camera, in her ear, when I was hugging her," he said. "Rosie was like, 'Don't worry, you're gonna be just fine. You got a lot of heart, kid.'"

Ritz, M.K., "Unreal TV" from *The Honolulu Advertiser*, pp. F1, F4, August 20, 2000. Reprinted by permission.

WRITING

What Is Real?

Plato's "Allegory of the Cave" is a philosophical dialogue that describes the life of a group of prisoners who are chained from birth in a fire-lit cave watching and interpreting shadows and forms projected upon the wall of the cave they constantly face. There are puppeteers behind the prisoners who carry the objects that cast the shapes and shadows on the cave wall. These shapes and shadows represent the whole of these prisoner's lives and experiences. They know of nothing except the sounds and images that they are experiencing in the cave. This is the life that is "real" to them—their reality.

The allegory is about perceptions, about what is perceived as "real" and what is, in Plato's opinion, truly *real*. It is about the purpose and process of education, about moving from ignorance to enlightenment, about the importance of perceptions, political leadership, and a host of other ideas.

You've read Plato's allegory and the article about a young musician from Hawaii with dreams of fame and fortune, about the world of TV and perceptions about what's "real" as opposed to what might be perceived as "real." There is a connection between Plato's 2,000-year-old dialogue and the newspaper article from August 2000.

Write a reflective response to the two readings about reality. Shape your paper any way you wish, but you might want to consider one of the following to get you started:

- Consider how the newspaper article relates to the allegory.
- Consider personal narrative versus scholarly narrative. How does the personal affect the scholarly?
- Reflect on the complexities faced by a "prisoner" who escapes, develops new perspectives/realities, and later returns to the cave to share new realities and discoveries. Can you think of any real-life examples of this kind of situation?
- Discuss other interesting parallels you may have discovered between Plato's discourse and the newspaper article.

Reality is not what it seems to be, nor is it otherwise.

—Tibetan Buddhist Teaching

How many of you have participated in chat rooms? E-mail? Discussion groups over the Internet? Virtual reality games? Which parts of what you are doing are "real"? With the ever-changing communication technologies affording us more and more computer interface and wider options of interaction, the place between real and virtual is blurred.

There is a serious conversation occurring between people who feel technology is a very positive force in our society and those who eschew technology and are afraid that it will alter humanity in a way that will make us sorry for what we lost. The next article is the introduction to a book, *War of the Worlds,* by Mark Slouka. He is concerned about our losing our individual status in society. Perhaps we will all become part of one big hive and let others think for us. Carefully read his criticism of the road he believes we're on.

The Road to Unreality

Mark Slouka

In 1990, a reporter for the *New York Times,* following the famous case of a man accused of murdering his pregnant wife and then blaming the assault on an unknown black assailant, asked a neighbor of the couple for her thoughts on the tragedy. Do you accept his story? she was asked. Does it seem possible to you, knowing this man, that he made up the whole thing? "I don't know," the woman replied, "I'm dying for the movie to come out so I can see how it ends."

I don't think this woman was joking. Or being cynical. Or even evasive. I think she simply meant what she said. For her, a TV movie about the tragedy would tell her—more accurately than her own experience—what to believe. It would settle for her what was real. Less than a year later, the made-for-television movie "Good Night, Sweet Wife: A Murder in Boston" presumably did just that.

I bring up this episode for the light it sheds on an important cultural trend, a trend so pervasive as to be almost invisible: our growing separation from reality. More and more of us, whether we realize it or not, accept the copy as the original. Increasingly removed from experience, over dependent on the representations of reality that come to us through television and the print media, we seem more and more willing to put our trust in intermediaries who "re-present" the world to us.

The problem with this is one of communication; intermediaries are notoriously unreliable. In the well-known children's game of telephone, a whispered message is passed along from person to person until it is garbled beyond recognition. If we think of that original message as truth, or reality, we stand today at the end of a long line of interpreters. It's a line that's been growing longer throughout the century. And now, accustomed to our place at the end of that line, we've begun to accept the fictions that reach us as the genuine article. This is not good news. For one thing, it threatens to make us stupid. For another, it makes us, collectively, gullible as children: we believe what we are told. Finally, it can make us dangerous.

When did we start accepting abstractions for the real thing? Most answers point roughly to the beginning of this century. Before 1900, daily life for the majority of individuals was agrarian, static, local—in other words, not that different from what it had been for centuries. The twentieth century, however, altered the pace and pattern of daily life forever. Within two generations, the old world (for better and worse) was gone. Its loss meant the loss of two things that had always grounded us: our place within an actual community and our connection to a particular physical landscape.

What started us on the road to unreality? Though the catalog reads like a shopping list of many of the century's most dramatic trends—urbanization, consumerism, increasing mobility, loss of regionality, growing alienation from the landscape, and so on—technology, their common denominator, was the real force behind our journey toward abstraction.

A single example may make my point. As everyone knows, unreality increases with speed. Walking across a landscape at six miles an hour, we experience the particular reality of place: its smells, sounds, colors, textures, and so on. Driving at seventy miles an hour, the experience is very different. The car isolates us, distances us; the world beyond the windshield—whether desert mesa or rolling farmland—seems vaguely unreal. At supersonic speeds, the divorce is complete. A landscape at 30,000 feet is an abstraction, as unlike real life as a painting.

It's an unreality we've grown used to. Habit has dulled the strangeness of it. We're as comfortable with superhuman speed—and the level of abstraction it brings with it—as we are with, say, the telephone, which in a single stroke distanced us from a habit as old as our species: talking to one another face-to-face. We forget that initial users of the telephone (our grandmothers and grandfathers) found it nearly impossible to conceptualize another human being beyond the inanimate receiver; in order to communicate, they had to personify the receiver and speak *to* it, as to some mechanical pet, rather than *through* it to someone else. Today, that kind of instinctive attachment to physical reality seems quaint.

We've come a long way, very quickly. What surprises us now, increasingly, is the shock of the real: the nakedness of face-to-face communication, the rough force of the natural world. We can watch hours of nature programming, but place us in a forest or a meadow and we don't know quite what to do with ourselves. We look forward to hanging out at The Brick with Chris on *Northern Exposure* but dread running into our neighbor while putting out the trash. There has come to be something almost embarrassing about the unmediated event; the man or woman who takes out a musical instrument at a party and offers to play is likely to make everyone feel a bit awkward. It's so naked, somehow. We're more comfortable with its representation: Aerosmith on MTV, Isaac Stern or Eric Clapton on CD.

And now, as we close out the century, various computer technologies threaten to take our long journey from reality to its natural conclusion. They are to TV or videoconferencing what the Concorde is to the car. They have the capacity to make the partially synthetic environments we already inhabit complete—to remove us, once and for all, from reality.

Let me state my case as directly as possible: I believe it is possible to see, in a number of technolo-gies spawned by recent developments in the computer world, an attack on reality as human beings have always known it. I believe this process has been under way for some time, that it will be aided immeasurably by the so-called digital revolution currently sweeping through the industrialized world, and that its implications for our culture are enormous.

I'm the first to admit that this may seem an absurd contention. Most of us, after all, have little trouble separating reality from illusion. We know, for example, that Homer Simpson is a cartoon character on TV, while our neighbor, however much he may act like one, is not; that the highway during our morning commute, the sky at noon, or the bird on the wire at dusk, are not hallucinations; that a drawing of a two-by-four does not a two-by-four make.

Within a few years, however, distinctions such as these will be less automatic. We'll be able to pick up an electronically generated two-by-four. Feel its weight. Swing it around. Whack somebody with it. And yet none of it—not the two-by-four, the person we hit, or the landscape in which this takes place—will be real, in the usual, physical sense. We'll be able to immerse ourselves in an entirely synthetic world, a world that exists only as a trick of the senses, a computer-induced hallucination. And when we emerge from cyberspace—that strange nonplace beyond the computer screen—all indicators suggest that we will find it increasingly difficult to separate real life (already demoted to the acronym RL on computer Nets around the world) from virtual existence. Or worse, that we will know the difference but opt for the digitized world over the real one.

However futuristic all this may sound, it's not all that new. In May 1938, in an essay written for *Harper's Magazine,* E. B. White predicted the encroachment of technology on what we might call the territory of the real. "Clearly," he noted, "the race today is . . . between the things that are and the things that seem to be, between the chemist at RCA and the angel of God." Already, he pointed out, sound effects had begun taking the place of sound itself. Television and radio were enlarging the eye's range, advertising an abstract place, an Elsewhere, that would grow to seem increasingly real. In time, he concluded, *representations* of life, seen on radio and television and in the movies, would come to seem more lifelike to us than their originals.

White called it perfectly. Only months after his prediction, citizens up and down the Eastern seaboard of the United States were heading for the hills, panicked by Orson Welles's radio adaptation of H. G. Wells's *War of the Worlds* into believing that sixteen-tentacled Martians had landed on Earth. It was a dramatic victory for the chemist at RCA and a defining moment for the New Age. For the thousands who rushed north to escape the Martians' onslaught, Welles's electronic illusion easily triumphed over common sense *and* reality.

The Martians (or the forces of electronic illusion) have been rolling on ever since. The war of the worlds—pitting physical reality against the forces of Elsewhere—continues, and reality continues to take it on the chin. In Yugoslavia recently, an actor who had portrayed the deceased dictator Marshal Tito in a docudrama found himself applauded, and reviled, by ordinary citizens on the streets of Belgrade. In Rio de Janeiro, when a soap opera villain murdered his co-star in real life, the actual homicide and the tortured plot of the *telenovela* fused seamlessly in the public mind. When the National Weather Service interrupted daytime programming to issue a tornado warning for a county in Kansas, the local TV station was flooded with phone calls from outraged citizens incensed over having to miss their soaps.

But television's transgressions on the territory of the real are just minor skirmishes compared to the all-out assault being conducted by the digital avant-garde. The race, you see, is no longer between the angel of God and the chemist at RCA. It's between the angel of God and the computer visionary at Microsoft. Or Apple. Or MIT. And he's not interested in imitating reality; he's out to replace it altogether. What the computer world is doing, says John Perry Barlow, Grateful Dead lyricist-turned-computer-cowboy, "is taking material and making it immaterial: Now is the flesh made word, in many respects."

Reduced to its essentials, it comes down to this: only a decade after White's death, we stand on the threshold of turning life itself into computer code, of transforming the experience of living in the physical world—every sensation, every detail—into a product for our consumption. "We now have the ability," says Barlow, "to take the sum of human experience and give it a medium in which to flow." What this means, simply, is that computer simulations may soon be so pervasive (and so realistic) that life itself will require some sort of mark of authenticity. Reality, in other words, may one day come with an asterisk.

None of which should come as much of a surprise. These, after all, are the days of miracle and wonder, of "telepresence" and "immersion technology" (which promise to submerge us in a fully sensual, synthetic world), of intelligent software, artificial life, and virtual damn-near everything. Entire virtual communities, some numbering ten thousand citizens and more, are now accessible

through the conceptual window of your computer screen. Many have homes, prostitutes, tree houses for your children. Within five years, according to John Quarterman, a cyberspace cartographer, the digital world will be inhabited by over a billion individuals worldwide. Those of us still on the outside, Professor Timothy Ferris of Berkeley informs us, will be able to "watch grandmothers be shot by snipers in Sarajevo from six camera angles" without leaving our couches.

Even for the technology literate, it can all seem vaguely surreal, a strange mixture of hard science and science fiction, binary code and bubble gum. Our home computers, to take just one example, will soon come with a face capable of responding to our expressions, understanding our gestures, even reading our lips. Its eyes will follow us around the room. We'll be able to talk with it, argue with it, flirt with it. We'll be able to program it to look like our husband or our child. Or the Holy See, I suppose. Will it have emotions? You bet. Scream at it and it will cower, or cringe. Maybe even cry. "What we want is not intelligence," says Akikazu Takeuchi, a researcher at the Sony Computer Science Laboratory, "but humanity."

What are we to make of this large-scale tinkering with the human mind and its time-tested orbit? What should those of us in RL make of the dizzying proliferation (and ever-increasing sophistication) of cyberspace communities—the so-called MUDs and MOOs and MUSHes? Or of the fact that an entire generation of *computerjugen* is now spending its leisure time in electronically generated space, experiencing what cyberspace theorists like to call "lucid dreaming in an awake state"? Or that cyberization—the movement to animate everyday objects in order to make them more responsive to our needs—is making rapid progress? In a word, how seriously should we be taking all this?

I'd like to suggest that we take it *very* seriously. Why? Because technology is never a neutral force: it orders our behavior, redefines our values, reconstitutes our lives in ways we can't always predict. Like a political constitution or a legislative act, as Langdon Winnder, professor of political science at Rensselaer Polytechnic Institute, has noted, technology establishes the rules by which people live. The digital revolution is technology with a capital T. And its rules, I suspect, may not be to everyone's liking.

Given the enormous effect the digital revolution may come to have on our lives (the digerati, as Steve Lohr has called them, routinely liken its impact to that of the splitting of the atom, the invention of the Gutenberg Press, and the discovery of fire), there is something downright eerie about the lack of debate, the conspicuous absence of dissenting voices, the silence of the critics. Congress seems uninterested; watchdog groups sleep. Like shined deer, we seem to be wandering en masse onto the digital highway, and the only concern heard in the land, by and large, is that some of us may be left behind. Under the circumstances, some caution is surely in order, particularly if we consider that the digital revolution is having its greatest effect on the young. Think of this book as a speed bump on the fiber-optic highway.

My gripe, I should point out, is not so much with the technologies themselves as with the general lack of concern over the consequences that many new applications may come to have. I'm a humanist, not a Luddite. Though I'll admit to a certain fondness for old-fashioned pastimes (I'll take a book or a musical instrument over a Mac and a modem), I'm not incapable of appreciating the contemporary wonders—from gene splicing to lasers—that everywhere crowd in on our attention. I'm not insensitive to the benefits and beauties of technology; without them, my wife and my son would have died during childbirth.

So let me be as clear as possible: I have no problem with what Andrew S. Grove, president and CEO of the Intel Corporation, has called "the ubiquitous PC." I own and use one. Nor do I have any argument, for example, with the millions of people who crowd the "chat groups" available on the Net (many of whom I've found to be no more or less decent and interesting than people in the real world). My quarrel is with a relatively small but disproportionately influential group of self-described "Net religionists" and "wannabe gods" who believe that the physical world can (and should) be "downloaded" into a computer, who believe that the future of mankind is not in RL (real life) but in some form of VR (virtual reality); who are working very hard (and spending enormous amounts of both federal and private money) to engineer their very own version of the apocalypse. As intelligent as they are single-minded, these people have been ignored by the majority of humanists for too long; it's time we started listening.

The *real* issue here, as the novelist and techno-evangelist Robert Coover has pointed out, is how we answer the question, "What's human?" For some, he explains, humanity "has to do with souls and 'depth' and the search for meaning and purpose; with tradition, ritual, mystery and individualism." For others, like himself, it has more to do with the spiritualism of the hive: the increasingly interlinked system of computers and computer technologies about to subsume (as Kevin Kelly, the executive editor of *Wired*

magazine, recently put it) the "millions of buzzing, dim-witted personal computers" (that's us) into one grand organism/machine immeasurably greater than the sum of its parts. For Coover (as for others, including Speaker of the House of Representatives Newt Gingrich), our "evolution" into this hive state is inevitable. "I regret," he says, "having to give up the comforting fairy tales of the past: I, too, want to be unique, significant, connected to a 'deeper truth,' canonized. I want to *have* an 'I.' Too bad."

Of course, shedding "fairy tales" like tradition, individualism, and identity, Coover admits, may have its downside. "If creatures of the past were hived under queen bees like Alexander the Great or Genghis Khan," he points out (quite reasonably, I think), "it seems unlikely that hived creatures of the future will escape their own hive-masters." And what, one might wonder, will happen to the "unhived"? "No doubt they will get stepped on," says Coover; "the Sophist principle 'knowledge is power' will make them mere meat at the fringe."

The expression "meat at the fringe," I think, comes close to explaining what this book is about. When a significant number of powerful individuals—scientists, academics, authors, engineers, computer programmers—following the scent of a potential $3.5 *trillion* industry begin referring to the human body as meat (the expression is a common one among the digerati), it's time for those still foolishly attached to theirs to start paying attention. When a subculture of enthusiasts yearning for the technological equivalent of rapture begins labeling the unhived (in a weak attempt at digital wit) PONAs (people of no account), the PONAs may want to start asking what counts and what doesn't.

"When the yearning for human flesh has come to an end," asks Barlow, referring to the human touch, not to cannibalism, "what will remain?" Good question. "Mind," he says hopefully, "may continue, uploaded into the Net, suspended in an ecology of voltage as ambitiously capable of self-sustenance as was that of its carbon-based forebears." To unhived PONAs like myself, this is hardly encouraging. I *like* my carbon-based body and the carbon-based bodies of my wife and children and friends. I like my carbon-based dog and my carbon-based garden. Nor, to pick up on Coover's "meat on the fringe" image, do I particularly fancy myself as roadkill on the digital highway.

My uneasiness with the new transcendentalists, I suppose, springs from my own instinctive allegiance to the physical world, to the present moment, to the strengths and limitations of the human mind. I'm suspicious of whatever tends to improve or displace these. I believe we all should be. I believe that tampering with the primary things in life (our sense of reality, for example, or individual identity) is not to be undertaken lightly, that technological progress sometimes is and sometimes ain't and that the cloak of inevitability (the technologists' time-tested method for steamrollering dissent or even debate) has been known to conceal both miracles and monsters.

Coover and Co. may find my timidity quaint, my values hopelessly sentimental. I can live with that. What it comes down to, it seems to me, is this: human culture depends on the shared evidence of the senses, always has; we can communicate with one another because a hurled rock will always break skin, a soap bubble always burst. A technology designed to short-circuit the senses, a technology capable of providing an alternate world—abstract, yet fully inhabitable, real to our senses yet accessible only through a computer screen—would take away this common ground and replace it with one manufactured for us by the technologists.

And this is not a good thing. Why? Because human history, in the largest sense, has been the record of our debate with the world. Because reality has been and continues to be the great touchstone for the world's ethical systems. Because, simply put, the world provides context, and without context, ethical behavior is impossible. It is the physical facts of birth and pain and pleasure and death that force us (enable us) to make value judgments: *this* is better than *that*. Nourishment is better than hunger. Compassion is better than torture. Virtual systems, by offering us a reality divorced from the world, from the limits and responsibilities of presence, offer us as well a glimpse into an utterly amoral universe. Consider an obvious example: in Night Trap, a CD-ROM video game recently popular among prepubescent boys, vampires drill holes into the necks of their barely clad female victims and hang them from meat hooks; virtual reality (coming soon to a modem near you) will allow you to *be* the vampire. To inflict pain. Without responsibility. Without consequences. The punctured flesh will heal at the touch of a button, the scream disappear into cyberspace. You'll be able to resurrect the digital dead and kill them again.

The implications of these new technologies are social; the questions they pose, broadly ethical; the risks they entail, unprecedented. They are the cultural equivalent of genetic engineering, except that in this experiment, even more than in the other one, we will be the potential new hybrids, the two-pound mice.

What will technologies that alter our sense of reality mean, in the long run? What will they do to us? No one knows. Ask the technovisionaries how human beings (who have evolved over millions of years in response to the constraints and pressures of the physical world) might respond to existence in aphysical environments, or to the wholesale cyberization of the human environment, and they'll fall over one another in their willingness to admit that they have no idea. Does this concern them just a little? Frighten them, maybe? Not a bit. "The best things in life are scary," Kevin Kelly told me recently, "I'm serious." Unfortunately for the rest of us, he probably is. So on we go, blindfolded, pedal to the floor, over the canyonlands.

Does my concern spring from a lack of vision? Apparently not. Not long ago, I asked John Perry Barlow what the advantages might be to leaving the physical world behind. "Damned few," he wrote back, "for any individual as presently configured. But advantage," he went on, "has nothing to do with it. There are many evolutionary forces at work here, most of them working against us. All of them inexorable." But what about all that business of leaving the flesh behind, I asked, of uploading ourselves into the Net? "Again," he answered, "it's less a matter of advantage than inevitability. It's happening and will continue to. If I could stop it I would." But what, I asked, would you say to those who might be terrified by this prospect (of transcending the meat, so to speak)? "They're right," said Barlow, wrapping up with a philosophical shrug. "But when you're about to be swept over the falls, you might as well try to enjoy the ride."

I am no Oliver Stone. I have no interest in conspiracy theories. Nor do I wish to gloss over the very real benefits the digital New Age may bring; technology, as I have said, is never a wholly one-sided affair. My concern, rather, is based on a small number of well-worn truths: that the free market can unleash forces difficult to control; that technological innovation has its own logic, often separate from questions of value and ethics; and that some technologies—particularly those that promise (or threaten) to transform human culture as we know it—bear watching.

TECHNOLOGY TOUCHES REALITY

Mark Slouka believes that many of us, if we are not already inside the cyberworld, are at its gates. He feels we must only enter if our eyes are wide open because there is a danger in confusing escape with salvation. He is concerned that the new machines are a dangerous attraction and offer people who are not content with the realities of their lives an illusion of escape from reality. Basically, Slouka warns against trying to escape reality. Perhaps he doesn't understand that humans always make their own realities.

We shall never be able to separate ourselves from our own inventions, and to try is only to take a step backward in the evolutionary sense. Technology is an extension of the human mind. Without technology, the distinction between humans and the animal kingdom would be lost. With the new emergent technologies, the definition of reality itself is in fact changing. Yet every person's reality is still different, and so we probably will need to define this "reality" in order for humanity to live together.

When you think about it, the new technologies are simply the creation of tools of a higher complexity. We don't ever want to go back to pre-wheel days, and we don't question the invention of electricity. All of the tools that have been created have been about adapting the world to our needs and wants. We seem to be generally content with our inventions. The Yanomamo of the Brazilian rain forest create better spears for warfare, and a scientist at a world medical conference might describe how some new substance will mimic muscle tissues. These are both tools we create.

What the new communication technologies allow is a compression of time and space. We can now beep, fax, finger, flame, modem, or page someone anywhere in the world and receive a reply in a matter of seconds. The world doesn't seem as large, because we can "walk" the entire globe and talk to anyone we want. What we have created is a new "place"—a condensed version of the world that is still vast and unexplored and draws us to discover. Humans are always enamored by the unknown. With cyberspace, we know more and less all at the same time.

So, the conversation about who we are as humans, about how to define community, about how to relate to nature, and other perennial issues that you will encounter during your liberal education is given a new twist by the emergence of this new "place." This new reality will affect how you conduct your life, and you should take special care to consider how you will merge with the technologies you create.

Journal Entry 15

A computer terminal is not some clunky old television with a type-writer in front of it. It is an interface where the mind and body can connect with the universe and move bits of it about.

Douglas Adams

There are some people who are very concerned that their children will not know what a real tree smells, feels, or looks like. They are concerned that the new virtual realities will take over what we know to be real and that we will lose something in the process.

Take time to ponder how you would feel if we moved from real to artificial—whether you're talking about sugar and artificial sweeteners, live or silk plants, or tomatoes grown in a garden or hydoponically. Are you concerned about these changes? Do you think we will ever turn into a totally humanmade world? Will we be using our tools, or will our tools be using us?

CASH IN ON EDUCATION

Linda Santos

Director, The Casey Family Program

In my family, going to college was an expectation, part of growing up, a continuation of a gradual emancipation process. My parents considered financing my education their responsibility, and my responsibility was to figure out what I wanted to be when I finished growing up and to work toward that goal. Neither of these responsibilities was easy for any of us. Deciding on my life's work in mid-adolescence, when boys, clothes, and having fun were uppermost in my mind, was a challenge. Having a strong family with clear values and solid support gave me the foundation to succeed in spite of myself. I was lucky.

When I was a junior in high school, my father must have noticed a lack of direction in my life. He pointed out that I needed to decide on a profession if I wanted to go to college. Being a flippant teen, I blurted out that since I was really mostly interested in my social life, I should become a social worker. And that is exactly what I did. Of course, the real reason had more to do with being brought up in a family whose values leaned in the direction of service to others rather than making lots of money. (My brother is a minister; my sister, a teacher.) The one significant event that was really the reason for my later decision was a car trip to Florida when I was 14. Driving through extremely poor areas of the southern United States was an exceptionally emotional experience for me. Seeing miles and miles of one-room shacks with bedraggled children playing in the dirt outside had a profound effect on me. Helping others not as fortunate as I seemed the only thing to do.

My undergraduate liberal arts degree prepared me to learn. Then I entered a master's program, in which I learned the specific skills needed to be a social worker. I view both phases of my education as equally important. In my undergraduate years, I learned more about life, matured, and learned to think. Of course, there were all those classes that seemed, at the time, irrelevant to everything, but I am sure who I am today includes a little piece of each of them. But again, the most significant experiences were when I was a Big Sister to a little girl who lived in a poor and neglectful home and the summer I spent working in a girl's reform school.

I truly blossomed in graduate school, finding that learning specific skills in helping others was stimulating and relevant. This also coincided with the latest step in my emancipation, having moved 5,000 miles away from my family.

It is clear to me that education is a multipronged experience. I would not have attained my position as director of a national program or my successful career if I had not had a sound academic education. I would not have had an enjoyable career if I had not had solid experiential learning. I would not have either if I had not had the opportunity to grow into myself.

CHAPTER SIX

Ways of Knowing

Objectives

- to grasp the four ways of knowing

- to explore the purpose of knowledge

- to discuss the nature of knowledge

"When the best dreams in your heart,
Overcome the fears in you, . . ."

Throughout our knowledge section, I have learned that some ways of knowing what we know as well as what is real are through personal experiences—our sensory perception, observation, and instinct, and through our education and training. I do not think I was even aware of how I know what I know, or how I know what is real or not, until we reached this section. I just thought everything was based on instinct and past experiences. The "Allegory of the Cave" was an interesting story because it made me realize that maybe I need to expand my horizons and see what other kinds of information I can get at other schools (maybe through an exchange program), and with that information I will have knowledge gathered at another place. With knowledge comes power and control of oneself, and the environment around oneself, and with the understanding of morals and society. Knowledge is power.

—April Centeno

TRAVEL ESSENTIAL

Information Literacy and Ways of Knowing

"I don't know how I know it; I just do." Actually, we receive information about the world around us in four standard ways. First, we can experience something, and that experience provides the information. I was driving my car and rear-ended another car. I can therefore tell you what happened, how it happened, what the results of the accident were, and even what I felt and thought. Experience is the most personal way of knowing.

Second, we can observe something. Observation as a way of knowing is based on our not actually being a part of the experience. Our distance from the experience can provide less personal and more evidence-based information. However, any police officer or lawyer can tell you stories of interviewing multiple observers of a car accident who report different versions of the same accident. Values and perspectives influence observation as a way of knowing as much as they influence experience as a way of knowing.

Third, we can gain information from other people. Authority as a way of knowing is the most common way students gain information for writing college papers. We select sources that our professors consider important to an understanding of a topic. We understand something by reading, listening, or viewing the opinions of others.

Finally, reflection combines the first three ways of knowing with our own ideas. Analysis occurs in which we consider our own experience and observation in relation to the perspectives of others to determine what is most "real" or significant.

Being information literate means you are able to determine what way of knowing is dominating the information source you are using. The way someone "knows" is a part of what forms that person's perspectives. Methodology is another way to understand ways of knowing. When you know the way of knowing, you are better able to determine how objective or subjective the perspective is and what evidence is being used. Being information literate means making clear what way of knowing you are using when creating information.

HOW DO YOU KNOW?

How do we come to believe anything? How do we know that our eyes are blue, that the earth is round, that milk turns sour, or that there has been an earthquake in some distant land? Most of you are probably thinking to yourselves, "Well, that's easy! We know it because we have seen it, or heard it, or just *know* it is true." And you would be correct. There are really only a few ways we know anything. Let's review them.

Experience. This is gaining knowledge from your own five senses. It is first-hand knowledge of something from direct interaction and involvement. You have seen, touched, smelled, heard, or tasted it. There is no training required; it just comes naturally and appears to be something you can trust.

"I know it because I saw it, heard it, tasted it, etc."

Observation. This is eyewitness testimony. You have not necessarily participated in an event, but you watched it and know it happened because of your observation. Your observation is the source of facts or knowledge.

"I know it because I watched someone else do it."

Authority. This kind of knowing is based on credible sources and expertise, credentials, and qualifications. You are relying on facts and knowledge that come from others. Part of this way of knowing is the scientific method or empiricism, an objective way of knowing that is subject to external scrutiny and systemat-

---

Data is not information. Information is not knowledge. Knowledge is not understanding. Understanding is not wisdom.

CLIFF STOLL AND GARY SCHUBERT

---

ic control of variables. The scientific method relies on sensory experience to collect observable data or facts, intuition helps develop a testable hypothesis about these facts, the use of logic develops a test or an experiment, and then sensory experience comes into play again to complete the test to discover the significance.

We also rely on other types of authority. For example, we often take someone else's word on something. We use time-tested advice and practice, traditions, rules, codes, norms, and values that are derived from cultures, religions, families, or communities.

"I tested the hypothesis experimentally and found it was true."

Reflection. This way of knowing combines experience, observation, and authority through analysis. Sometimes we observe or experience something ourselves and then later read an account of the same activity in a book or article. Have you ever done so and not really understood the significance until much later? One day you are mulling over some memory and you finally "get it!" You come to understand the meaning behind the activity in a way you have not done so before. Perhaps this is an intuitive reaction, but most likely it has to do with your being able to "reflect"— to ruminate, speculate, and deliberate, to think. Taking the time to step back from a situation, a piece of information, or an event and actually give it some careful thought is a way of knowing, of giving meaning to what you know.

"I spent some time thinking about the situation and the facts involved and figured out why we were having the dilemma."

WRITING

Experience

Practice the concept of knowing something through experience. Send an e-mail to your instructor that describes your experience of a celebration.

Include the following:

What	describe the celebration you experienced
When	describe when it occurred, the situation, the time of year, and so forth
Where	describe the setting for the celebration
Why	describe why the celebration was occurring, the purpose of the celebration
How	describe the sequence of events

Be as specific, detailed, and thorough as possible. All of this information should come from *your* experience of the celebration.

This activity should follow your written "experience" of a celebration. This time, pick a celebration you can observe, but one in which you are not a participant. Use the *what, where, when, why,* and *how* questions from your experience journal entry to help you portray this celebration.

Procedure:

- Pick a partner for this activity.
- Each of you should choose a celebration to observe or one you have observed at some time in your life.
- Make a list of words to describe this celebration.

- Answer the what, where, when, why, and how questions.

- Exchange observations with each other.
- Write at least two questions about the celebration your partner has described.

- What could your partner have said that would have explained the celebration to you more clearly?

- If you have time, exchange your descriptions with other students so that when you receive yours, you will have many questions and comments on how the celebration you observed might have been described in more detail.

WRITING

Authority

Let's continue the theme of celebration to have you practice another way of knowing. You have already sent an e-mail to your instructor about a personal experience regarding a celebration. Then you did a class activity about observing, but not participating, in a celebration. Now, for this assignment, you will explore how various *authorities* might describe a celebration.

Pick a celebration, one you know or one you don't. Use four different sources from the following categories:

books	World Wide Web
magazines	interviews
journals	video/TV/movie/film
newspapers	government publications

Let's say you have decided to research a corn festival in Iowa. You might choose to read a *book,* to *interview* a relative, to watch a *film,* and to read an article in a *journal.* Those four sources would be the authorities you would use to describe the celebration itself and its significance.

The final few paragraphs of your paper should address the differences you see between a "story" that came from experience or observation and one that was constructed from sources of authority. What did you discover?

Journal Entry 16

Knowledge is better than riches.

African Proverb

Certainly the ways of knowing described in the previous pages are an oversimplification of the process. Entire books have been written on knowledge and knowing, but it isn't necessary for purposes of this book to delve into the inherent complexities. You should have a fair understanding of how you know something.

Therefore, let's take this a step further and ponder what the purpose of "knowing" anything might be. For this journal entry, write lists of words that describe for you the purpose of knowledge. Perhaps it will be easiest to just jot down key words that describe what *you* know and then separate those into categories that might help you figure out the purpose of knowing what you know. Good luck.

THE PURPOSE OF KNOWLEDGE

Now that you've learned about the various ways of knowing, let's address why knowing anything is important at all. What, after all, is the *purpose* of knowledge? Let's review five reasons that knowledge is significant and crucial to our lives.

First, knowledge is necessary for *survival*. You must know certain things for basic living. This includes how to make or find shelter, gather food, keep warm, locate clean water, and so forth. Without knowing how to do these very basic tasks,

---

The mountain remains unmoved at seeming defeat by the mist.

RABINDRANATH TAGORE

---

you would not survive for very long. In fact, if you think about the animal world, parents consistently model survival behaviors to their young before casting them out on their own. There is another layer of survival—common sense. You need to know when stores are open, where to buy gas for your car, how to navigate through a particular town, when not to walk down certain streets in the dark, and many more day-to-day activities. All of this knowledge helps you survive.

Second, knowledge contributes to *self-realization*, knowing more deeply about yourself. For instance, you know you like music but don't really know much about it. Learning about it gives you a deeper appreciation of music. Another example might be studying about families in crisis and understanding the sociological reasons behind certain economic problems similar to your own. This gives deeper meaning to your own life.

A third purpose of knowledge is *power*. Power really is about competition. "I know something you don't know" means "I can do something you can't do" or "I can do it first" or "better." This power is found in corporate secrets, military advantage, espionage, scientific endeavors, or something as simple as access to the game plans of an opposing team. If you know more than someone else, or a whole group of people, then your knowledge gives you an edge and can be translated into a kind of power.

Understanding your place in comparison to others—your *context* in society—is a fourth purpose of knowledge. Who are you? Where do you come from? What do you know about your heritage? How does your small town fit into the history of your state, which is part of the United States? What place does the United States have in the world? Another example might be understanding that you have a medical condition and how it plays out in the greater picture of your health. For instance, you may have diabetes and need to know how to manage it, how others might have done so, who is doing research in the area, how you should approach food because your body functions differently, and what does it mean overall to be diabetic? This kind of knowledge helps you put your life's experience in context; you understand that you are part of a greater whole in all aspects of your life.

Finally, knowledge informs *values*. You make decisions, moral and otherwise, based on what you know. The more you know about any issue, the more likely you will be to develop a value system based on that knowledge. If you learn about the water shortage in your neighborhood and are asked to conserve, you might do so or you might not. However, if you are able to have all the facts that led to your water department asking for conservation—the water table is low, drought conditions have been pervasive, you will lose indigenous plants and animals, your neighborhood will lose real estate value—you might make your decision to conserve water voluntarily based on this knowledge. You benefit from making informed decisions. These cannot be made unless you have adequate information with which to work.

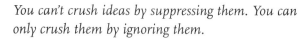

You can't crush ideas by suppressing them. You can only crush them by ignoring them.

—Ursula K. LeGuin

In the next article, "The Hazards of Science," Lewis Thomas explores the power of knowledge. He suggests that there are some kinds of information that might be dangerous and he poses the idea that human beings are better off not knowing various things. Read the article carefully, and then reflect on what he says.

The Hazards of Science

Lewis Thomas

The code word for criticism of science and scientists these days is "hubris." Once you've said that word, you've said it all; it sums up, in a word, all of today's apprehensions and misgivings in the public mind—not just about what is perceived as the insufferable attitude of the scientists themselves but, enclosed in the same word, what science and technology are perceived to be doing to make this century, this near to its ending, turn out so wrong.

"Hubris" is a powerful word, containing layers of powerful meaning, derived from a very old word, but with new life of its own, growing way beyond the limits of its original meaning. Today, it is strong enough to carry the full weight of disapproval for the cast of mind that thought up atomic fusion and fission as ways of first blowing up and later heating cities as well as the attitudes which led to strip-mining, offshore oil wells, Kepone, food additives, SSTs, and the tiny spherical particles of plastic recently discovered clogging the waters of the Sargasso Sea.

The biomedical sciences are now caught up with physical science and technology in the same kind of critical judgment, with the same pejorative word. Hubris is responsible, it is said, for the whole biological revolution. It is hubris that has given up the prospects of behavior control, psychosurgery, fetal research, heart transplants, the cloning of prominent politicians from bits of their own eminent tissue, iatrogenic disease, overpopulation, and recombinant DNA. This last, the new technology that permits the stitching of one creature's genes into the DNA of another, to make hybrids, is currently cited as the ultimate example of hubris. It is hubris for man to manufacture a hybrid on his own.

So now we are back to the first word again, from "hybrid" to "hubris," and the hidden meaning of two beings joined unnaturally together by man is somehow retained. Today's joining is straight out of Greek mythology: it is the combining of man's capacity with the special prerogative of the gods, and it is really in this sense of outrage that the word "hubris" is being used today. That is what the word has grown into, a warning, a code word, a shorthand signal from the language itself: if man starts doing things reserved for the gods, deifying himself, the outcome will be something worse for him, symbolically, than the litters of wild boars and domestic sows were for the ancient Romans.

To be charged with hubris is therefore an extremely serious matter, and not to be dealt with by murmuring things about antiscience and anti-intellectualism, which is what many of us engaged in science tend to do these days. The doubts about our enterprise have their origin in the most profound kind of human anxiety. If we are right and the critics are wrong, then it has to be that the word "hubris" is being mistakenly employed, that this is not what we are up to, that there is, for the time being anyway, a fundamental misunderstanding of science.

I suppose there is one central question to be dealt with, and I am not at all sure how to deal with it, although I am quite certain about my own answer to it. It is this: are there some kinds of information leading to some sorts of knowledge that human beings are really better off not having? Is there a limit to scientific inquiry not set by what is knowable but by what we *ought* to be knowing? Should we stop short of learning about some things, for fear of what we, or someone, will do with the knowledge? My own answer is a flat no, but I must confess that this is an intuitive response and I am neither inclined nor trained to reason my way through it.

There has been some effort, in and out of scientific quarters, to make recombinant DNA into the issue on which to settle this argument. Proponents of this line of research are accused of pure hubris, of assuming the rights of gods, of arrogance and outrage; what is more, they confess themselves to be in the business of making live hybrids with their own hands. The mayor of Cambridge and the attorney general of New York have both been advised to put a stop to it, forthwith.

It is not quite the same sort of argument, however, as the one about limiting knowledge, although this is surely part of it. The knowledge is already here, and the rage of the argument is about its application in technology. Should DNA for making certain useful or interesting proteins be incorporated into *E. coli* plasmids or not? Is there a risk of inserting the wrong sort of toxins or hazardous viruses, and then having the new hybrid organisms spread beyond the laboratory? Is this a technology for creating new varieties of pathogens, and should it be stopped because of this?

If the argument is held to this level, I can see no reason why it cannot be settled, by reasonable people. We have learned a great deal about the handling of dangerous microbes in the last century, although I must say that the opponents of recombinant-DNA research tend to downgrade this huge body of information. At one time or another, agents as hazardous as those of rabies, psittacosis, plague, and typhus have been dealt with by investigators in secure laboratories, with only rare instances of self-infection of the investigators themselves, and no instances at all of epidemics. It takes some high imagining to postulate the creation of brand-new pathogens so wild and voracious as to spread from equally secure laboratories to endanger human life at large, as some of the arguers are now maintaining.

But this is precisely the trouble with the recombinant-DNA problem: it has become an emotional issue, with too many irretrievably lost tempers on both sides. It has lost the sound of a discussion of

technological safety, and begins now to sound like something else, almost like a religious controversy, and here it is moving toward the central issue: are there some things in science we should not be learning about?

There is an inevitable long list of hard questions to follow this one, beginning with the one which asks whether the mayor of Cambridge should be the one to decide, first off.

Maybe we'd be wiser, all of us, to back off before the recombinant-DNA issue becomes too large to cope with. If we're going to have a fight about it, let it be confined to the immediate issue of safety and security, of the recombinants now under consideration, and let us by all means have regulations and guidelines to assure the public safely wherever these are indicated or even suggested. But if it is possible let us stay off that question about limiting human knowledge. It is too loaded, and we'll simply not be able to cope with it.

By this time it will have become clear that I have already taken sides in the matter, and my point of view is entirely prejudiced. This is true, but with a qualification. I am not so much in favor of recombinant-DNA research as I am opposed to the opposition to this line of inquiry. As a longtime student of infectious-disease agents I do not take kindly the declarations that we do not know how to keep from catching things in laboratories, much less how to keep them from spreading beyond the laboratory walls. I believe we learned a lot about this sort of thing, long ago. Moreover, I regard it as a form of hubris-in-reverse to claim that man can make deadly pathogenic microorganisms so easily. In my view, it takes a long time and a great deal of interliving before a microbe can become a successful pathogen. Pathogenicity is, in a sense, a highly skilled trade, and only a tiny minority of all the numberless tons of microbes on the earth has ever been involved itself in it; most bacteria are busy with their own business, browsing and recycling the rest of life. Indeed, pathogenicity often seems to me a sort of biological accident in which signals are misdirected by the microbe or misinterpreted by the host, as in the case of endotoxin, or in which the intimacy between host and microbe is of such long standing that a form of molecular mimicry becomes possible, as in the case of diphtheria toxin. I do not believe that by simply putting together new combinations of genes one can create creatures as highly skilled and adapted for dependence as a pathogen must be, any more than I have ever believed that microbial life from the moon or Mars could possibly make a living on this planet.

But, as I said, I'm not at all sure this is what the argument is really about. Behind it is that other discussion, which I wish we would have not to become enmeshed in.

I cannot speak for the physical sciences, which have moved an immense distance in this century by any standard, but it does seem to me that in the biological and medical sciences we are still far too ignorant to begin making judgments about what sorts of things we should be learning or not learning. To the contrary, we ought to be grateful for whatever snatches we can get hold of, and we ought to be out there on a much larger scale than today's, looking for more.

We should be very careful with that word "hubris," and make sure it is not used when not warranted. There is a great danger in applying it to the search for knowledge. The application of knowledge is another matter, and there is hubris in plenty in our technology, but I do not believe that looking for new information about nature, at whatever level, can possibly be called unnatural. Indeed, if there is any single attribute of human beings, apart from language, which distinguishes them from all other creatures on earth, it is their insatiable, uncontrollable drive to learn things and then to exchange the information with others of the species. Learning is what we do, when you think about it. I cannot think of a human impulse more difficult to govern.

But I can imagine lots of reasons for trying to govern it. New information about nature is very likely, at the outset, to be upsetting to someone or other. The recombinant-DNA line of research is already upsetting, not because of the dangers now being argued about but because it is disturbing, in a fundamental way, to face the fact that the genetic machinery in control of the planet's life can be fooled around with so easily. We do not like the idea that anything so fixed and stable as a species line can be changed. The notion that genes can be taken out of one genome and inserted in another is unnerving. Classical mythology is peopled with mixed beings—part man, part animal or plant—and most of them are associated with tragic stories. Recombinant DNA is a reminder of bad dreams.

The easiest decision for society to make in matters of this kind is to appoint an agency, or a commission, or a subcommittee within an agency to look into the problem and provide advice. And the easiest course for a committee to take, when confronted by any process that appears to be disturbing people or making them uncomfortable, is to recommend that it be stopped, at least for the time being.

I can easily imagine such a committee, composed of unimpeachable public figures, arriving at the decision that the time is not quite ripe for further exploration of the transplantation of genes, that we should put this off for a while, maybe until next century, and get on with other affairs that make us less discomfited. Why not do science on something more popular, say, how to get solar energy more cheaply? Or mental health?

The trouble is, it would be very hard to stop once this line was begun. There are, after all, all sorts of scientific inquiry that are not much liked by one constituency or another, and we might soon find ourselves with crowded rosters, panels, standing committees, set up in Washington for the appraisal, and then the regulation, of research. Not on grounds of the possible value and usefulness of the new knowledge, mind you, but for guarding society against scientific hubris, against the kinds of knowledge we're better off without.

It would be absolutely irresistible as a way of spending time, and people would form long queues for membership. Almost anything would be fair game, certainly anything to do with genetics, anything relating to population control, or, on the other side, research on aging. Very few fields would get by, except perhaps for some, like mental health, in which nobody really expects anything much to happen, surely nothing new or disturbing.

The research areas in the greatest trouble would be those already containing a sense of bewilderment and surprise, with discernible prospects of upheaving present dogmas.

It is hard to predict how science is going to turn out, and if it is really good science it is impossible to predict. This is in the nature of the enterprise. If the things to be found are actually new, they are by definition unknown in advance, and there is no way of telling in advance where a really new line of inquiry will lead. You cannot make choices in this matter, selecting things you think you're going to like and shutting off the lines that make for discomfort. You either have science or you don't, and if you have it you are obliged to accept the surprising and disturbing pieces of information, even the overwhelming and upheaving ones, along with the neat and promptly useful bits. It is like that.

The only solid piece of scientific truth about which I feel totally confident is that we are profoundly ignorant about nature. Indeed, I regard this as the major discovery of the past hundred years of biology. It is, in its way, an illuminating piece of news. It would have amazed the brightest minds of the eighteenth-century Enlightenment to be told by any of us how little we know, and how bewildering seems the way ahead. It is this sudden confrontation with the depth and scope of ignorance that represents the most significant contribution of twentieth-century science to the human intellect. We are, at last, facing up to it. In earlier times, we either pretended to understand how things worked or ignored the problem, or simply made up stories to fill the gaps. Now that we have begun exploring in earnest, doing serious science, we are getting glimpses of how huge the questions are, and how far from being answered. Because of this, these are hard times for the human intellect, and it is no wonder that we are depressed. It is not so bad being ignorant if you are totally ignorant; the hard thing is knowing in some detail the reality of ignorance, the worst spots and here and there the not-so-bad spots, but no true light at the end of any tunnel nor even any tunnels that can yet be trusted. Hard times, indeed.

But we are making a beginning, and there ought to be some satisfaction, even exhilaration, in that. The method works. There are probably no questions we can think up that can't be answered, sooner or later, including even the matter of consciousness. To be sure, there may well be questions we can't think up, ever, and therefore limits to the reach of human intellect which we will never know about, but that is another matter. Within our limits, we should be able to work our way through to all our answers, if we keep at it long enough, and pay attention.

I am putting it this way, with all the presumption and confidence that I can summon, in order to raise another, last question. Is this hubris? Is there something fundamentally unnatural, or intrinsically wrong, or hazardous for the species in the ambition that drives us all to reach a comprehensive understanding of nature, including ourselves? I cannot believe it. It would seem to me a more unnatural thing, and more of an offense against nature, for us to come on the same scene endowed as we are with curiosity, filled to overbrimming as we are with questions, and naturally talented as we are for the asking of clear questions, and then for us to do nothing about it or, worse, to try to suppress the questions. This is the greater danger for our species, to try to pretend that we are another kind of animal, that we do not need to satisfy our curiosity, that we can get along somehow without inquiry and exploration and experimentation, and that the human mind can rise above its ignorance by simply asserting that there are things it has no need to know. This, to my way of thinking, is the real hubris, and it carries danger for us all.

Journal Entry 17

Human history becomes more and more a race between education and catastrophe.

H. G. Wells

In the end, Lewis Thomas does defend scientific inquiry, if only for purposes of understanding nature. Before you write this journal entry, take the time to chat with two or three of your classmates about Thomas's idea that "some kinds of information" might not be good for us to know. Then write your own reaction to the article and see if you can list information you wish humans didn't know that we already do. Also, complete a list of possible information we might garner in the future that would be detrimental to our lives.

Once you have done this, decide whether all information should be available to all or if humankind should put a stop to inquiry in some areas. Be sure to explain why you feel the way you do.

There are no facts, only interpretations.

—Friedrich Nietzsche

The concept of knowledge is actually quite complex, as you are coming to discover. We have the variety of "ways" we know things, the myriad of "purposes" for which knowing anything might be useful, and then the construct that whatever we know and however we might have gotten to know it, it still is only "interpretation."

Read the next article, by Daniel Goleman, and see if his opinions about an "intelligent filter" ring true to you.

The Intelligent Filter

Daniel Goleman

What words do these fragments suggest to you?

    s-x

    shi-

    f-k

Reading these, you should have no trouble completing them, more likely than not, as suggestive or off-color words. But imagine yourself in a room with a stranger, repeating aloud the words you make of these fragments. Your responses might take another turn, if only to avoid embarrassment. Your thoughts might, too.

Over more than two decades following World War II, researchers conducted a gargantuan number of studies to test ways in which what one perceives can be muted or heightened depending on its emotional salience. Several hundred published studies dealt with this question, for the most part without resolving anything. The problem was not so much with the studies themselves, as with the then-current understanding of how the mind processes information.[1]

Take the words in the list above. If I ask you to complete the fragments and you tell me they represent the words, "six," "shin," and "fork," I can surmise that you either did not allow yourself to *perceive* the more suggestive alternatives, or that you suppressed *reporting* them to me. In more technical terms, the question is one of the locus of bias: is it in perception or in response?

If the bias was in your response, then I can assume the suggestive words came to mind but you quickly thought of more acceptable alternatives. But if the bias was in your original perception and you *never* were aware of the suggestive words, your mind somehow engineered its censorship outside your awareness.

The implications for how the mind's workings are orchestrated are quite different for each of these alternatives. Bias in response suggests that this is merely an instance of social dissembling—nothing very startling. But a bias in perception implies an unconscious center at work in the mind, imposing its judgments on all we perceive, shaping our experience to fit its priorities.

For many years these two possibilities vied with each other as mutually exclusive alternatives. An exhaustive review in 1966 of two decades of experimental results pro and con was unable to resolve the debate.[2] The reviewer's conclusion, after failing to settle the battle, was a conciliatory suggestion: since the two possibilities are not incompatible, perhaps, just perhaps, both may be correct. There may be censors in perception as well as in response.

That suggestion fits well with what is today the commonly accepted view of how information moves—and fails to move—through the mind.

There was a half-century lapse before experimental psychologists seriously addressed the proposals Freud made in the seventh chapter of *The Interpretation of Dreams.* From the 1920s on, the ascendancy of behaviorism made what went on within the mind a taboo topic for most psychologists. When the mechanics of mind finally re-entered psychological research, one immediate impetus was most unlikely: the rise of aviation.

The next major volley in the debate over how the mind handles information was fired in 1958 by Donald Broadbent, a British psychologist.[3] His interests were very different from Freud's. Broadbent worked with the British Royal Navy in the years after World War II. Because of the explosive growth of aviation in that era, the volume of air traffic besieged controllers. The controllers, Broadbent realized, took in far more information through their eyes and ears than they could deal with. He wondered just how the mind sorted out this barrage.

Broadbent, like Freud, used a flow chart to describe how the mind handles information. His chart showed that people receive more data through the sense than they can handle (see Figure 1). This information gets to a short-term store—akin to the sensory store—and then flows on to a "selective filter," where most of it is weeded out. This filter somehow blocks all but those messages that merit fuller attention. The passage is seemingly instantaneous. But the few thousandths of a second it takes allow ample time for the mind to sort through the mass of data in sensory storage and filter out irrelevancies before the information passes into conscious awareness.

Broadbent assumed that the mind needs to filter the information that impinges on it through the senses because it has only a limited capacity. The selective filter, he believed, is essential here because of a bottleneck: there is a sharply limited channel capacity at the next stage of processing, often called "short-term" or "primary" memory.

Primary memory is the region of perception that falls under the beam of attention. For our purposes we will call it "awareness." The contents of the zone of awareness are what we take to be "on our minds" at a given moment; it is our window onto the stream of consciousness. This zone is quite fragile, its contents fleeting.

The traffic between awareness and long-term memory is two-way, according to Broadbent's model; what is in long-term memory can be called into awareness, what is in awareness finds a place in memory. Only information that reaches awareness, he proposed, will be retained for very long—that is, we remember only what we first pay attention to. Awareness, then, is the gateway to memory, and a filter controls what enters awareness. But what controls the filter?

For Broadbent, only the gross physical aspect of a message—its loudness or brightness, say—determined whether it would get through, not its meaning. That view was put to rest soon after he proposed it by experiments on the "cocktail party effect." At a cocktail party or in a crowded restaurant there is typically a din of competing conversations, all carried on at high volume within earshot of the others.

Contrary to Broadbent's prediction, you don't hear simply the loudest voice. For example, if you are stuck listening to a bore recount the gruesome details of his last vacation, rocky relationship, or nearly consummated deal, it is easy to tune him out and tune in on a more interesting conversation nearby—particu-

Figure 1. Broadbent's model of the mind, slightly modified: Sensory stimuli are analyzed as they reach the sensory store and sorted and filtered on their way to awareness (or short-term memory).

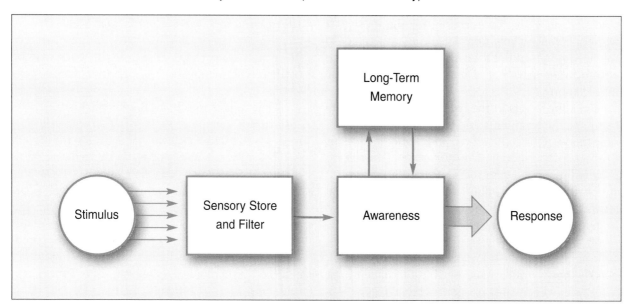

larly if you hear you own name mentioned. During the course of these turn-outs and tune-ins, the *sounds* coming to your ears may be identical in volume. What changes is the focus of your *attention*.

This means that information is scanned for *meaning* before it reaches the filter, contradicting Broadbent's assertion that the filter tunes in or out based solely on physical aspects of a message. The filter seems to have some intelligence; it is tuned by the importance to a person of the message.

This has major consequences for how the mind's architecture must be arranged. In order for an intelligent filter—one that reads meaning—to operate during the few moments of sensory storage, the arrangement of the mind's elements must be modified in a critical fashion. If the filter is intelligent, then there must be some circuit that connects the part of the mind that cognizes—that recognizes meanings—with the part that takes in and sorts through initial impressions. A simple, linear model such as Freud and Broadbent proposed would not work.

Meanings are stored in long-term memory. What is required is a *loop* between long-term memory and the earlier stages of information processing. That loop is shown in Figure 2. Such a feedback loop allows for the sensory store to sort its contents by drawing on the vast repertoire of experience, on the meanings and understandings built up over a life span, stored in long-term memory. The judgment "salient" or "irrelevant" can be made only on the basis of the knowledge in long-term memory.

With access to the mind's lifelong store of experience, preferences, and goals, the filter can sift through the mass of impressions that assail it at each successive moment, and immediately tune in or out what matters.

Indeed, contemporary theorists now assume that information passing through the sensory store is subjected to scrutiny and filtered on the basis of its meaning and relevance. "Essentially," sums up Matthew Erdelyi, a cognitive psychologist, "long-term memory itself becomes the filter, deciding what to block from short-term storage (and therefore awareness), thereby determining indirectly what to accept for eventual storage in long-term memory itself."[4]

That means the contents of awareness come to us picked over, sorted through, and pre-packaged. The whole process takes a fraction of a second.

There are compelling reasons for this arrangement in the design of the mind. It is much to our benefit that the raw information that passes from sensory storage to awareness sifts through a smart filter. The region of consciousness would be far too cluttered were it not reached by a vastly reduced information flow. While the information in consciousness seems limited, it also seems to be the case that before getting there, that information— and an even vaster amount left behind, seemingly to evaporate—has gone through a massive amount of analysis.

The more thoroughly information in sensory storage can be sorted out, the more efficiently the next way station—awareness—can operate. If too

Figure 2. A simplified model of the mind, loosely adapted from Donald Norman: Memory screens perception at the earliest stage of information flow, filtering for salience what is allowed through to awareness.

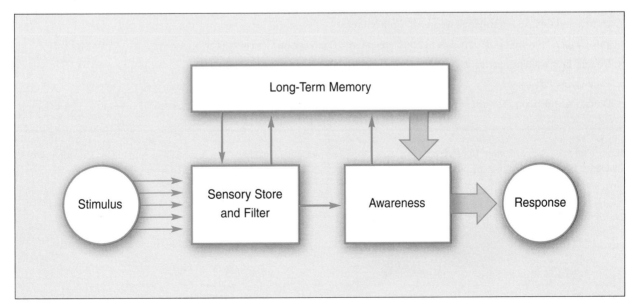

much gets through, awareness is swamped. . . . It is of critical import that this filter operate at a peak, in order to save us from continuous distraction by a mass of irrelevant information. If the filter were much less thorough we might literally be driven to distraction by distractions, as happens in schizophrenia.

The idea that information passes through an intelligent filter led to what has become the prevailing view of how information flows through the mind. The most commonly pictured flow chart was proposed by Donald Norman in 1968; Figure 2 is a simplified version of his model.[5] In this model what enters through the senses gets a thorough, automatic scan by long-term memory—specifically by "semantic" memory, the repository of meanings and knowledge about the world. For example, every bundle of sounds automatically is directed to an "address" in semantic memory that yields its meaning. If you hear the word "grunt," semantic memory recognizes its meaning; if you hear a grunt, semantic memory also recognizes that that sound is not a word.

All this filtering goes on out of awareness. What gets through to awareness is what messages have pertinence to whatever mental activity is current. If you are looking for restaurants, you will notice signs for them and not for gas stations; if you are skimming through the newspaper, you will notice those items that you care about. What gets through enters awareness, and only what is useful occupies that mental space.

Perception, says Norman, is a matter of degree. In scanning incoming information, semantic mem-

ory need not go into every detail; it need only sort out what is and is not relevant to the concern of the moment. Irrelevant information is only partly analyzed, if just to the point of recognizing its irrelevancy. What *is* relevant gets fuller processing. For example, if you casually scan a newspaper page and suddenly see your name, it will seem to "leap out" at you. Presumably the words you saw as you skimmed were partly processed and found irrelevant; your name—which is always relevant—rated full processing.

This model of the mind has several important implications. For one, it posits that information is screened by memory at every stage of its processing, and that memory scans information and filters it for salience. All this processing goes on *before* information enters awareness; only a small portion of the information available at a given moment filters through to consciousness.

That is not to say that attention is entirely passive. We can, after all, decide to scan for something, and so awareness can modify how the filter operates. But awareness does so indirectly, through the services of long-term memory: the activity of the filter is never directly evident to awareness. We can, however, bring information into awareness from long-term memory. There is two-way traffic, then, between awareness and long-term memory, but there is only one-way traffic between the filter and awareness. There is a very real sense in which long-term memory—the sum total of experience one has about life—has a more decisive say in the flow of information than we ordinarily realize.

1. The best review of this saga and the issues dealt with in modeling the mind is in Matthew Hugh Erdelyi, "A New Look at the New Look: Perceptual Defense and Vigilance," *Psychological Review* 81 (1974), 1–25. Also recommended: Colin Martindale, *Cognition and Consciousness* (Homewood, IL: Dorsey Press).

2. R.N. Haber, "Nature of the Effect of Set on Perception," *Psychological Review* 73 (1966), 335–351.

3. Donald E. Broadbent, *Perception and Communication* (London: Pergamon Press, 1958).

4. Erdelyi, op. cit., 19.

5. Donald A. Norman, "Toward a Theory of Memory and Attention," *Psychological Review* 75 (1968), 522–536.

W R I T I N G

Taking the Personal into the Scholarly

Most people are mirrors, reflecting the moods and emotions of the times; few are windows, bringing light to bear on the dark corners where troubles fester. The whole purpose of education is to turn mirrors into windows.

—Sydney J. Harris

Pick a topic of personal interest. This should be a topic with which you have had some experience and for which you have had the opportunity to develop some interesting observations and opinions. Possible areas of interest include:

> hobbies, sports, issues (such as environment, law, poverty, adoption, homelessness, censorship), movies (ratings, stars), dance (types, importance, history), travel (places you have been, want to visit, are of significance to your family), theater (individuals, personalities), music (types, instruments, performers), inventions, technology (computer games, artificial intelligence), careers, politics (role models, privilege)

Four-Part Paper

1. Write two paragraphs describing your personal *experience* with your chosen topic.

2. Write two paragraphs describing what you have *observed* about this topic.

3. Develop a list of 12 questions about your topic. Go beyond the who, what, why, where, when, and how. Think about more complex questions, such as *who might, what did, why was, where could, when were, which did,* and *how many.*

4. Look at your 12 questions and write a final *reflective* paragraph describing the "problem" or "central question" that comes up about your topic. In other words, if you were to do some research on this topic, what would you be looking for?

5. Refer back to Goleman's article, and pinpoint places in your paper where you think a filter might have influenced the facts, information, or knowledge you reported.

CASH IN ON  EDUCATION

Kevin Kemper
Business Manager, CableRep Advertising

Having been out of college for a decade, I look back on those years as some of the best in my life. Not only did I receive an education, I also laid the blocks for becoming a true adult.

While preparing for college and during college, the primary focus seemed to be earning the almighty degree. Once in the "real" world, that focus is not as important as it was made out to be. Obviously, certain degrees are required and very specific for a selected career, such as a lawyer or doctor, but even those degrees have latitude. My degree is in cinema–television production, a very specific field with a very specific career path. Am I doing something today with my degree? No. I'm a business manager in an advertising agency. Is there anything I learned in college that I'm using today in my career? Yes and no. I'm not editing film or writing scripts, but in terms of dealing and working with other people, I draw from my college experience every day. I also learned how to get things done, accomplish tasks, meet deadlines, and manage my time. These weren't things you learned in a class in college; you learned by doing.

What the college experience comes down to is the experience of college itself. It's not the books, the lectures, or the papers; it's the process of how you go about it. College is the time to try new things, to grapple with new problems in different ways. It's about the social interactions and dealing with many types of people all at once.

I chose to go to a university out of state for very specific reasons—I wanted to expose myself to different types of people, situations, and geography. This gave me a way to live in another area of the country yet not be bound to stay there. I knew that after four years, I could stay in the city I graduated from, I could move back to my hometown, or I could move to an entirely different part of the country. I grew up in a small community (roughly 40,000 people), and I went to college in Los Angeles (roughly 7 million people). Where I grew up you could leave your car doors unlocked when you went into the store. Not to say that there wasn't any crime or problems where I grew up, but moving to LA certainly opened my eyes. I looked at it as part of my education. I felt that if I could learn to live in LA, I could move anywhere. Living in a new city was intimidating and challenging; however, it was always comforting to know that if I ended up not liking my surroundings, I could make a change after attaining my degree.

I also knew that because I had a college degree in hand, it spoke for my experience and education. I am now on the other side of the interview table, and I have seen how the companies that I've worked for interviewed potential candidates. They would look to see if the candidate had a degree; however, the college or field was not vital. What was important was that a degree proved to the company that this person could commit himself to something and complete it. In fact, you could even equate it to the good housekeeping seal of approval! This person has proof that he knows how to learn.

Besides preparing you for your career life, college prepares you for the social world. In the first year, you are thrown together with people from all over the world. They are in the same situation you are in, living away from home for the first time, away from family and friends. This creates a situation in which you make a new family. The friends and people I met in college have become lifelong friends; we went through similar experiences together, which creates a bond. I have more friends that I keep in touch with from college then I do from high school. Not that I don't like my high school friends or that I dismiss the important experiences with them, but the challenges I went through during college are what made me the adult I am. In the end, the college experience wasn't about getting straight As or mastering your degree; it was about who I became during the process. Like so many things in life, "what you put in, is what you get out."

CHAPTER SEVEN

Information
and Knowledge

Objectives

- to grasp the differ-ence between information and knowledge

- to understand the nature of a scholarly narrative

- to discover the variety of knowledge products

- to learn how to gather information

"Then you step beyond the road,
Where your feet are always
sure, . . ."

I learned that in order to get the information that you want, you need to know how to ask for it. Searching for sources is a skill that you need to master. I have to keep reminding myself that it's not the computer's fault. It is just doing what I am telling it to. I used to give up really easily if searching took too long, but looking for sources for the capstone project made me more patient when locating information. It helped me to see that every search engine is different and that if you know the shortcuts, it's not all that bad.

I also learned a different mentality when going through the information I had gathered. I usually thought that the book with the most chapters pertaining to my specific topic was the best one. It was usually moved to the bottom of the "useful" list if only a couple of chapters mentioned the subject I was looking for. But I learned that, at least when writing a scholarly narrative, there aren't always going to be sources that directly pertain to my topic. I need to use the discourse of other people and draw my own conclusions. I actually need to think for myself (imagine that!). I need to make connections between variables and discover the relationship between them for myself. This wasn't always an easy task, especially when a lot of the scholars used such difficult sentence structure and hard words. But in the end, I felt like a detective trying to find all the pieces of a puzzle.

—Anna Baguio

Information Literacy and Knowledge

Information is data, and applying information to a story you are telling creates knowledge. Information without a story doesn't tell us much. For instance, when we hear that 50 percent of marriages in the United States end in divorce, we have no context or story for that data until we give it some context. A context is reached when we start asking ourselves the following: "So what does that mean?" "What could it mean?" "What do I want it to mean?" The last question might be better understood as "What story do I want to tell with that piece of information?" If we looked for information about the history of divorce in the United States, we might tell a story about how the divorce rate has changed. We might analyze why people divorce in order to tell a story about why that 50 percent divorce rate occurs. By telling either of those stories we are giving context to the data; we are telling a story that has meaning. The story is the knowledge.

In order to make knowledge from information, we have to be able to find information. We have to know how to use databases, how to search the Web, how to find journal articles or books in a library, and how to find experts who can tell us about a topic. What we discover, though, is that in the majority of cases we aren't just finding information; rather, we are finding stories that use information to communicate knowledge. Another way to think of knowledge is as meaning. When we read a magazine article about divorce, we are given information but also an interpretation; we are given meaning.

To be information literate is to know how to use the information and knowledge of others to create our own story. Our story integrates our own information that we have from the ways of knowing, from our values, and from our perspective with these other stories, which come from the ways of knowing, values, and perspectives of others.

Knowledge is stored in standard places that can be thought of as "knowledge products." Certain categories of knowledge products contain particular types of knowledge or stories. For instance, journal articles contain stories by experts in a particular field or discipline, such as sociology. These stories are told in a particular way that is acknowledged as "good storytelling" for that field or group of experts. The stories are told from a particular perspective.

Government documents are "official" government reports or studies sponsored or conducted by government agencies. Books focus on stories that provide more of a historical context. Magazine articles tell descriptive stories emphasizing current events. Videos tell stories that use visual images and include perspectives with emotional content that helps us "feel" the story. Recordings provide stories that allow us to "hear" the story.

An information-literate person understands that creating knowledge requires one to find information in appropriate knowledge products that enables one to integrate the stories of others with the story one wants to tell. Information literacy is about choosing the best sources for your story, not the first story you find or the easiest story to find.

Journal Entry 18

Everybody gets so much information all day long that they lose their common sense.

Gertrude Stein

What is the difference between information and knowledge? Reflect on something you know, and see if you can divide your "knowing" into two sections. First would be a list of facts (information) about something. Second would be a few sentences creating a story (knowledge) out of those facts. Use the blank space in your journal to make the list, and then write out the "knowledge" in the lined section.

INFORMATION AND KNOWLEDGE

The mind thinks with ideas, not information. A computer thinks with information, not ideas. (Although, if the proponents of artificial intelligence are correct, perhaps our machines will be thinking like us any day now!) So, what is an idea? Think about the following three statements, and consider what information would create the ideas behind them:

Man is a rational animal.

Life is a pilgrimage.

The mind is governed by unconscious instincts.

When you consider these "ideas," you have to *assume* (and trust) that someone's experiences, observations, understanding of authoritative sources, and analysis thereof led to making these broader statements. For instance, the concept of being governed by unconscious instincts as something we "know"

It is possible to store the mind with a million facts and still be entirely uneducated.

ALEX BOURNE

(knowledge) must have been developed by studying human behavior, physiology, and so forth. The "facts" (information) consist of experimental data, observations, and other data and led to the story (or scholarly narrative) that begins with "The mind is . . ."

Thus, a scholarly narrative is a story that has been constructed by gathering information and making it into knowledge. Examples of how these "stories" are written and how you can find them will be found later in this chapter. What is important to remember now is that these scholarly narratives are not so unlike your personal ones.

The simplest way to get a handle on the difference between information (facts) and knowledge (narrative or story) is to create the distinction yourself. This activity should be done in groups of three or four students.

1. One member of each group should volunteer to tell a story derived from some experience. (I was walking across the street, two people came running from around the corner and knocked into each other, one was unconscious, the other had spilled a milkshake all over herself . . . etc.)

2. The other members of the group should listen to this story and write down a list of "facts" from the story (people walking across a street, people running, someone was unconscious, someone was drinking a milkshake, one person was wearing a red hat).

_____

_____

_____

_____

_____

_____

_____

_____

_____

_____

3. Once each of the groups has a list of "facts," these should be traded so that each group has a list of facts about which they did *not* hear a story.

4. Each group should now look at this new list of facts and compose a "story" with the facts. Given the list, what do *you* think happened?

_____

_____

_____

_____

5. When finished, groups should share their stories with one another to see how close the contrived stories are to the actual ones.

SCHOLARLY NARRATIVES

Before we analyze scholarly narratives let's go back to personal stories or narratives. These have simple components. They usually have a main character involved in some kind of event. This event usually has a crisis point that leads to some kind of insight, which is followed by a conclusion or affirmation. For example, your little sister (main character) is a member of a soccer team that is about to play in a championship game (event). The best player, who happens to play the

---

If you have knowledge, let others light their candles in it.

MARGARET FULLER

same position as your sister, is injured (crisis), leaving your sister to take her place. She does so and is quite good. You think about the season and realize she probably should have been a starter all along (insight). The game goes into overtime, and she kicks the winning goal (conclusion). This is a simple story, but it follows the typical path of a personal narrative.

Now let's look at how a scholarly narrative might be similar though different. The elements of a scholarly narrative are as follows:

- Theory/hypothesis
- Literature review
- Methodology
- Data
- Interpretation/meaning/conclusion/ramifications/significance

What kind of parallels can we find between these two types of narratives?

Personal Narrative	Scholarly Narrative
Main character	Theory/hypothesis
Event	Literature review and methodology
Crisis	Data
Insight	Interpretation and meaning
Affirmation/conclusion	Conclusion/significance

For now, let's just look at the simple definitions of these elements. They will be explored in more detail later.

Theory/hypothesis: a topic, the questions being asked about a topic, a problem that is seen within the scope of a topic, or the relationship between two or more variables

Literature Review: the study of what other people in authority have already discovered about a theory or a hypothesis

Methodology: the way in which data/information is gathered for the specific study

Data: who, what, when, where, and all the ways of knowing something

Interpretation/meaning: finding a consistency between your study and others, discovering a dominant perspective, or pinpointing a clear relationship between variables

Conclusion: a summary of what the findings might mean and what the significance of these findings might be to other knowledge being created

Journal Entry 19

Do not believe in anything simply because you have heard it. Do not believe in anything simply because it is spoken and rumored by many. Do not believe in anything simply because it is found written in your religious books. Do not believe in anything merely on the authority of your teachers and elders. Do not believe in traditions because they have been handed down for many generations. But after observation and analysis, when you find that anything agrees with reason and is conducive to the good and benefit of one and all, then accept it and live up to it.

Buddha

Read the above quote several times. Reflect on what it means and then write a few paragraphs explaining the quote and what significance it might have when you deal with scholarly narratives.

KNOWLEDGE PRODUCTS

Types of Knowledge Products

Stories (narratives), both personal and scholarly, are found many places. For purposes of this book, we'll call these places *knowledge products*—the places you go to find information or knowledge. You are probably familiar with most of these—books, journals, magazines, newspapers, films, videos, television, the Internet, conversations, government publications, documents, and diaries. You find different kinds of knowledge and information in each of these sources.

- **Books**—history, pictures, overviews
- **Journals**—research studies, opinions by experts, analysis, lists of other information sources
- **Magazines**—basic information, recent information, pictures, reviews
- **Newspapers**—very recent information, information about a specific place, reviews
- **Films/videos/television/music**—pictures, speeches, sound
- **Internet**—current or historical information from a variety of sources or individuals, data or commentary compiled by individuals or specific organizations, graphics, sound, music, moving images, pictures
- **Conversations/interviews**—opinions, direct experience, personal viewpoints, attitudes, history
- **Government publications**—reports, studies, statistics, laws, regulations
- **Documents**—reports, laws, statistics, facts
- **Diaries**—personal stories, history, opinion, reflection

Finding Knowledge

Where is knowledge kept? The most familiar place is the library. To date, this has been the place where we go to find information. In the library, there is a specific method to finding what you need. This includes a variety of database structures that can be accessed by using key words, author names, titles, or subjects. Of course, the way we search in libraries is changing continuously as new computer technologies afford us easier access and multiple databases. Some databases are simple, merely giving you a call number and place to find a book or document. Other databases offer the full text of journal articles and more.

However, the library is not your only source of knowledge. You need to be aware of experts, institutions, individuals, various disciplines, your community, and so on. Be sure to ask the following four questions when looking for information:

1. What knowledge resource(s) is best for my need?
2. What is the discourse?
3. What type of knowledge product best meets my need?
4. How credible and valid is my knowledge?

GATHERING INFORMATION

Database as Story

Databases tell stories. They contain records that describe information sources (books, journals, magazines, newspapers, and so forth) on many topics. Most important, they tell stories. You can find out about the history of baseball or the development of cancer therapies. Perhaps you want to see what kinds of stories have been told about reforestation or water conservation. All of this information can be found in a variety of databases, and it is all the basis for stories told over time by many people.

The universe is made of stories, not atoms.

MURIEL RUKEYSER

When you search a database, you retrieve sources to see which ones are most relevant to your topic. However, be careful how you define "relevance." What you may be doing is looking only for items that discuss your topic in the *way* you understand your topic. Stop! Instead, spend a few minutes examining the list of sources you have found before you choose anything. Try to decide what stories are being told about your topic. Remember, any topic can have many stories told about it. If you had been interested in cancer therapies, for example, you would have found sources that focus on the medications being used. Other sources would focus on the patient's well-being, and still others might focus on FDA regulations regarding experimentation with new chemicals. As you look at the titles, think about what the different perspectives might be. What points of view or different ideas did you find? Then compare the stories being told by this list of sources to the story *you* want to tell. What perspectives should be included from the list that will make your story a more complete, more interesting, more persuasive story? How do the stories in the sources you have found complete the story you want to tell?

Databases retrieve a list and display it in an order showing the most current items first. The farther down the list you go, the older the items will be. What you are seeing, then, is a history of what has been written about the topic in that particular database. Don't just choose the current items. Sometimes, older sources give you a perspective, context, or background that is vital to making your story complete.

Finding Information

The descriptions in these databases are made up of some fundamental information. For a book, you will find the author(s), title, place of publication and publisher (example: New York: Basic Books), year of publication, and total number of pages. For journals, magazines, and newspapers, additional elements are included, such as name of the journal/magazine/newspaper, volume number, issue number, and a more specific date of publication (day, week, month, or quarter). Many databases also include specific library locations for the items. For videos and CDs, the length of the recording is often included in the record information.

Finding information resources is about making choices from thousands of possibilities. The Internet is a vast and ever-changing repository of resources, but it can be challenging because no one is really in charge of it. Using search engines can give you a smaller array of possibilities, but they don't help you sort those possibilities very well.

The Library

Libraries have created Web pages that act as guides not only to the Internet but to resources that scholars more commonly use. Become familiar with the location and control of your library's Web page. What databases can you reach? What search engines do they recommend? What full text sources have been made available online? What does the library catalog tell you? The library's Web page is your information organizer. It is usually available 24 hours a day from any computer. When you are asked to explore a topic or select a scholarly story to tell, go first to this organized site of the information world.

Libraries are structured for exploration. Once you have an idea of what questions you are asking, you can begin exploring those questions without searching any database or library catalog. Most academic libraries are organized by classification schemes. Each item gets a call number—a number or a letter/number code. There are lists of these codes in every library and often on the library's website.

These classification schemes parallel the way courses are organized at your university or college. Just as there is a psychology department, there is a classification for psychology materials. For most academic libraries the classification code for psychology is "BF." To begin exploring what questions you could ask, you can go to the BF section of the library and look at what is there. Use the library structure to introduce yourself to what questions have been asked and answered already. In other words, what stories have already been told about your topic? Many databases even allow you to search by classification code. You could search the library catalog by looking for all the books in the BF section.

Search Commands

Most important to your gathering of information is that you know that all records are assigned a controlled vocabulary of subject words that describe formally the subject of the item. Thus, when you search a database, you are asking the computer to find specific items on the basis of what is actually in the record. Each database may have a different way to find records. These are called *search commands*. To search successfully, you should use more than one *search strategy*, or way to search. There are numerous ways to search a database:

- Key word
- Subject
- Different key words
- Different subject words
- Combining key words (and, or, not)
- Author name
- Title

Developing a Strategy for Searching Databases

Begin by identifying one of the following: a topic, a set of questions, a problem, or a theory/hypothesis. For instance, let's say you choose jazz as your topic of interest. You now have to do some *question analysis* using the following strategies:

- Key words
- Synonyms
- Narrow terms
- Broader terms
- Database language (controlled vocabulary)
- Boolean logic

How do you do this? Well, begin with a *key word*. Jazz. OK, now think of some synonyms that would work for jazz. Maybe blues? How about a narrower term? Miles Davis? A broader term? American music? What language does the particular database you are searching use for music and jazz and so forth? This is the controlled vocabulary you are looking for; these are the words that will lead you to your required information.

Boolean logic is helpful for searching databases because it uses the operators *and, and not,* and *or.* Here's an example of how it works. You have asked for a hamburger with cheese and onions but without mayonnaise and lettuce. Here's how your order will look using Boolean operators: hamburger AND cheese AND onions AND NOT mayonnaise AND NOT lettuce. A search engine would interpret this Boolean expression in the following way: *The user wants me to show her links to all the pages that include the word "hamburger" as well as the word "cheese" and the word "onions," but she wants me to subtract pages that include the word "mayonnaise" or the word "lettuce."*

This is logical and it works, even if it appears to be a bit clunky. The operator AND means that the word that follows has to be in the text of the pages that are to be listed in your search. Pages including the words following AND NOT will not be listed.

If you aren't completely certain about what kind of cheese you want, you could use the operator OR. Then you could ask for Cheddar OR Swiss. That way your search would come up with all the pages with Cheddar, all the pages with Swiss, and all the pages with both Cheddar and Swiss. If you take out the operators and just type in "hamburger cheese onions mayonnaise lettuce," you will come up with pages that include all of these words. And that isn't what you wanted, right? You didn't want mayo and lettuce. However, most search engines interpret spaces between words as AND, so you get it all.

Unfortunately, this rule doesn't hold for every search engine. Some on the Internet, such as Excite and Infoseek, interpret the space between words as OR. So you get pages with any of those words on it and may find all kinds of irrelevant pages on the cultivation of onions!

One thing is certain: it is good to become acquainted with the protocols for the various search engines or databases you use when you do your research. If you don't take the time to find out how they work, you can be spending hours of frustration searching through pages and pages of information that is only distantly related to your topic.

Example: Doing the Search

You can always search for more than one word at a time; however, how you put the words together means something for what you will find. For instance:

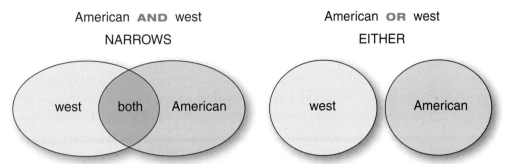

American **AND** west

NARROWS

west | both | American

American **OR** west

EITHER

west | American

W R I T I N G

Books as Information Sources

The man who does not read good books has no advantage over the man who can't read them.

—Mark Twain

Books can be personal or scholarly narratives. *Personal narratives* discuss the subject from the perspective of *experience* the author has had with the subject. *Scholarly narratives* incorporate the elements of *hypothesis, literature review, methodology, data, interpretation,* and *significance.* For this assignment, pick a topic of interest and find a book that follows the pattern of a scholarly narrative.

Your success in finding relevant resource material depends on two things: (1) the *search terms* you use and (2) the *actual content* of the materials themselves. There are several ways to explore the contents and establish the potential usefulness of a book without reading it from cover to cover.

For this writing assignment, do the following:

1. At the top of your first page, type a proper MLA or APA citation for the book.
2. Find a book that you think covers the topic you have chosen, and examine the table of contents, index, and chapter headings. After looking at these, write a one-page discussion of the most relevant portions of the book for your topic. Answer the following questions in this one-page discussion:
   - What sections of the book are most important to your topic? Why?
   - What sections will best help you answer the questions you are asking about your topic?

3. *Skim* the book to see if you can get a clear sense of its potential as an information source for your topic. Write a one-page reflection about locating books in databases. Describe your experiences, and comment on your successes, challenges, and frustrations. Describe what parts of a book give you the best clues as to its usefulness.

4. Conclude with a final one-page description of a book you wish you could have found! Make up a title and create a table of contents for this imaginary book.

5. Finally, make a list of key words, synonyms, and narrow and broad terms that would help someone find a good source on your topic.

What's In a Database?

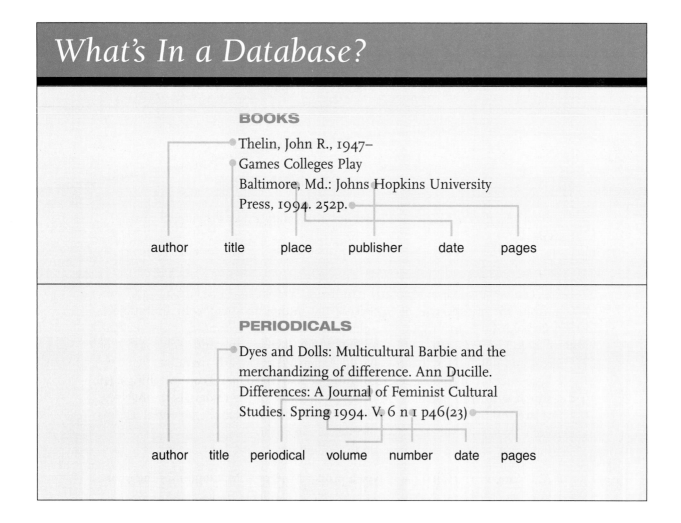

BOOKS

Thelin, John R., 1947–
Games Colleges Play
Baltimore, Md.: Johns Hopkins University
Press, 1994. 252p.

author · title · place · publisher · date · pages

PERIODICALS

Dyes and Dolls: Multicultural Barbie and the merchandizing of difference. Ann Ducille. Differences: A Journal of Feminist Cultural Studies. Spring 1994. V. 6 n 1 p46(23)

author · title · periodical · volume · number · date · pages

Think of a topic that interests you. It doesn't matter what you choose as long as it's simple. Then do the following:

1. Choose two databases in your school library that have records of journal articles.

2. Describe the contents of each database (its purpose, subject coverage, size, who produced it—anything that explains what your chosen database covers).

_____

_____

_____

_____

_____

3. Describe how you search each database (what commands are used, what words did you use, what steps you took to find articles on your topic).

_____

_____

_____

_____

4. Choose two articles from each database, and identify the following:

Author(s) _____

Title of article _____

Journal name _____

Volume number, issue number, date _____

Pages _____

Call number _____

Author(s) _____

Title of article _____

Journal name _____

Volume number, issue number, date _____

Pages _____

Call number _____

Many other sources of information and repositories of knowledge will be useful to you. One such source is a museum, a place that contains visual representations of ideas or knowledge. Many scholars research particular topics for years and then, with the help of museologists, choose a method of displaying this knowledge visually in a manner that appeals to and educates their audience. Though you more than likely have visited some kind of museum in your lifetime, be it a zoo, an arboretum, or a science or art museum, you probably have never analyzed what you are observing.

For this activity, do the following:

1. Go to a local museum, and choose one exhibit to analyze.

2. Make sketches in your journal to help you remember what you see and what you have experienced at this exhibit.

3. Describe in some detail the "story" that the exhibit tries to tell. In other words, what is the main or overall message of the exhibit?

4. What was the most interesting part of this particular exhibit? Why?

5. For what main audience was this exhibit created?

6. What were the goals and objectives of this exhibit?

7. Were the goals achieved? Why? Be specific.

Journal Entry 20

Now that we have all this useful information, it would be nice to do something with it. (Actually, it can be emotionally fulfilling just to get the information. This is usually only true, however, if you have the social life of a kumquat.)

Unix programmer's manual

Think of a time you required some information for a project that you needed to complete quickly. Did you know instantly where you would go to get the information? Did you try to find information in multiple sources? Were you successful? Were you impatient with the task? Were you satisfied with your search?

For this exercise, answer the above questions and then jot down a list of knowledge products you have used over your lifetime in school. Be sure to include all of the sources you have ever used to gather information. In fact, you can do this as a mind map, if you wish.

This activity is designed to help you do some research on the elements you will find on Web pages. You will also learn to use several search engines to see the differences in the kinds of information you find.

Search #1—Your Name

Write your name (first and last): _____

A. Using Yahoo!

1. Put *your name* in the space for searching in Yahoo!

2. How many entries did you find? _____

3. Skim through some of the entries and pick three that interest you (not just the top three that come up).

4. Make some observations on two of the three that you liked.

1a. URL: _____

What was interesting about this site? _____

_____

_____

1b. URL: _____

What was interesting about this site? _____

_____

_____

B. Using Excite

1. Put *your name* in the space for searching in Excite.

2. How many entries did you find? _____

3. Skim through some of the entries and pick three that interest you (not just the top three that come up).

4. Make some observations on two of the three that you liked.

1a. URL: _____

What was interesting about this site? _____

_____

_____

1b. URL: _____

What was interesting about this site? _____

_____

_____

Search #2—Your Hobbies

List two hobbies: _____   _____

A. Using Yahoo!

    1. Put *your first hobby* in the space for searching in Yahoo!

    2. How many entries did you find? _____

    3. Skim through some of the entries and pick three that interest you (not just the top three that come up).

    4. Make some observations on two of the three that you liked.

       1a. URL: _____

       What was interesting about this site? _____

       _____

       _____

       1b. URL: _____

       What was interesting about this site? _____

       _____

       _____

B. Using Excite

    1. Put *your second hobby* in the space for searching in Excite.

    2. How many entries did you find? _____

    3. Skim through some of the entries and pick three that interest you (not just the top three that come up).

    4. Make some observations on two of the three that you liked.

       1a. URL: _____

       What was interesting about this site? _____

       _____

       _____

       1b. URL: _____

       What was interesting about this site? _____

       _____

       _____

continued

Search #3—Occupations

List two occupations you are considering for yourself:

_____   _____

A. Using Yahoo!
    1. Put *your first possible occupation* in the space for searching in Yahoo!
    2. How many entries did you find? _____
    3. Skim through some of the entries and pick three that interest you (not just the top three that come up).
    4. Make some observations on two of the three that you liked.
       1a. URL: _____

       What was interesting about this site?

_____

_____

       1b. URL: _____

       What was interesting about this site?

_____

_____

B. Using Excite
    1. Put *your second possible occupation* in the space for searching in Excite.
    2. How many entries did you find? _____
    3. Skim through some of the entries and pick three that interest you (not just the top three that come up).
    4. Make some observations on two of the three that you liked.
       1a. URL: _____

       What was interesting about this site?

_____

_____

       1b. URL: _____

       What was interesting about this site?

_____

_____

CASH IN ON EDUCATION

College: The Trek to Self-Discovery

Dr. Linda Andrade Wheeler
CEO, Successories of Hawaii, Inc.

As a young girl growing up in Puunene, Maui, the largest sugar plantation town on the island of Maui, I dreamed of many things—meeting new people, seeing different places, learning more stuff, and certainly imagining the very best for myself. My elementary school years at Puunene School shaped in part the person I was to become. I knew I had the capability to be a high achiever, but I always chose to focus on "living in the moment" with my classmates, doing things I really enjoyed. I loved creating new ideas, thoughts, or things. That was far more interesting to me than having to learn that which was already known. I was always out for the experience, rather than the grade, for any of my classes.

When I continued my schooling at St. Anthony Girls' School, I quickly discovered that I had to learn to discipline myself to focus on academics and redirect my creativity in ways that were more aligned with subject content. At first, it was difficult for me to learn to adapt to a more academically oriented educational setting. However, in high school I gained a sense of confidence for what I wanted to do in my life and the understanding that competence was pivotal in doing it well.

College was where I expected to learn my craft well—what I was to do in life and the degree of personal excellence I could attain in that chosen path. And although I did gain the knowledge, skills, and attitudes to become an educator, what I acquired in the context of learning my craft has made more of an impact on my life than learning any subject content.

I never expected that in the context of learning I would discover more about myself as a human being. I never expected to learn to discern what was important to me in the world and worthy of my time and attention. I never expected to acquire the discipline to focus my energy on those things that mattered most in my life. I never expected to learn how to go about the discovery of truth—in other words, how to think . . . and how to apply that to my life in ways that would make me a better person. These are things I never expected from my college education. Nevertheless, these lessons were priceless, and they formed the solid basis from which I practice my craft.

As a first-year college student, expect that you will be given numerous opportunities to discover the best in yourself. Remember that your greatest asset is your uniqueness. That is what you will bring to whatever career you choose. You will bring meaning to whatever you do in life, but before that can happen, you must first find meaning in your life. College is an important time of self-discovery as you explore truth. Remember, everything in life teaches; it all depends how much you want to learn.

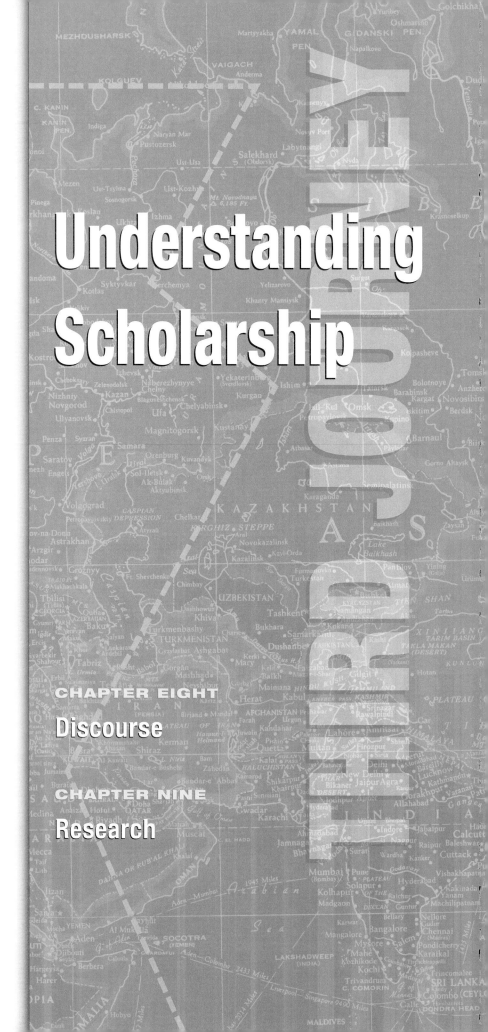

SOUVENIR:

How He Got His Grades

The concept of scholarship is daunting to most first-year students. You may not usually fashion yourself to be a scholar, and perhaps most of the scholarship you have encountered has been unreadable, hard to understand, and maybe even a bit boring! This perspective can get in the way of being successful in your college work. Sometimes you may feel this way about anything academic because you have never been challenged to do the work yourself from a place of understanding.

I had a student—let's call him Gary—a few years ago who was totally scared of learning in a college atmosphere. We were in the third week of school when he came to me with feelings of frustration and fear. Gary stated that he didn't think he could make it and didn't know how he even got to college. As a member of his high school football team, he assumed he was given whatever grades he needed to stay eligible, but he didn't think he was responsible for any of the grades himself. Now, in college, with no high school teachers to help him along, he was scared of failing.

THIRD JOURNEY

Understanding Scholarship

CHAPTER EIGHT

Discourse

CHAPTER NINE

Research

Introduction to the Third Journey

There is a term—"walkabout"—that is considered a derogatory expression coined by white men in Australia to describe what they considered to be laziness on the part of Aboriginal people. Originated in the late 1800s, when Aborigines were working on farms, the term referred to times when Aborigines left the farm and disappeared into the bush. Non-Aborigines viewed this act as lacking a work ethic or a commitment to one's job. However, Australian Aborigines had been nomadic for thousands of years and were used to moving camp often. Perhaps they left these jobs to follow food and cultural cycles. Often spiritual, these journeys were for attending corroborees (celebrations), initiations, and ceremonies.

In Aaron Fletcher's book *Walkabout,* a young white boy named Jeremy runs away from home and meets an Aborigine named Jarboe. Jarboe explains the term "walkabout" to Jeremy. He says that it is the time when people "go to the place they belong. . . . Perhaps a place they've never seen. . . . The one place where they belong in every way." This is a favorable way to think about *walkabout*—a journey toward learning about who you are in context of your world. In many ways, your experience in college is like a walkabout.

In the first two journeys, you learned about narratives, both personal and scholarly. You discovered that all of knowledge is, in a manner of speaking, a story. It is probably much easier to understand scholarship if you think of it as a story. Engage yourself in your years in college as though you are on a walkabout, absorbing as many of the "stories" that are being told around you. This is a time to learn as much as you can from the experience itself. Be open to the stories told by anthropologists, which tell you the story of humans, be they from the mountains or the islands. Listen to the stories told by historians as they explain the past to help you understand the future. Pay attention to the stories that scientists tell because these will explain your physiology as well as the black holes found in the distant universe. Study the stories you see embedded in art and sculpture with an appreciation of how they represent ideas over time. Read stories written by people, which will touch your heart, make you think, make you angry, and make you laugh.

All of these stories inform your education. The scholarly ones, as well as the personal, help you begin to construct your own stories. But first, let's understand the term "scholarship." What makes a sociologist's story scholarly? Why does a scientific article in a journal qualify as a scholarly story?

In the Third Journey, you will see how the kind of story that is told in a scholarly manner is actually a conversation, one that takes place over time. This is called *discourse.* Approaching

I suggested he pay close attention to what we were doing in class, ask for help whenever he felt lost or confused about the work, and trust that he had the ability to succeed. He agreed to work with me, but he still was not convinced that he could make the grade.

A couple of months later, during midterms, I asked the class about their exams. Most groaned and some were just glad they were over, but Gary smiled and exclaimed "I did great!" The student next to him punched him in the arm and said, "Yeah, great. . . . Jeez, you got a C. What's so great about that?"

Gary just looked at him, shook his head, and said, "Yes, I got a C!" I understood. It was *his* C. He had earned it. He knew now that he was responsible for his own work and that he could succeed. I was happy for him and knew that he would make it—which he did.

scholarship from this standpoint allows you access not only to information but to those who have researched a particular topic and now voice their findings, opinions, perspectives, and conclusions. To join this discourse, people do research, pull the information they find into a cohesive package, and then tell their own story. In the following two chapters, you will learn more about discourse and will practice jumping into scholarly conversations to see what it means to tell a story over time. After this, you will be given the tools to do your own research, adding a bit of your own story to the larger conversation.

So don't let the concept of scholarship overwhelm you. Keep in mind that you are on a walkabout listening to many stories to learn more about the whole of life.

COMPASS

"I had never volunteered in my life before this. It made me understand the common struggles in people's lives. . . . It made me understand and realize each person makes a difference in someone's life and future. It also made me more patient with the human race."

—*First-year student*

Include some form of service learning in each of your semesters. Find an agency to help out, work with children in a school, help out at the humane society, work with the elderly, do a special project for your neighborhood board, care for people in a hospital. All of these activities will be helpful to your community; however, even more important is how useful the time spent will be to your own growth and understanding. For example, when you listen to a child tell you about her home life and the lack of comfort found there you will automatically reflect on your own upbringing. When you help an elderly person tell his or her life story, yours will become more focused. When you help your local food bank feed the hungry, your own nourishment will be more evident.

Service learning is more than service. It is learning about yourself as reflected by others.

CHAPTER EIGHT

Discourse

Objectives

- to learn that discourse is a conversation over time

- to determine how to ask questions

- to understand the concept of question analysis

"Till you see that new horizon, You have never seen before."

Imagine trying to create a paper on a topic that you love. In this paper, you must remember everything you've learned through your years of schooling. This paper has to be the best because you should know a lot about your subject. However, there are always going to be things that you haven't learned about something. Your job is to figure out what you don't know. You want to reach that scholarly narrative peak while writing this paper. The only problem is you don't know how to start.

Let me ask you a question. What do you do when you are lost? You ask yourself, what is one way I can solve this problem? Although it may not seem like much, this is a great start. Asking questions is the key to finding answers. To begin your paper, you must first ask the question "Who?" Who is the paper about? Who might this topic affect? Who causes this topic to be what it is? Who is it that I'm trying to convince with this topic? These are just some of the questions I ask myself when beginning a paper. It gives you a better understanding of who you are and whom it is that you are trying to attract with this topic.

My next question would be "What?" What is this about? What do I expect to gain from this topic? What is it that I'm trying to express? Asking these questions helps you understand what your topic is about.

—Nikki Debebar

TRAVEL ESSENTIAL

Information Literacy and Discourse

"That was a great conversation; I wish I knew what they were talking about." Imagine that you are at a party that started about an hour before you arrived. You know some people at this party but not everyone. You want to join in the fun, so you walk up to a group of five people, two of whom you know. You greet them and start listening to what they are talking about. As you pick up the threads of the conversation topic, you begin to make your own comments, becoming a part of the conversation. After a while, you decide to move on to another group and repeat the process of joining. You might stop by the food table on your way. This experience is discourse.

Discourse is a conversation over time about a particular topic. People have contributed to this conversation in various ways, just as in a conversation at a party. Discourse contains different opinions, various perspectives, alternative information (data), and different stories about a topic. Discourse is the bigger story made up of smaller stories created by different storytellers. It is the broadest level of knowledge.

When you use a database, you are seeing discourse. A database lists the different voices in a conversation chronologically, usually from the most recent article (voice) to the older articles. How old an article can be depends on the database.

Discourse is also represented in a references list of a journal article, in the back of a book, or on a website. Authors reveal the other stories that are important to their story by "citing" other sources of information on the topic. The context for understanding any one story is created in this way.

An information-literate person is able to better understand a particular source by being able to find sources that came before or after that source. We know something now because we learned something else first. When we learn something new, it can change what we thought we knew before. We know that there could be different ways of looking at something. Discourse involves different perspectives, different interpretations. The more completely we understand the conversation on a topic, the more complete a story we can create.

WRITING

On Time

The kind of research you did during your high school years might be called a "stab in the dark" formula. You picked a topic, did some quick research, and wrote a paper. But did you ever really look at the discourse on the topic you chose? Did you ever study the changes over time in perspectives, available data, and discovery?

Let's go back to the kind of research you are acquainted with and have some experience actually doing. This will ease you into the world of research and scholarship on familiar territory and will prepare you to step out of your comfort zone and try your hand at finding the smaller stories within the larger, broader ones.

For this paper, take a look at the following clichés:

> Time waits for no one. Father time. Time frame. Time is money. Time to go. Time's up. Overtime. About time. Howdy Doody time. Time zone. Miller time. What time is it? Wasting time. Out of time. Time capsule. Time is at a standstill. Time warp. Time management. Time to act. Time out. Time in. Good times. Timing is all off. As time goes by. Hang time. Time to eat. Daylight saving time. Time to go. Time and time again. Air time. Don't let time pass you by. Quality time. Time travel. Time lapse. Time period. Behind the times. One time. Time trials.

You could probably add a few of your own to this list. The meaning you attribute to any of these phrases might differ or even be completely meaningless depending upon your culture. For this paper, you will discover a particular culture's perception, use, explanation, definition, or attitude about time. Do the following in your paper:

1. Describe a particular cultural perspective on time. Indicate the culture and why you chose it.

2. Include at least five sources as references. Use MLA style when documenting your sources. Your sources can be books, journals, magazines, interviews, videos, or websites.

3. Do something out of the ordinary—for example, accompany your paper with photos, drawings, music, or graphics or arrange your paper in such a way that it illustrates your chosen culture's perspective on time.

DISCOURSE

As discussed previously, discourse is a conversation over time. Scholarly discourse is done by scholars, in chronological order, using primary and secondary resources. These scholars have credentials that stem from their education, prior research and work, and validation by others in their field. They create the discourse through connections to others in their field through reviews of the literature, questions they ask of one another, and contributions they then make to the conversation.

The reverse side also has a reverse side.

You will most easily access discourse at the library. You could call a library an "archive of discourse." It is organized by departments, such as reference, collections, and instruction. The materials are organized by call numbers that relate to various disciplines.

Scholars use information to answer one or more questions inspired by a topic of interest. Usually, a scholarly question identifies a problem and a solution. Such questions are most often written in the form of a *hypothesis,* a statement about the relationship between two things that (1) identifies a problem and (2) identifies an answer or a solution. The standard questions should be familiar to you: *why, what, who, when, where,* and *how.* You might make your own list by adding such words as *is, did, can, will, might, are, do, does, won't, could, should.* This enables you to see questions that begin with *who could, when should, who is,* and so forth.

The following three examples illustrate the kinds of hypotheses made by scholars and what questions are being asked.

1. Stern, Susan R., Smith, Carolyn A., and Jang, Sung Joon. "Urban Families and Adolescent Mental Health," *Social Work Research, Vol. 23(1):*15 (1999).

Abstract/Summary/Hypothesis

The study discussed in this article investigated the effects of social and economic disadvantage on parent distress, family processes, and adolescent mental health in a longitudinal, multiethnic sample of 800 urban adolescents and parents. The findings support the hypothesis that poverty, life stressors, and isolation affect parent mood and disrupt family processes, which, in turn, are linked to adolescent externalizing and internalizing problems. The findings illustrate the importance of integrating an understanding of family process and context in assessment and intervention directed at adolescent mental health problems. (Copyright © 1999, National Association of Social Workers, Inc., Social Work Research.)

Questions

a. *How does* social and economic disadvantage affect parents?

b. *Why do* adolescents externalize or internalize problems?

c. *What can* be done about adolescent mental health problems?

2. Kammer, C. Scott, Young, Craig C., and Niedfeldt, Mark W. "Swimming Injuries and Illnesses." *The Physician and Sportsmedicine, Vol. 27(4):31* (1999).

Abstract/Summary/Hypothesis

Swimming has a distinct profile of injuries and medical conditions. Common problems seen among swimmers include "swimmers shoulder," an overuse injury that causes inflammation of the supraspinatus or the biceps tendon; overuse injuries of the elbow, knee, ankle, and back; such medical conditions as asthma, folliculitis, and otitis externa; and problems associated with overtraining. Swimmers are more likely to comply with treatment plans that minimize time spent out of the water. Prevention and treatment of musculoskeletal injuries often focus on proper stroke mechanics. (Copyright © 1999 by *The Physician and Sportsmedicine*. Reprinted by permission of McGraw Hill.)

Questions

a. *What kinds* of injuries are most common for swimmers?

b. *How should* these injuries be treated?

c. *Why don't* swimmers follow treatment plans?

3. Kosasa, Karen K. "Pedagogical Sights/Sites: Producing Colonialism and Practicing Art in the Pacific." *Art Journal, Vol. 57(13):46* (1998).

Abstract/Summary/Hypothesis

Students in art are routinely educated to associate the beginning of their creative efforts with blankness—the white sheet of drawing paper, the gessoed canvas, the blue screen of the video monitor. But what if this surface and space, identified as empty, were already filled with something that our artistic sensibilities and aesthetic schema are unable to detect? According to Henri Lefebvre, the primary misconception about space in Western society is that it is empty. For Lefebvre, space is always filled with the unseen social relations of people; it is produced by social relations and embodies them. We fail to see the historical and contemporary relations of people because we are taught to use particular conceptual strategies and categories in Western culture that ignore these interactions and therefore allow space to appear empty to us. The social, political, economic, and historical relations that actively produce the world and shape the way we live in it are not immediately visible. Ideology and power thus remain largely unseen in daily life. (Copyright © 1988 by *Art Journal*. Used by permission.)

Questions

a. *Who is* Henri Lefebvre?

b. *How does* Western culture define space?

c. *Where do* other cultures exist that view space differently?

d. *Why are* cultural differences about space important?

Understanding that research topics are established by asking questions helps you know what information you need. Thus, when you think up a topic, begin jotting down questions. In fact, the more questions you ask yourself, the more easily you will be able to make a list of words to use in your search for information. Take a look at the sources you find, and gather the questions that were being asked by the scholars about your topic. What kinds of questions are they? Are any of them similar to what you are looking for? You will find an endless array of questions to be asked about any topic.

WRITING

The Socratic Method

The Socratic method of teaching is to teach by asking instead of by telling. This method, which uses questions to teach and to evaluate the performance of students, is derived from Socrates, the Greek philosopher and teacher who was a mentor for both Aristotle and Plato. In fact, you read a long discourse between Socrates and Glaucon in Chapter Five. If you look back at Plato's "Allegory of the Cave" in that chapter, you will see that the entire conversation was in the form of questions. Socrates was teaching by asking questions.

Actually, teaching by asking questions is also a form of learning. In many cases, asking questions sheds new light on a particular subject. Sometimes a question comes from a different angle than expected. Varied perspectives also inform the questions, and the answers are sometimes startling and certainly always illuminating. Asking questions produces new answers, which creates thinking and expands everyone's knowledge or view of a subject.

As two people, sometimes a teacher and a student, interact, they discover more about the topic at hand. They become part of the learning process.

For this writing assignment, you will design a set of at least 20 questions that you will be asking a faculty member. You want to find out what makes a particular professor credible and able to teach a college-level course. In other words, what has this person done to warrant the position of professor in his or her academic discipline? Design your questions to get the maximum information from the person you choose to interview.

Hand in both the list of questions and the answers. Then write a reflective piece about what you learned. Did you discover anything new? Did the interview go as you had expected? Was the person you were interviewing reluctant to answer any of your questions? If so, why? What kind of conversation did you have with this person? Did any of your questions lead to longer discussions? Do you wish you had asked other questions?

From the library, select a journal article about something you know *nothing* about. For instance, if you know nothing about nursing, then choose a nursing article; if you know nothing about engineering, then pick out an article in an engineering journal.

Hint: Look for a publication that has either the word "journal" or the name of a discipline in the title—for example, the *American Sociological Review* (discipline name) or the *Journal of Microbiology* ("journal" in the title). Remember, you are looking for a scholarly journal article.

Once you have your article, photocopy it. Read the article carefully, and then do the following:

1. Identify the hypothesis of the article. In other words, find the summary of what the article is researching.

2. Write *five* questions that you need to have answered in order to understand what the article is researching. For instance, if the article is about a new procedure for nurses to work with cancer patients, do you understand the type of cancer the article is talking about? Do you understand the previous procedure for caring for patients that the article discusses? What else do you need to know? These are the kinds of questions you will need to write down.

QUESTION ANALYSIS

Remember the search strategies discussed in the previous chapter? To use the variety of databases available to you when you search for information, you must use a question analysis design to do your searching. Here is a simple chart to help you make a list of words whenever you are about to do research.

Computers are useless. They can only give you answers.

PABLO PICASSO

QUESTION ANALYSIS WORKSHEET

Key Words
What are the main words that describe your subject, and what do you want to say about it?

_____

_____

_____

Synonyms
What other words can you use that mean the same thing as your key words?

_____

_____

_____

Narrow Terms
What are some specific things you want to know about your key words or synonyms (time, geography, location)?

_____

_____

_____

Broad Terms
What larger subjects include your key words or synonyms?

_____

_____

_____

In Activity 8.1, you were asked to locate and read a journal article about something you knew nothing about. Part of the assignment was to write five questions about the article that, if answered, would help you understand the article. This next activity will help you practice how to use your question analysis strategy to find information.

1. Choose one of the questions you wrote in Activity 8.1.

2. Fill in a question analysis chart with key words, synonyms, and narrow and broad terms.

3. Use all that you have learned about finding sources to find three information sources (books, magazines, videos, journals, government documents, newspaper articles, recordings) that will answer your question. You will need to use databases, look on library shelves, and use reference books and indexes. Use all of the research skills you have learned.

4. During your search for three sources, take notes about how you decided to look, where you looked, and how you looked. Tell the story as *specifically* as you can of how you found the sources that answered your question. Tell where you looked, why you looked, what words you used to search, what you had to do to find the sources, and what you did that did not work.

Journal Entry 21

The only interesting answers are those which destroy the questions.

Susan Sontag

Draw a picture of your search for the answers to the question you chose in Activity 8.2. Then write a short description of how you felt when you were filling in the question analysis chart as well as when you were actually searching for the information. Be truthful. Were you annoyed? Did it take too long? Was it stressful? Was there any trick you discovered that made it easier?

READING

The following article was written in 1939. Read it carefully, and jot down such information as the hypothesis, the data, the methods used by the author, Samuel Haig Jameson, to get his information, and the conclusions he draws.

Certain Adjustment Problems of University Girls

Samuel Haig Jameson

A girl entering the university is an unknown, but a knowable quantity. An inventory of her experiences, desires, ambitions, habits of thought and action would enable her educational advisers to utilize appropriate techniques for her conditioning. Whatever may be the ultimate objectives of the university, such objectives cannot find realization without an analysis of the students who come to the institution as raw materials, to be transformed into certain finished products. Without this finishing function, the university could not justify its existence. Rightly or wrongly, such results are expected, particularly in a state university.

In order to ascertain those areas of experience in which freshman women found difficulty in adapting themselves to the aims of the university, and in gaining satisfaction of their wishes and wants from the university, and to discover the range of intensity and the extent of the problems of these freshman girls who found it difficult to make the anticipated adjustments, 341 freshman girls were interviewed. These girls told, in their own language, and without any suggestion on the part of the interviewer, their problems of personal adjustments since coming to the university; but in order to assure some semblance of uniformity for comparison later on, the interviewer asked a series of questions touching on certain special areas of university adjustment experiences. The volunteered expressions and the direct answers to the questions were recorded after the student left the room. All the necessary precautions were taken to reproduce their statements as accurately as possible in terms of incidents cited by the students and their reac-

tions to both specific and general situations. After going over these 341 case records, the types of problems elicited were specified. Seeming duplications were eliminated. Out of these types of problems, a questionnaire covering fifty-six areas of experience was prepared which could be answered by yes and no.

The next year, 1932–33, in the fall term, the study was carried a step further. One hundred and seventeen Freshmen for that year, representing both the dormitory and sorority groups, were interviewed first, and then the questionnaire prepared at the end of the previous year was submitted to them. Our purpose in doing this was twofold: to standardize the test, and to see what changes had occurred in the range of maladjustment experience areas of the freshman girls during these two successive years. Those problems which reappeared as constants were tabulated in this study. The rest were dropped out. Moreover, during 1933, of the initial 341 freshman girls 113 were again interviewed as Juniors in the University, and the questionnaire was also submitted to them. Our purpose was to discover the extent of solution of the problems during their travel from the freshman to the junior years, the emergence of new problems, the techniques of adjustment, and the validity of the initial interview by checking the answers through their answers to the questionnaire.

Some social scientists question the value of the interview technique. With respect to this study, however, we have become confirmed believers in its validity. Out of 113 Juniors only one case admitted that during her freshman interview she did not tell the facts. Our checking of the interviews with the yes-and-no questions brought the same result. Willful misrepresentation happens in less than one per cent of the cases. The administration of the questionnaire as a supplement to interviews was necessary as a double check. The questionnaire not only served to bring to mind problems the girl had faced, but enlightened her as to the breadth of problems which could be included among adjustment problems. Obviously, only those problems which weighed heavily upon the student's mind as needing adjustment were voluntarily expressed to the interviewer. Undoubtedly many of the girls because of established complexes, lack of support, and fear of ridicule, and the like, have concealed some of their major adjustment problems. The data presented in this study are decidedly student-centric; they reveal the problems which have come to the threshold of their awareness, and for which they have sought some answer. A few of them are presented here, therefore, from the student's point of view, no matter how much we ourselves may remain unaware of their existence.

In this study we have endeavored to focus attention on the local instead of the extramural problems. No doubt, several of the fifty-six adjustment situations elicited exhibit out-of-university forces and factors.

Nevertheless, they are manifestations within the university while the students are carrying on activities to adjust themselves to the direct and the indirect, overt and subtle demands of the academic world. Of the fifty-six adjustment areas covered in the study, only four are included in this paper. These four are grouped together because they deal strictly with academic and scholastic pursuits.

Universities indulge in advertising as do business firms. No educational institution can perpetuate itself without loyal graduates, and graduates are possible only when students enroll, and the enrollment increases by selling university education to ambitious men and women.

During this process of salesmanship some prospective students underestimate the financial cost of the anticipated degree. Although the university catalogues devote pages to the minimum and maximum cost per year of each specific course, students discover that the minimum specified is not sufficient to carry them on throughout the academic year. Moreover, there are students with different standards of living who only after their sojourn on the campus for a while discover that their education is going to impinge upon their funds more than they ever anticipated. Certainly there are students who after once putting their hands to the plough do not

turn back, but others offer sets of rationalizations in terms of the high cost of education in the university. Some leave the institution because they find the financial strain greater than their endurance; others stick by in spite of greater financial investment than they expected to make. The conflict arising out of this financial incompatibility is not a minor one for the girls of the three groups. For the Freshmen of 1931, the rate of incidence is 18 per cent; for the 1933 Freshmen, 21 per cent; and for the Juniors, 35 per cent. Apparently the longer the students stay in school, the more they realize the weight of their financial burden. Thus, with a constancy of 18 per cent, it becomes an important problem in the mind of the students, although a 4-per cent increase in 1933 over the 1931 period appears negligible.

It is unnecessary to present many illustrations here. The fact is selfdeclaratory. One student says:

> My dad interferes with all of my plans. He preaches *little money* all the time. He thinks that college is costing too much, so I never get anything I want or need!

Another, speaking of her predicament, states:

> I would like a change if I thought I could possibly make it financially!

Still another admits:

> Finances are now my biggest worry and have been for some time. I hope to make it through by next year.

A fourth, much discouraged, reveals the frustration of her family plans:

> Finances kept us from going to Washington, D.C. I've had to be careful this year. I hope to return next year. This place has cost more than my dad thought it would.

And finally one bemoans:

> I have no money for extras or for clothes. . . . I wish someone would tell us what to bring to college by way of clothes. I wasted a lot of good money buying things the salesladies said I would need. Now I am holding the sack. . . . My parents say I can't have any more. Who would have thought that college would cost a fortune!

These sundry illustrations offer only introductions to several parts of the problem. Each one of these parts is an individual matter, yet the experiences take place according to a social organizational setup which perturbs minds and creates maladjustment situations; and no matter how vociferously college and university presidents advertise the value of higher education in terms of financial returns after graduation, some students are still of the opinion that the investment they must make during the four years is more than they can manage. A few students go further and criticize the lack of financial equalization for the students in a state university, and their criticisms find supporters among the rank and file of the labor groups throughout the country. Equalization of the costs of higher education calls for a planned system for the youth of the state as a whole. If one third of the Juniors and one fifth of the Freshmen find it too expensive to procure an education in the university and become disgruntled, the matter deserves careful consideration by the taxpayers of the state and their special representatives engaged in the administration of policies in the field of higher education.

Item 46 in the questionnaire, related in part to secondary-school experiences where the technique of learning is on a different level, occupies the third place as far as frequency in incidence is concerned. Recitational method with dependence upon a textbook, coupled with the dogmatism of a teacher because of limited range of familiarity with the field, is somewhat incompatible with the university professor's seeming profundity of specialized knowledge. In the university, lectures take the place of recitations; formidable lists of references are substituted for a single textbook; instead of being exposed to the views of one person, the student is expected to familiarize herself with many diverse opinions; instead of lingering on one item until even the mentally slowest understands it, the lecturer states the point and passes on; instead of pointing out the important concepts by underlining them in the textbook, the professor leaves the girl to separate the wheat from the chaff for herself. Note-taking, classification, description, and impartial presentation are all new ideas. The university teacher is not hired to teach the technique of study as applied to his own field. As he has learned it by the method of trial and error, he leaves the pupil to grope for herself until she arrives at the promised land or perishes by the wayside. It is not surprising, therefore, to note that 42 per cent of the 1933 Freshmen felt themselves maladjusted because of their inability to know in advance the way to study their assignments. Neither does this situation tend to show much improvement after the students reach the upper-division level. Forty per cent of the Juniors for 1933 believe that they suffer because of inadequate techniques of study. What could be considered

more aggravating and perturbing to a freshman girl than the inability to study? And this problem shows 12-per cent constancy.

Here is a major problem worthy of the attention of the faculty and the administration. The present high rate of mortality during the first two years in college may be attributed, at least in part, to this indifference of the instructional staff. A few typical illustrations should be sufficient to give a glimpse of the reactions on the part of the girls. The Juniors admit:

"I think I still have a hard time budgeting my time for study. I didn't know how to study—really."

"I still do not know how to study. I think that that should be learned in high school. It's a waste of time, energy, and money to have to learn here."

"I haven't really learned to study even yet. This is my biggest problem right now."

"As for knowing really how to study I don't even today. . . . I can concentrate better now since I have been forced to study."

"I didn't know how to study. I didn't know how to divide my time. Study table merely antagonized me. I really haven't adjusted to this yet."

As for the Freshmen, the following are self-revelatory:

"I haven't made my grades and my sister has. I just don't know how to study."

"I have found my biggest difficulty was not knowing how to study.

"Of course my grades suffered. I don't know how to study."

"With no preparation for self-dependence in studying, it is hard for a girl to get along her first year. I hope it won't be so hard next year."

"My principal problem is working out my budget of both money and time and of concentration. I didn't learn to study when I was in high school."

Whether a new set of required courses in the technique of studying should be initiated in the university in order to tackle this problem, or whether the responsibility should be expected of the secondary schools, is to be determined by the judges of these two—interdependent educational administrators and curriculum-makers. Meanwhile, realizing that only a fraction of the secondary-school pupils ever go to institutions of higher learning, it becomes the task for the latter rather than for the former. The predominant attitude of the students, however, appears to shift the responsibility to the schools.

The questions, Are class discussions a particular problem to you? Do they really bother you? elicited 12-per cent frequency among the 1933 Freshmen, 14 per cent for the Juniors, and none for the 1931 Freshmen in the winter and spring terms, but for the fall term, 45 per cent. Apparently most of the Freshmen pass through a crisis period in the fall term when everything is new. Especially open discussions on taboo literary works, the theory of evolution, the mysteries of heredity and variation, and contemporaneous social problems offer novel intellectual food for thought which, because of previous biases and rationalizations, open the floodgates of emotional-reaction patterns. That free discussions on the part of the instructor and certain sophisticated members of a class are really emotionally disturbing features on the campus is well substantiated by the students. Here are a few of the statements taken at random:

"I am bothered when the 'prof' talks on sex matters. I am so embarrassed."

"Large classes are all right, but I hate like Hades to talk in them on certain matters. They deal too much with personal things."

"Large classes and their discussions bother me."

"I have had a hard time in my classes because there is so much discussion. . . . I wasn't used to boys either and to find them in my classes was hard at first. I didn't want to recite. . . . I'm doing better now."

"I am not used to seeing boys in my classes. I went to a boarding school before I came here. It is so very different. I feel very embarrassed sometimes when I go to recite."

"My third major problem was having boys in the class. The frankness of professors before men floored me for a while."

"I had a very difficult time with large literature classes. . . . I could not bring myself to recite as I should."

"I disliked reciting in classes and large classes bothered me."

"Frankness of professors bothered me at first. Then I knew them and I have not minded it since."

These statements suggest a variety of problems: subject-matter, frankness on the professor's part, size of classes, and coeducation. Some of these are reme-diable. For instance, one of the girls who was much bothered with the frank discussion on sex matters claims that "dating" with boys cured her. Others get used to the presence of the male sex in the classroom within a short time. Still others learn to take the discussions impersonally, abstractly, objectively; therefore they no longer suffer from self-consciousness. Hence, most of these problems of temporary maladjustment solve themselves with the widening of the student's range of mental and social horizon. The size of classes, however, presents an almost insurmountable barrier. This, too, could be handled by dividing the classes into smaller groups, but mass education is still the rule. There is the angle of per-unit cost of instruction to consider, and the administrators have not become enlightened enough pedagogically to introduce the necessary adjustments in the size of classes. It is not a matter of concern only to the students who find difficulty in adjusting themselves to large-sized classes; it is a real problem to be faced by the administration, parents, and particularly by the tax-payers. This problem invites more than passing notice on the part of the various groups.

Area 12 deals with the problem of disillusionment in college. Perhaps there are as many expectations from college life as there are students. Each girl has her fancies, her wishful thoughts, her ideals concerning the college atmosphere as a whole and the college man in particular. When actualities fail to measure up to expectations, disillusionment is inevitable. The question, Have you had an adjustment to make because college is not what you thought it to be? has elicited the following: 12 per cent of the 1931 Freshmen, 17 per cent of the 1933 Freshmen, and 20 per cent of the Juniors are disappointed in college life. The reasons for their disillusionment are legion, but from the quotations presented one may discern the range of the problem:

"Is college life worth while? I have begun to ask the question to myself. . . . There is so much emphasis on the social side of it to the exclusion of intellectual development. It is much more than disillusioning."

"My classes are too elementary for me; they are not stimulating enough. High-school stuff! I thought I would learn something new in college, but I don't seem to. You know, my father is a professor."

"I am not satisfied in college and am quite disillusioned with everything."

"I am disappointed in university life. I often want to go home to stay. I am bothered by cliques in the house."

"I am terribly disillusioned in college. It is not what I dreamed it would be like at all."

"I am terribly disillusioned in school, especially fraternities. I think this is a snobby campus. . . ."

"I think many Freshmen are disappointed in college, don't you? I mean that they dream of college being quite different from what it is and rush-week meets the illusion perfectly."

"I've found college different from what I expected. I found that my high school activities didn't help me to be more popular in college. . . . The house hasn't pushed me as they have other girls. . . ."

"I am a little disappointed in that. . . . I build up a 'castle' of what I thought life would be like here, but having to get good grades, etc., has taken all the gilt from my dream."

"I expected much bigger things than I've found here at the university. I built a dream which was unreal, I guess. . . . I am disappointed in my department. I don't want to return next year."

Expressions from the Juniors further supplement this dominant reaction pattern. For instance:

"I don't care about my course or my activities. I don't like this school. In fact I am terribly disillusioned. . . . I came here only to be away from home."

"I was not a leader in high school and had dreamed of being one in college. I was quite disillusioned in my dreams."

"I am quite disillusioned in school, and in people. . . . I was disillusioned in men my first year on the campus. These men expected nothing less than 'all.'"

"I have been terribly disappointed not to have been recognized in the house by being given an office this year. . . . I am so disillusioned in school and in people in general. I don't want to come back next year."

"College is an awful bore! Professors, students, and subjects. . . . Everything bores me. . . . The campus is snobbish."

"My biggest comedown was in my dreams of college when I pictured myself as the 'belle of the campus.'. . . I had practically no dates. The boys didn't fall for me. . . . I had been the rival of many girls in my home town—and such a comedown here was indeed hard."

These Juniors, after having had at least two years of opportunity to orient themselves with the objectives of the institution, still feel disillusioned and disappointed. Each and everyone of these represents a type. They reveal some of the causative factors in the disillusionment process of the girls in general. Some girls state clearly that the disappointments go to the extent of abhorring the university atmosphere altogether. A thorough analysis of these typical causative factors and a systematic approach for their alleviation might change the attitudes of these girls who otherwise will nourish an anti–higher education complex as prospective tax-paying citizens.

With the hope of adding flesh and blood to skeletal quantitive data based on returns from 341 of 1930–31, and 117 of 1932–33 Freshmen, and 113 out of the 1933 junior class, direct statements by these girls in personal interviews were offered. This illustrative material substantiates the quantitative results revealed in this study.

A university or college administration handles diversified issues according to a unified educational policy. The many girls and boys, each with specific problems, are to be handled in conformity to some system. The four areas of adjustment cited here could be treated configurationally only by those who consider the system of higher learning as a unit. Be it the president, the deans of men and women, the personnel office, or the whole faculty, each must have a clear-cut conception of a university's role in the preparation of future citizens. Administrative cross-purposes accentuate the problems of the individual students. A unified administrative front might be able to offer concrete criteria to attack the emergence and the incidence of the individual student's problem.

It is always amazing to see how much ideas and perspectives have changed over time. Certainly, in the previous article, the attitudes about women in college and notions of their inability to cope are dated and come from a time in which women were viewed differently than they are today.

For this activity, use a database to find an article written in the past 10 years about women in college. Then do the following:

1. Read the article

2. Write down the hypothesis.

_____

_____

_____

3. Get together in class in small groups, and share the various hypotheses of your articles. Then answer questions 4–6 in your group.

4. What method was used by the author to do the research?

_____

_____

_____

5. What were the conclusions drawn by the author?

_____

_____

_____

_____

6. What differences could you see between the article written by Jameson and the ones found in your group?

_____

_____

_____

_____

WRITING

Discourse

You are now ready to do your own study of discourse as a conversation over time.

Assignment: Trace the development of discourse on a controversial subject over the past four decades, and show how the discussions have evolved over time.

1. Find a very recent article on some controversial issue that interests you. For this, use the Expanded Academic Index, in which you can obtain the entire text of the article you find.

2. Find at least two articles for each decade that are about your chosen issue. You will have a minimum of eight sources for the paper.

3. Compare the methods used in the various sources you find.

4. Discuss the perspectives of each of the authors.

5. Discuss how the data was used by each author to support his or her arguments.

6. Summarize how perspectives regarding your controversial issue changed (or did not change) over the decades.

7. Use the following list of sources to help you find your eight sources.

List of Sources to Examine

1990s

    Expanded Academic Index

1980s

Expanded Academic Index	Sociofile (sociology)
Psychlit (psychology)	Social Work Abstracts
MLA Bibliography (literature)	ERIC (education)
ABI/Inform (business)	Newspaper Abstracts

1970s

Humanities Index (history)	Social Sciences Index
Art Index	Psychlit
ERIC	

1960s

Humanities Index	Art Index
Social Sciences Index	ERIC
Reader's Guide (general magazines)	

By now you should have a decent idea of how discourse is a conversation over time. You should also understand that when you insert yourself into the middle of the conversation, you are getting the information only from that particular time, space, and perspective.

Go back to the original article you found on a controversial subject. Note the date it was published and do the following:

- Find a source that is published *after* your source—one that adds new information to your topic.

- Find a source published *before* your source that helps you understand your topic.

- Find a source that *supports* the information, opinion, or perspective of your original article.

- Find a source that *disagrees* with the information, opinion, or perspective of your article.

- Find a source that was written by the same author of your article on the same or related topic, or find another author who has written about your topic more than once.

List these five new sources in MLA format, and write at least one paragraph about the information found in each source. Include in your paragraph how these new sources add to the information you had originally.

CASH IN ON EDUCATION

College and Me, Fifty Years Later

David Wolsk

Ph.D., Allegheny College Class of 1951

I recently returned for my 1951 graduating class's 50-year reunion. It was a unique experience that initiated much contemplation about how those four years had fitted into the rest of my life. We were a class of about 275 freshman, most living on campus, on the edge of a small town in northwestern Pennsylvania. Seventy-eight of us returned, almost all of whom I had no contact with in the interim.

By the end of the second day, it was as if those 50 years had been greatly compressed. Each morning as I walked alone from my dorm room to breakfast, I asked myself: what was it really like for me then? As a 17-year-old raised on the East Coast, I began to think back, with pride, of my exploits that first year of dorm and classroom and social life. I was part of the rebellion about the freshman rules, especially mandatory wearing of a beanie hat. And, in our dorm room, there was conflict with the dorm administrator about added furniture. So, although I obviously had propensities for not just accepting rules that seemed unjustified, both the social context of this small liberal arts college and the writing, philosophy in literature, and introductory psychology courses all kept my mind busy looking for answers. This was two years postwar, with a number of World War II veterans attending on the GI Bill, so there was a climate for questioning the past and looking ahead creatively.

The small size of the campus and student body along with spending four years together meant that I was actively participating in a broad range of social relationships. Although I also had a small group of friends, I wasn't able to hide myself within that mutual admiration society. I also had to deal with what the broader college group knew and felt about me. If I couldn't get a date for a big Saturday night dance, I was aware lots of students would know of my failure. So, I had to face up to it. There's a lot of character building within that context.

I also went on a European tour the first summer and worked the three others, along with occasional work while at the college. This combination now seems important for providing a reality base and broadening perspectives from textbooks and course reading lists.

Looking back on some of the papers and articles I wrote for the college literary magazine and my classes, I'm amazed at how much seems like something I could be writing today. Obviously, those four years became a major part of forming the rest of my life. Since I'm very pleased with how my life unfolded, those walks to breakfast filled my head with a heady sense of how much this campus had meant to my whole life. I could now easily understand how quickly our group of 75 returning classmates became like one big happy family, as we all shared those crucial four years.

Thus, my advice to the freshman of today is to avoid trying to learn reality from books. There is no teacher like the real world of real people making decisions for their jobs and life. Also, try to avoid getting swamped in a sea of faceless fellow students and impersonal websites. Instead, get engaged with your community and travel to explore other communities, other worlds.

CHAPTER NINE

Research

Objectives

- to learn about research methodology

- to recognize scholarship

- to identify credible and valid sources

- to do scholarly writing

"We may stumble through a storm,
With no compass but our own, . . ."

The concept of formulating my very own hypothesis that *no one* had attempted to prove was quite intriguing to me. I had never thought that I could create a paper in which I pointed out the problem and then answered it using my own observations and knowledge learned from different sources that I read. As it turned out, it was pretty difficult to come up with a really good hypothesis that would be provable and realistic. I didn't want to seem ridiculous or fanciful; in the end, I felt that I had come up with a respectable hypothesis.

I found that it was very difficult to locate sources that dealt directly with my topic. Instead, I found many sources about the general topic, but I had to try and connect the information to my hypothesis somehow. For example, I found many sources that talked about the history of the guitar. Since my topic was the guitar and its significance and contributions to society, I had to find a way to connect the historical information that I found in the sources with my topic. I decided that by showing how the guitar was used throughout ages past, it would be easier to prove that the guitar took part in shaping and molding society as we know it today.

Also, finding journal articles using the online databases was harder than I expected. I thought that it would be like finding a book in the library, but I was wrong. The results that came up were sometimes not even remotely close to what I was looking for. For example, when I was searching for sources on the construction and design of the guitar, journals that were simply instructional lessons for guitar playing came up all over the place. It was a bit frustrating to go through each one to find that one really good source.

I also learned the importance of using every single tool possible when searching for online resources. The Boolean logic helped me so much when searching. When I typed in "guitar history" initially, tons of results were simply about history in general or the history of a completely unrelated object. But when I typed in "guitar AND history," the majority of the results related to the topic. This saves time and energy and makes researching much more efficient and quick. Also, when using Web search engines such as Lycos or Webcrawler, always try to use the "advanced search" option. I never used to choose that option until I learned what a significant impact it can make when searching for a specific topic. All of these new tools that I learned to use through this unit about scholarly narratives and research will most definitely help me with my future research endeavors.

—*Matt Evans*

TRAVEL ESSENTIAL

Information Literacy and Research

Question: "Where do you want to go?" Answer: "I'm not sure." Response: "Then it doesn't much matter what direction you take."

Research is exploration. Research is about finding possible answers to questions. Questions are at the center of research. Most of us think research is about finding answers, but research is more about the questions we are asking that lead us to those answers. Researchers are evaluated as much for the questions they ask as for the answers they find. They are even evaluated for the way they found the answers, the methodology that they used.

Good research starts with good questions. The first mistake we make is thinking that the information we are after can be found by stating a topic: I want information about sexually transmitted diseases. I want to know about Jane Austen's writing style. I want to know about the effects of light on plants. Because all knowledge is formed through a process of integrating information into a story that brings together ways of knowing, values, and perspectives, our first step ought to be: What questions can I ask about my topic?

Articulating what we are researching in the form of questions helps us better know what answers we are seeking. For instance, what is it about Jane Austen's writing style that makes her different? Did her writing style change over time? What influenced her writing style? What are the distinctive characteristics of her style? Are there other writers who had styles similar to hers? These questions help us sift through all of the information that exists about Jane Austen so that we can better select those stories that are most relevant to our research.

A standard form of research used by journalists is the who, what, where, when, why, and how questions. A journalist seeks the answers to these questions to write a complete story that is thorough and provides context for whatever point the story

has. Formal research has an established form for asking questions: the hypothesis. A hypothesis is really a question asked in the form of a statement that identifies variables—for instance, reducing the amount of light a plant receives diminishes the amount of leaf production of a plant. One question here is, what is the effect of light on plant leaf production? Another question is, how much light makes a difference to leaf production?

Researchers ask themselves a series of questions, create a possible answer in the form of a hypothesis, and then begin a process of gathering information with a methodology. Finally, they use the ways of knowing to determine if their question has been answered either by the answer they thought of in their hypothesis or with some new answer they discovered. Often researchers answer a different question than the one they originally asked!

If we understand how important questions are to doing research, we are then better able to determine how credible and valid the information sources we use are. When evaluating sources we can ask: Why should I believe this author? What does he know that makes him someone I should pay attention to? We are deciding about credibility. We can also ask: What did the author do to convince me her answer is the correct answer? What evidence did she provide? Did the evidence really match the question the author was asking? Is there enough evidence? We are asking questions about validity.

An information-literate person knows how to ask relevant questions about a topic and understands that there are many questions that can be asked. Information literacy is the ability to evaluate sources on the basis of what questions were asked, determining if those are the best questions to ask, being able to assess if the answers offered really answer the questions, and deciding if the author is prepared to answer those questions well. Finally, being information literate is to understand that the information sources we select are the ones that best answer the questions we want answered.

RESEARCH METHODOLOGY

What Is Research?

Research is a part of life. You need to "look things up" whenever you need to find a hotel in a new city, want to bake a new dessert, or need to find the definition of a word. All of this is part of asking a question and then answering it. Scholarly research is telling a scholarly story, complete with all of the components mentioned in Chapter Eight. Research can be defined as activities that produce new knowledge. It is a critical process for asking and attempting to answer questions. However, it is not timeless. There will always be new research that contradicts,

---

It is the mark of an educated mind to be able to entertain a thought without accepting it.

ARISTOTLE

---

changes, modifies, adds to, or merely refocuses the answer to a question. Why? Well, questions change. What was once the best question to ask may no longer be the case. New questions bring new light to bear on any topic or issue. Consider the way we have controlled the use of pesticides—we've gone from acceptance to shock and horror at some of the side effects. Another example might be the changes in attitude toward affirmative action. New questions are asked, and therefore new answers are given.

Research is everywhere and has affected all of us in ways we don't think about. We all accept certain things as fact. For instance, how do we come to believe such things as "three out of four dentists recommend . . ." or "McDonald's french fries are preferred three to one over . . ." or that "heroin is addictive" or that "putting infants in car seats prevents fatal injuries" or that "drinking while pregnant can be harmful"? It is amazing how many questions people ask which lead to serious research. Thank goodness there are people who are interested in the breeding habits of a teensy fly in South America. Why? Because, recently, the knowledge of how this particular fly's hearing operates has spawned new research on how to create better hearing aids. What a wonderful bit of information to have!

Knowing about the methods used to do research will help us understand how we come to know what we know. Obviously, someone was interested in knowing the answer to a particular question, planned a research study, and then publicized the findings. Sometimes the results of a research study lead to incredible discoveries, such as the development of a more functional hearing aid. Other times, the findings serve a purpose for marketing or for further study in a specialized area.

So, if you read about those McDonald's fries, do you believe they are the best? Or are there other people who might have done research on french fries and discovered that Burger King's fries are better? When making up our own minds which study to believe, we should know what kinds of methods the researchers might have used. How many people did they ask? How representative was the sample? In other words, did they only ask patrons of one or the other establishment? Or, what about the concept of alcohol and pregnant women? Did researchers make pregnant women drink alcohol and then find out later that the fetus was damaged? Was there another method employed to find out this information? You would certainly want to know before making up your own mind about what to believe.

What Is Research Methodology?

Research methodology is a system of applying scientific procedures toward acquiring answers to questions. It is an orderly approach to problem solving and gathering useful data, using such strategies as interviews, public documents, review of historical documents, surveys, testing, and experiments to answer questions.

What Might Affect Methodology?

Remember reading about values and perspectives in Chapter Four? You studied these from a variety of points of view, such as gender and culture. The methods used by researchers come from a frame of reference that affects the way the researchers look at data. This might be their system of values, their philosophy of life, or the knowledge and perspective of their particular academic discipline or field of study. Sometimes you can find that perspective hidden in the hypothesis or basic research question. For example, if the hypothesis reads "Use of cell phones while driving affects accident rates in cities," you can assume that these researchers are already somewhat on the side of the fact that cell phones *do* have some effect on the cause of accidents. The researchers will be looking for evidence to prove their theory. This approach is acceptable. But would you look at the hypothesis differently if the researchers worked for large communications companies that produced cell phones? What would their bias be? Would their methods of research perhaps differ?

What Kinds of Research Exist?

Exploration. Does something exist? This could be an event, a thing, or an idea. For instance, you want to know whether men or women are more likely to sit in the front of a classroom. This kind of exploration might be done for purposes of a study on differences between male and female academic scores. Or, perhaps, you might like to know what causes you to have blue eyes and your brother to have brown ones. What happens genetically to make this kind of difference occur in siblings? This is exploratory research.

Descriptive. This research defines something by describing characteristics, behaviors, and actions. For example, to describe the population of America, researchers rely on census statistics. With such data, they can compile facts about single-family households, numbers of children, populations of rural areas, and so on. Descriptive research might also be used to show the mathematics behind the existence of a black hole in the universe.

Prediction. This kind of research identifies relationships that make it possible for us to speculate about one thing by knowing about something else. By looking at the descriptive data discovered by those doing the census, for example, another group of researchers might formulate theories based on that information—perhaps theories not about numbers of single-family households but about why so many of these households exist in one particular part of the country. Prediction could also be used, for example, to study high school GPAs and make a relationship between them and success in college.

Explanatory. This type of research examines cause-and-effect relationships—for instance, caffeine seems to keep people awake. Another theory that has come from explanatory research is the concept that smaller dogs are less likely to have problems with their hips. Why? Well, someone notices something—such as coffee keeping folks awake—then does some research on it and comes to the conclusion that caffeine has some effect on people's ability to stay awake. In the case of the dogs, statistics on breeds of dogs have probably helped explain the occurrences of hip dysplasia.

Action. This is research done specifically to solve a problem. This would include everything from doing research studies to finding a cure for cancer to developing ways to conserve water in times of drought. In other words, the research is intended to be useful right away.

Overall, research is about gathering information you need to answer a question and to help you solve a problem. Most important, remember that research equals evidence (authority). Otherwise, what you have is only observation and experience.

What Is Scientific Method?

Scientific method is thinking according to a set of rules, searching for the truth in the process. This methodology guides much of research. Scientific method does not rely on speculation or argument, methods of research usually found in the humanities, to create a scholarly story. Instead the components of the scientific method can be described as follows:

Empirical. Scientific method relies on observations of phenomena by the senses—touch, sight, hearing, smell, and taste, not unlike the "ways of knowing" you learned about in Chapter Six. Some scientists also deal with things we cannot sense, such as black holes or subatomic particles. Even these are conceivable through mathematics, however.

Verifiable. Research findings must be confirmed by others doing the same research. Otherwise, a study sits out there alone with no supporting evidence other than its own. Merely experiencing and observing something by yourself is not going to make the grade as scientific method. Therefore, you must hope that someone else can replicate your study and reach the same findings.

Cumulative. Scientific method relies on your adding research to that of others. This continues the discourse on a particular subject, so it is assumed that you relied on the work of those coming before you, that your research is using their information, and that now you are suggesting a new approach or some new evidence.

Self-correcting. This means that your research is open for further review. How this is stated is by using the phrase "evidence strongly suggests" in your research. You can see that by saying this you are not closing the door on others (maybe even yourself!) doing another study and countering your current findings. In fact, you will see that statement over and over again in studies you read. It is a way for researchers to keep themselves from being the final word on a topic.

Deterministic. Whatever you have discovered always has a cause. Scientific method does not rely on the magical or the supernatural. The use of scientific method presumes that events do not happen by themselves. Thus, the study of astrology or paranormal activities would not count in the realm of scientific method.

Ethical. This means that your research is value-free and that your own ideology does not influence what is being studied. It is assumed that if you are conducting a valid, objective, and legitimate research study, you are complying with the general ethical considerations inherent in your field.

Statistical. Scientific method subjects data to statistical analysis, such as averages, percentages, or more complex analysis.

Experimental. Because it deals with observable information, scientific method always has a component that is experimental in nature.

READING

This article by David Witthaus attempts to document the disappearance of a genetic trait for ugliness. Read the article with an open mind, paying special attention to Witthaus's hypothesis, methodology, and results.

The Ugly Gene

David Witthaus

Following in the footsteps of a multitude of prominent researchers we elected to examine the characteristics and practical consequences of a readily observable genetic trait. In this paper we describe the nature and inheritance of the ugly gene. Although research on the ugly gene is sparse, we found that research into the absence of the ugly gene (namely beauty) is extensive (Diamond, Bolton, Presley, Sinatra). Although a number of researchers have investigated this trait, the gene remains poorly understood and its evolutionary aftermath unexplored.

We propose that a gene deletion of the ugly gene gave rise to the relatively common trait known as beauty. This characteristic appears to be the fortuitous consequence of a spontaneous genetic event. An unexpected finding of our research was the establishment of the approximate date of the gene deletion which was the genesis of beauty.

Research describing the ugly gene's phenotypic expression is incomplete, however it is clear that the gene manifests itself in a variety of ways. Our research documented a number of the gene's physical manifestations (discolored skin, sagging skin, lack of muscle tone, sagging jowls, bags under eyes, unpleasant body configurations, a variety of nose conditions, double chins, moles, and blemishes).

As a number of colleagues have noted, individuals expressing the ugly gene are likely to encounter severely limited opportunities for procreation, thus a natural selection advantage may be conferred on those lacking the gene. Our research focused on confirming and documenting such an advantage and on analyzing the societal impacts of such a process.

We recognized that cultures portray their most ideal (beautiful) members through popular media (*Vogue, Cosmopolitan, Vanity Fair*). Historically this media has included sculpture, literature, painting and more recently photographs. By examining images produced over several centuries we hoped to reveal important information on the course of modern human evolution.

Our examination of early painting and sculpture was instructive. In these images the ugly gene appears to be expressed with a 100% frequency. We found this to be true through the 14th century. The images depict individuals with a variety of unpleasant personal anomalies. Even the 14th century works of artists such as Pietro Lorenzetti and Simone Martini reveal a complete absence of individuals lacking the ugly gene. Although the specific physical manifestations of the ugly gene were catalogued, the true significance of our observations is that individuals portrayed were uniformly ugly. This finding suggests that the gene deletion of the ugly gene had not yet occurred in the 14th century.

Examination of images from 15th and 16th century artists reveals the emergence of individuals lacking the ugly gene (Botticelli 1477, Da Vinci 1465, Zenale 1480). These images suggest that the ugly gene deletion occurred in the early to mid 15th century.

In an attempt to confirm the time of the gene deletion we examined historic literature. Biblical accounts do not refer to the ugly trait. This is to be expected in a culture that is uniformly homozygous for the gene. Furthermore the concept of ugliness could not be conceived until the gene deletion occurred. It is significant that by the 17th century literature by Shakespeare includes numerous references to the ugly trait. Because these works bracket our proposed gene deletion date we accept this as independent confirmation of the event.

Our research confirms that individuals expressing the ugly gene encounter limited mating opportunities. In addition to the competitive advantage in mating, absence of the ugly gene appears to provide other more subtle advantages. Evidence of this advantage is clearly evident today. Upper level positions in many fields are dominated by those lacking the gene (politics, marketing, cheerleading). Principles of natural selection indicate that in the absence of some offsetting advantage provided by the ugly gene it will decline and disappear.

Our research suggests a rapid disappearance of the ugly gene from the species. We were surprised by the magnitude of the advantage conferred on those lacking the gene. Although estimates by our research team vary, the current percentage of the population lacking the ugly gene appears to be between 30% and 50% (considerable regional variation was noted). In the short span of roughly 16 generations, it appears that the gene deletion occurred and spread to its current frequency of approximately 40%. This rapid conversion hints at an unprecedented advantage offered by the gene deletion. The pace of this evolution greatly exceeds any heretofore described.

Our research revealed an unexpected deviation from mating patterns predicted based on the presence of the ugly gene. Initial observations of the patterns of mate selection appeared to the research team to be complex; additional study revealed that simple patterns are present, but that a significant skewing of the natural selection process is mediated by wealth. In many cases wealth appears to mitigate the effects of the ugly gene. Although the mode and action by which wealth skews mating behavior is unclear, targeted observations confirm it is so (see Lyle Lovett and Bill Gates case studies).

We conclude that a gene deletion in the 15th century gave rise to individuals lacking the ugly gene. The gene has conferred such a competitive advantage that the purging of the ugly gene from the species has progressed with incredible speed and is likely to progress unabated.

In light of the evidence regarding the practical consequences of the ugly gene we can forecast societal impacts of the phenomena of gene clearance and phenotype concentration. As the gene clearance progresses, concentrated pockets of individuals expressing the ugly gene will further develop in response to intense competition for mates in gene-poor areas. Additionally, we anticipate further concentration of wealth among individuals expressing the ugly gene as this will be a key determinant of mating success for those possessing the ugly gene in largely gene-poor populations.

Our research provides a message of hope for our progeny. Not only will their generation be more beautiful (less ugly) than ours, those individuals retaining the ugly gene will almost certainly be filthy rich.

References

1. N. Diamond, *Beautiful Girl*, Electra, 1996
2. M. Bolton, *A Love So Beautiful*, Colombia, 1988
3. E. Presley, *Beautiful Baby*, Sun Records, 1962
4. F. Sinatra, *The Beautiful Strangers*, Reprise, 1969

From "The Ugly Gene" by David Witthaus, *The Journal of Irreproducible Results*, Vol. 45(3), May/June 2000, p. 11. Reprinted with permission of *The Journal of Irreproducible Results*.

Journal Entry 22

Learning is not compulsory. . . . Neither is survival.

W. Edwards Deming

The article "The Ugly Gene" mimics a scholarly narrative. For this journal entry, go back to the article and see if you can find the hypothesis, the methods of research used, the data discovered, and the findings and conclusions. Can you find evidence of these aspects of a scholarly narrative? Where? Is there anything wrong with this article? Was the author convincing? Why or why not?

LET'S DO RESEARCH

You've now read enough about scholarly narrative and should have some experience reading scholarly narratives. It is time for you to actually do the research yourself, to go through the components of research to really understand what they entail. What's first? A topic.

Picking a Topic

Perhaps one of the hardest parts of research for a first-year student is choosing an interesting topic. In high school, you were often given a list of topics from which you could choose. Those weren't always the most exciting topics! Now that you will be doing some writing of scholarly narrative, you have the option of choosing anything with which to work. However, to help you out, below is a sample list of questions you might ask yourself.

The initial mystery that attends each journey is: how did the traveler reach his starting point in the first place?

LOUISE BOGAN

There are many ways of thinking about a topic. Pick something, anything (music, a politician, a social issue, food, a sport), and ask some questions. Let's say you picked music. Here are some questions you would ask.

- What does music mean?
- What is the function of music?
- What is the value of music?
- What is the significance of music?
- How is music made?
- What causes music to happen?

Don't forget all those questions you learned about earlier. Use the *who, what, why, when, where,* and *how,* and add the other words—*might, could, can, should, will, must, did,* and so forth. That way you can begin to ask good questions that will help you narrow your topic. For example, you could ask: How might this music change? What could happen to this music? Who will play this music? How did this music come about? Why should we listen to this music? Now, pick a topic and fill in the following.

Researcher's (Your) Name:

Topic:

Three Main Questions about the Topic:

Moving from a Question to Its Significance

1. *Name your topic:* _____

   I am studying . . . _____

In the earliest stages of a research project, when you have only a topic and maybe the first glimmerings of a few good questions, try to describe your work in a sentence like this: *I am learning about/working on/studying* _____.

2. *Suggest a question:* _____

   _____

   because I want to find out who/how/why . . . _____

   _____

As early as you can, try to describe your work more exactly by adding to that sentence an indirect question specifying something about your topic that you do not know or fully understand but want to: *I am studying X because I want to find out who/what/when/where/whether/why/how* _____. When you can add that kind of clause, you have defined both your topic and your reason for pursuing it.

3. *State the rationale for the question:* _____

   _____

   in order to understand how/why/whether _____

   _____

   _____.

There is one more step. It is a hard one, but if you can take it, you transform your project from one that interests you to one that may interest others. It becomes a project with a rationale explaining why it is important to ask your question at all. To do that, you must add an element that explains why you are asking your question and what you intend to get out of its answer. In step 3, you add a second indirect question: *I am studying X because I want to find out who/what/when/where/whether/why/how X in order to understand how/why/whether X.*

Beginning the Research

Remember key words. Go back to your question analysis worksheet, and fill it in for your new topic.

- **Key words:** the main words that describe your topic
- **Synonyms:** other words that mean the same thing as your key words
- **Narrower terms:** more specific things you want to know about your key words (time, geography, population)
- **Broader terms:** larger subjects that include your key words

Remember Boolean logic. For many kinds of information searches, it is important to analyze and develop relationships between the concepts or key ideas that you are using. This is especially important in computer-assisted searching, either online or on CD-ROM. Once you have identified concepts and selected suitable key words or phrases, you can establish the relationships that most clearly define or limit your search. For most electronic searching, three words—*or, and, not*—are used as logical operators in a system developed by George Boole, a mathematician. The basic uses of these Boolean operators are briefly defined again below. The diagrams used to illustrate these logical operators are called Venn diagrams.

Search Question: How does electronic media affect student and faculty communication?

OR. Used for synonymous terms; you want information on either topic.

electronic media OR telecommunication

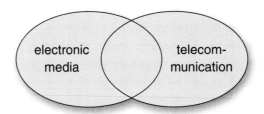

AND. Used to connect two terms or ideas; you want only the information that contains both concepts together.

electronic media AND faculty

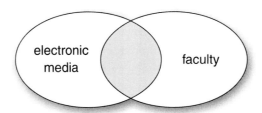

NOT. Used to exclude a term or idea; you do not want this topic.

electronic media NOT radio

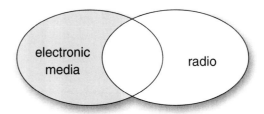

WRITING

Locating Sources for Your Research

1. Identify below some of the key words that describe your topic:

   _____

   _____

   _____

   _____

2. State your hypothesis. Then write a few sentences explaining what your intentions are in your research.

   _____

   _____

   _____

   _____

   _____

   _____

   _____

   _____

3. Find five sources that you will use to help you with your topic. These sources should include:
   - One journal article from the Expanded Academic Index
   - One magazine article from the Expanded Academic Index
   - One book
   - One source from the ERIC database
   - One website

4. Do your citations in MLA format, and write at least one paragraph as an annotation of each source (see the box on annotations on the following page.)

5. Indicate where you found each source.

Annotations

An *annotation* is simply a descriptive paragraph telling a reader what can be found in a particular source. Focus on the main point of a source, and include a sentence about whatever conclusions were drawn. For a book, you might write an annotation in the following manner:

Bibliographic entry in MLA style

Paragraph about the source

9.1 DETERMINING CREDIBILITY AND VALIDITY

What are your definitions of *credibility* and *validity*? What indicators do you use to decide? Look at the various sources in the chart below, and think about what would make the source credible and the information valid to you. Fill in the chart accordingly.

Source	Credibility	Validity
story from a friend		
story you tell someone		
television program		
website		
nonfiction book		
novel		
magazine article		
newspaper article		
journal article		

EVALUATING SOURCES

You have now found the first five sources for a research proposal you will be writing later in this chapter. However, for now, you need to learn about the concepts of validity and credibility. Remember reading the article entitled "The Ugly Gene"? Did you have any notion that the article might have been bogus from the start? What made you think so? What was missing? Could you have verified that research? It is a good idea to understand how to assess both the validity of a study and the credibility of those who conducted it.

Validity

There are at least five ways to check the validity of a particular piece of scholarly narrative. Was the study:

1. Based on empirical evidence (experiments)?
   A. Can you find contradictory or confirming experiments?
2. Based on authority?
   A. Can you find evidence that contradicts the authority?
   B. Does the authority not take your evidence or ideas into consideration?
   C. Is the topic out of the authority's standard expertise?
3. Based on prior systems of knowledge and beliefs (assumptions)?
   A. Is the evidence not applicable in this particular situation?
   B. Are the two situations not really the same thing?
4. Based on cultural evidence?
   A. What assumptions have been made about what is true?
   B. Have the values or the situation changed?
5. Based on methodology?
   A. Was the method chosen the best method to use?
   B. Was the method accurate (large enough, thorough, comprehensive) for the hypothesis?

It is even necessary to ensure your own validity. You should always be prepared for *rebuttals*. Therefore, in your research, you can address possible objections and questions. Second, you can make *concessions*. In other words, if you can't rebut an objection or question, admit it. Finally, state the *limitations* of your knowledge. This means that you can give conditions—what has to happen for what you say to have it be valid. You can direct the scope of your research by using such words as *widely, one of, especially, among those, often, good, tend to be, may have, significant, key aspects, many of, weight of, suggests,* and *probably.*

Credibility

Another check you need to do when using sources is to evaluate the authors. Are the authors experts on the topic? Do they have credentials to write on this particular topic? Are they published in this or related fields sufficiently often for their opinions to be believed? Here are ways to find out how credible a particular author might be:

1. Do an author search in various databases. (What else has the author written about this or other subjects?)

2. Look for book reviews or journal articles by others commenting on the author's work. Do a subject search by the author's name to find commentary by others about the quality of the author's work or ideas.

3. Find biographical reference books that may give information about the author.

Another way to find out if the sources you are using are sound is to look into the discourse on a particular subject. Ask yourself if the content or the nature of the discussion has changed over time. Find out how your particular source fits into the overall conversation. Use these methods as ways to find out:

1. Do a subject search by key words in databases for the subject of the author's writing, noting the nature of the discussion and the time periods.

2. Note the reputation of the publisher. Is it a major journal or discipline? A university press? Or is it a press that concentrates on publishing a particular type of work? Maybe it is a press with a questionable reputation (such as a vanity press)?

Finally, look at the methodology of the work. How does the author support opinions found in your source?

1. Examine footnotes and references.

2. Examine evidence given by the author for opinions.

3. Determine if the methodology supports the opinion. (Is the sample size large enough? Was the theory actually proven?)

4. Compare these results to the results of your author credibility search and your look into the discourse.

www.Tips

Evaluating the World Wide Web

Try to answer the following questions about a website you have found:

1. Who is responsible for the site? (Who is the author?)

2. What can you find out about the responsible party?

3. Where does the site's information come from (opinion, facts, documents, quotes, paraphrasing, excerpts) ?

4. What are the key concepts, issues, and "facts" of the site?

5. Can the key elements of the site be verified by another site or source?

	CREDIBILITY (BELIEVABLE)	VALIDITY (EVIDENCE)
Author	degrees, experience, affiliation (where author works), recognition (awards)	credentials relate to topic, bias toward or against a particular perspective
Source	affiliation with university, professional association, government; reputation for accuracy	presence or lack of bias toward a particular perspective
Methodology	experiments; data; analysis of personal knowledge; analysis/ interpretation of other research, writing, or documents, not just opinion	accurate methodology (large enough samples); thorough, comprehensive, relevant sources; appropriate methodology
Discourse	context (of topic or author), reputation (what others say about author's work or ideas)	appropriate sources, contradictory and/or confirming sources
Content	intended audience identified, currency, fact and opinion differentiated, discourse used	assumptions, questions unanswered, alternative perspectives, evidence provided, conclusions logical

How to find credibility and validity indicators:

1. Read.
2. Think.
3. Search databases/websites for discourse (look for supporting and critical sources).
4. Search databases/websites for author (both by and about).
5. Examine footnotes and references.
6. Look at biographical reference books/websites.

This is an opportunity for you to practice finding out the credibility of an author.

1. Work in pairs.
2. Choose one of the following names:

Maya Angelou	literature
Neil Postman	education
William F. Buckley, Jr.	politics
George Stephanopoulos	politics
Deborah Tannen	psychology
Ronald David Laing	sociology
Dinesh D'Souza	sociology
Joseph Klein	journalism
Barbara Tuchman	history
Wayne Booth	literature
Frank Kermode	literature
Allan Bloom	education
Martin E. Marty	religion
Roger Ebert	film

3. Identify the person's expertise (credibility) as much as possible in the following categories:

Degrees:
_____

Work Experience:
_____
_____
_____
_____

Publications:
_____
_____
_____
_____
_____

REVIEW OF LITERATURE

What Is a Literature Review?

A literature review finds, evaluates, and integrates past research. It is a critical synthesis of the research literature that:

- Shows how previous studies relate to one another
- Shows similarities and differences between studies
- Discriminates between relevant and irrelevant information
- Indicates weaknesses in previous work

The purpose of the literature review is to synthesize many specific events and details into a comprehensive whole. This may involve featuring a problem or an issue and a consideration of what the relevant literature may say about this problem or issue. Synthesis results from weaving together many smaller generalizations and interpretations into a coherent main theme.

Writing a Literature Review

A literature review is always a required part of any research proposal because its purpose is to analyze critically a segment of a published body of knowledge. You will do this through summary, classification, and comparison of prior studies, reviews, theoretical articles, and other historical information. A good review encompasses the following:

1. Start the introduction by describing the problem area or issue; gradually shift your focus to the specific research hypotheses, purposes, or questions.
2. Explicitly state the significance of the topic in the introduction.
3. Use of the first person is acceptable when it helps smooth the flow of the introduction.
4. Present the review as an essay, not as an annotated list.
5. Emphasize the findings of previous research.
6. Point out trends and themes in the literature.
7. Point out gaps in the literature.
8. Feel free to express opinions about the quality and importance of the research being cited.
9. Use the review to establish the need for more study, including the object of data collection, how the data (information) will be collected, how it will be analyzed, and what results or conclusions you expect to reach.

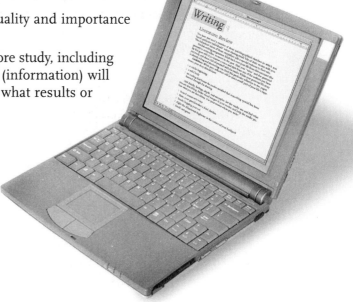

Which of the following resources will provide you with the most information sources about your topic? Mark each resource that you think is better for finding information on your topic.

- ☐ Books Databases
- ☐ Video/film Databases
- ☐ Expanded Academic Index
- ☐ ERIC (education-related articles)
- ☐ ABI/Inform (business-related articles)
- ☐ Internet websites
- ☐ Psychlit (psychology-related articles) (CD-ROM)
- ☐ MLA Bibliography (literature-related articles) (CD-ROM)
- ☐ Sociofile (social issues–related articles) (CD-ROM)
- ☐ Social Work Abstracts (social issues) (CD-ROM)
- ☐ Newspaper Abstracts (CD-ROM)
- ☐ America: History and Life (reference)
- ☐ Historical Abstracts (reference)
- ☐ Humanities Index (history, art, architecture, philosophy, religion)
- ☐ Social Sciences Index
- ☐ Religion Index
- ☐ Reader's Guide
- ☐ Art Index
- ☐ TV Schedules (for programs related to your topic)
- ☐ Interviews (with people knowledgeable about your topic)

Plagiarism

Definition: to present the ideas or writings of another person as your own
   You are plagiarizing if:

1. You use substantive words, phrases or structures from your source without documentation. Whether you "lift" one or two words or a whole page, you are plagiarizing.

2. You use any ideas that are clearly *not* common knowledge (for example, milk comes from cows) without citing your sources.

3. You copy from any source without the use of quotation marks or citations.

Journal Entry 23

But it is better to fail in originality than to succeed in imitation.

Herman Melville

Think about the last time you wrote a research paper or any paper at all for which you had to use sources. Were you aware of how easy it was to pick words off the pages and use them in your own writing? Did you make a conscious effort to give proper citations to all of the information you might have "lifted" from other work?

Take a moment to reflect on your experiences with research for writing and what decisions you had to make about using and citing sources. Include in this journal entry your notion of when you are taking someone else's work for your own. Is it only when you use direct quotes? Think about it.

WRITING

Scholarly Narrative

The capstone project for this Third Journey is to create a pathfinder for your topic. A *pathfinder* is a list of resources created to help individuals locate relevant materials on a particular topic. This assignment will mirror the elements of scholarly narrative and will ask you to describe in detail the process you went through to research your chosen topic.

1. *Hypothesis.* Make a statement that describes your central question or problem as a relationship between two or more variables. List at least three questions that you asked that helped you create your hypothesis.

2. *Methodology.* Describe at least four places that you looked for information. Include the following:

   a. The name of the databases or search engines you used and a general description of their contents.

   b. The key words or search commands you used to find sources in each database and search engine.

   c. The best terms to look under in each database and search engine.

3. *Literature Review.* Make a bibliography in correct MLA citation style of your sources for your research topic. Include at least *two books, three journal articles, three magazine or newspaper articles,* and *two websites.* (If you found more than these 10 references, list all of them.) Write a summary paragraph (annotation) for each of your sources describing the contents of each source. This annotated bibliography is your "topic pathfinder."

4. *Interpretation.* Discuss the most important knowledge you learned about your topic from all of your sources.

5. *Significance.* Describe the process of locating information to develop your research topic. Provide advice to other researchers about how to find information effectively and efficiently for this topic.

6. *Conclusion.* Write a summary paragraph about the answer you discovered for your hypothesis. Conclude with at least three questions that your research did *not* answer that still need to be researched.

7. *Reflection.* Write a short, two-paragraph reflection that describes what you have learned about scholarly narrative and how you think your writing and reading have changed.

CASH IN ON EDUCATION

Tod Benedict
Golf Pro

I spent 22 years as a naval officer, retiring in 1996 as a commander. I spent the first 12 years on submarines and eventually became a commanding officer of a sub. I then worked for 10 years in the Navy as a meteorologist and an oceanographer, including a stint as chief tropical cyclone weather forecaster for the Pacific and Indian Oceans. I finished my career as an oceanographer for the Pacific Submarine Force.

After retiring, I pursued a career in the golf industry, where I am now employed as the head golf professional at Rolling Hills Golf Club in Longwood, Florida. It is a 300-member private club and as far as I could get from Navy life!

Thoughts on education: I owe everything I have done in my life to my teachers and instructors. Regardless of what individuals may think as they progress through their lives, things do not come naturally! I was not that interested in books and learning as I went through high school. I had enough intelligence to get by without much effort; however, reality hit once I got into college. My fellow students were actually as smart as I was! I now had to work to keep up! The instructors challenged you, and you had to respond or get left in the dust.

I thought college was tough, but then I was commissioned in the Navy. The best students from all over the country were thrown together by a common dream—to defend their nation. Oh, how I wished I had applied myself more when I was in school and under the security blanket of receiving an education. Now I was expected to respond to real-life situations in an intelligent manner on an $800 million submarine with 150 people's lives depending on me.

Study habits developed in college helped me get by, and eventually it all became second nature as training and real-life experiences progressed. However, I know it would have been much easier had I challenged myself in college with harder, more advanced classes and not taken the easy route to a degree.

When it came time for me to retire from the Naval Service, I reflected on all of the things my education had brought me—the opportunity to travel around the world and visit six of the seven continents; the chance to command a ship at sea; and the chance to meet people and make friends all over the world. These are all things I never could have done had I decided to blow off school!

When I began my search for a new challenge in life, what did I do? I went back to school! I pursued a career as a professional golfer, went to a professional golf management school for two years, graduated first in my class (I had learned my lesson about applying myself in school!), and got a job in the industry, which blossomed into a lifelong dream: being a head golf professional at an exclusive private country club.

Education is about sacrifice. If you're willing to take advantage of the opportunities the educational system provides you, when your time comes you will be ready. . . . I know I was!

SOUVENIR:

Opening Night Hula

Over the years, I have had many students who displayed anger at the program I direct. One such student—let's call her Maile—exhibited this kind of discontent and anger often. She was upset at working in groups and was irritated at the projects we were doing for the end-of-semester capstone. She didn't see what possible sense it would make for her to continue in the program, so she got up the gumption to come into my office and spill her heart and frustration in my lap.

She marched in, resolute, arms folded ready for defense, and sat down. She talked. I listened. She complained about various aspects of the course that had gone wrong. I agreed. She talked some more and indicated that she was going to leave the program for the spring semester. I told her that was fine but asked if she would listen to my side for a moment before leaving.

I spent some time telling her about the reasons behind the program's activities. I suggested that much of what we were doing was preparing students to contribute what they know and learn to the rest of their community. I agreed with her notion that what we were doing was uncommon, out of the

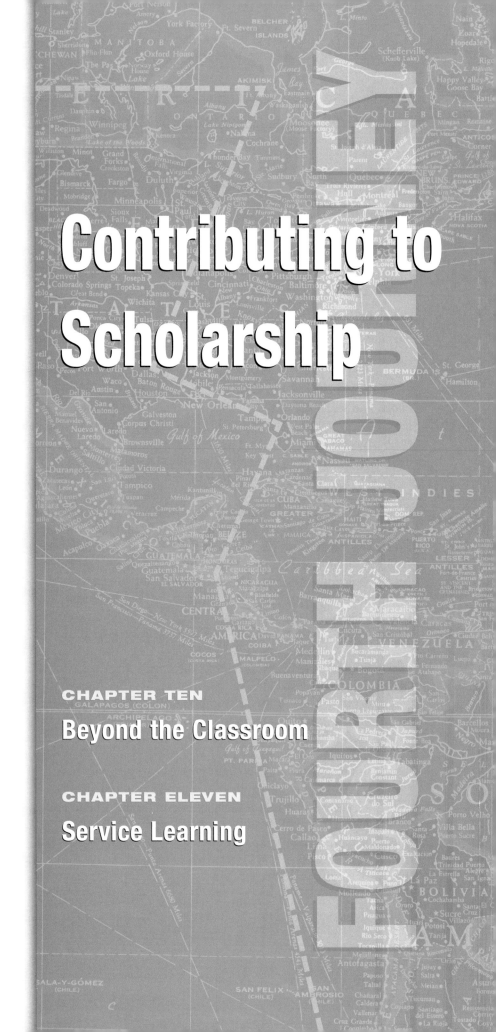

Contributing to Scholarship

FOURTH JOURNEY

Introduction to the Fourth Journey

For the past 20 years or so, educators have been discussing the "how" and "what" of educational practice. In other words, they have had conversations about the best ways to teach students—content, skills, ideas, perspectives, whatever. They have also been arguing about exactly what these elements might be. Should you only be reading philosophy from Western civilization? Is it necessary to include readings on the Holocaust? Should Native American stories be essential to literature classes? Does every student need to know how to create a spreadsheet? Should all students have equal access to the Internet's sources? Whose perspective on a particular event in history should be given the most time in a class?

All of these questions and the answers to them have guided your educational experiences until now. The general core of courses that you will need to take before graduating from college are just another attempt to deal with these issues of "what" to teach. You probably are not aware that most colleges have workshops and training sessions available to faculty to help them improve, change, augment, and develop their teaching skills—the "how" of teaching the "what."

But what about the "why"? Much of this book is about answering the "why" of your education. The first three journeys have attempted to connect your personal narratives with your academic experiences in order to help you connect with why college is an essential experience. In this Fourth Journey, "Contributing to Scholarship," you will begin to see even more clearly why you need an education to create for yourself a rich and full life.

First, you need to be *involved*—with your fellow students, with faculty, and with the rest of the community. Second, you will need to build the capacities for *tolerating* and *resolving* the differences between your own and other ways of thinking. This ability is crucial to living in a community. Finally, you have *civic responsibility*. Your education needs to foster participation and a sense of commitment to the larger community, encouraging you to take an active voice in shaping ideas and values throughout your life.

Ultimately, you need to be prepared to see that your learning unfolds in a public way. As teachers become more like expert designers of your intellectual experiences, you become more responsible for turning these experiences into something that helps bring solutions, meaning, the creation of products and, of course, understanding.

In the beginning, you do this in small ways, preparing you for a lifetime of applying your knowledge. Keep in mind that scholarly activity has three basic components. We touched upon the first two earlier in this text: (1) the creation

ordinary and, yes, different from her other classes. And I convinced her that it might benefit her to stay.

Six months later, at the end of the spring semester, Maile was still in the program. We were working on our end-of-semester capstone project, a museum exhibit, and she had chosen to dance a hula that she composed herself. Up until this moment, Maile hadn't talked with me too much. She had reluctantly decided to stay but wasn't going to give me the time of day—until the hula.

The moment she raised her hands to the heavens to begin her dance, the entire year came back to both of us. She knew I had gone out of my way to adjust the program to her needs; she was now going to pay me back with her dance.

The beautiful music quieted the audience, Maile's brown eyes met mine, her dance was mesmerizing, and I knew she was saying "thank you."

of knowledge by scholars (the writing of scholarly narratives) and (2) the preservation of this knowledge in some form by making a place for these "stories." The third component is the scholar's job to transmit information to others, which is what this journey is all about—contributing to scholarship.

In the next two chapters, you will find a variety of ways you can transform and extend your learning into meaningful and practical activities. Chapter Ten addresses the concept of being both a teacher and a learner—a teacher as you exhibit your work in a variety of ways, a learner as you intern or apprentice for purposes of attaining more experience and knowledge. Exhibiting your work can be as simple as publishing an article in a school paper or as complex as installing a museum exhibit in your community. Internships and apprenticeships require a commitment away from your academic institution to spend the necessary time to gain useful experience. In Chapter Eleven, you will learn about service learning. This is a two-way street—you give and get equally from the experience. Service learning, you will discover, is much more than merely doing community service on an ad hoc basis. It can be thoroughly integrated into your academic activities to help you discover the relationship between theory and practice.

Be responsible and take pride in your ability to share your learning with others. Step off the road you know and test the waters. Be different. Make a difference. Understand the "why."

COMPASS

She started telling me about how her father was in jail and how he gave her gifts that he made in prison. It was so weird to actually hear a real-life story like that. She is so young, yet she knows so much about such a harsh life.

—First-year student

Sometimes educators view today's students not as being *disenchanted* (apathetic and disengaged) but as being *unenchanted* (never being passionate about anything at all). This is not necessarily an indictment against a generation but more an impetus for creating academic environments that might create passion. Perhaps it is the bleak economy, the instability of the environment, the fragmentation of the world, the dissolution of families, or the violence in city streets. But something has indeed created a vacuum. If part of the task of higher education is to pass on the social, cultural, and political heritage to students, then time in college needs to be a time of training not only for a career but for life.

You can expect, then, that your time in college will often be geared toward helping you understand your communities, both global and local. This will occur in some form of service learning. This call for service is both a call for practical experience to enhance your learning and a reinforcement of moral and civic values inherent in serving others. To do this, it is necessary to teach students the scope of values and perspectives that guide decision making across different cultures, age-groups, religions, and so forth. Service learning is one way to provide the kind of academic environment that encourages students to reach out and grasp new ideas, experiences, and meanings. Service learning offers you the opportunity to go outside of the classroom, learn about the "others" in the world, find out about their lives, thoughts, and struggles, reflect on what these mean to your own life, and then integrate this knowledge into the rest of your learning.

CHAPTER TEN

Beyond the Classroom

Objectives

- to discover the value of exhibiting knowledge

- to become acquainted with internships

- to understand the value of sharing knowledge with the wider community

"But, we'll still make it, arm-in-arm, Down this road we've never known, . . ."

215

The guns exhibit was the most poignant for me because it was the most shocking. What do I mean by shocking? It exceeded surprise. More than challenging intellectual preconceptions by displacing the participant into a new, unfamiliar microcosm, the guns exhibit pissed me off, saddened me, and titillated my machismo. In short, it emotionally confused me.

Other exhibits were emotionally provoking. The AIDS Quilt invoked sorrow—it seemed side conversations subsided while those transparencies were up and students knew they were expected to feel (and consequentially behave) differently. But the guns, and particularly the obviously phallic one, shocked me. At first I laughed—good classic bathroom humor, I think. Then I thought, this is calling me a schmuck (literally) because I'm a guy and I'm not totally sensitive to the disadvantages women have in our culture. Other thoughts popped into my head, such as STDs and rape, contrasted with the idea that the penis really should be a symbol of life because of its part in reproduction. And though I hate to admit it, I felt more powerful—some sort of "I'm a guy's guy and why don't I own a gun" feeling that I can't quite explain.

So when the instructor said that maybe an exhibit shocking its participants was a good idea, I immediately disagreed. If the exhibit makes viewers feel emotionally convoluted, how are they going to expand intellectually? How are they going to truly evaluate and discern ways to improve their lives and the lives of others?

Sure, people are often rationally inaccessible when they are emotionally shocked. I was confused. I was experiencing emotion that I don't find acceptable to myself, that I deny even having. But I remembered what I saw, and a few hours later I realized that if you want to suggest true change to the participants, maybe shocking them isn't such a bad idea, and that involving them on an emotional level as well as an intellectual one is a necessity.

—*Benjamin Chaffin*

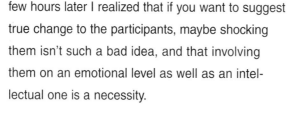

TRAVEL ESSENTIAL

Information Literacy and Contributing to Scholarship

Contributing to scholarship is not reporting. When a student writes a paper for a class, the most common strategy is to find the number of sources required by the assignment and report what they said. This process is not telling the student's own story but is simply stringing together the essence of the stories of others. It is regurgitation, not a contribution to scholarship.

Contributing to scholarship integrates your story with the stories of others so that something new is created, a new perspective, a new insight, a different story (discourse). You want to know what others have said so that you can use that as the context for your own perspective.

Because information literacy is about connecting the internal and external worlds through the ways of knowing, the information-literate person is constantly creating relevant connection and scholarship. You can experience and observe, identify authority needed to better inform yourself, and then reflect to create meaning.

Writing a paper is only one form of scholarship. Discourse isn't only a written form of conversation. Any interaction that connects the personal, internal world and the external world adds to the discourse of what is known about a topic. Knowing what questions to ask, when information is needed, how to find information, and how to evaluate it is a way to live one's life as an informed person.

Museum exhibits, discussions over dinner, chat rooms and listservs, and the creation of anything that informs and illuminates are acts of scholarship. A scholar is always being informed, informing, and creating in an ongoing way that is constantly contributing to scholarship. Really, you can live as a scholar.

Journal Entry 24

There's a statistical theory that if you give a million monkeys type-writers and set them to work, they'd eventually come up with the complete works of Shakespeare. Thanks to the Internet, we now know this isn't true.

Ian Hart

Have you ever contributed to scholarship? Have you ever wished that the project or paper you were completing for some course had more value than just the grade it might receive? Have you ever displayed, published, talked about, or presented any of your own work?

For this journal entry, discuss ways you might have contributed to scholarship over time. Then outline for yourself ways you might like to contribute to scholarship.

EXHIBITIONS

Many possibilities exist for exhibiting work you have done in a college class. Obviously, some of the choices you might make will be in response to whatever your instructors want to do. The levels of contribution can be just for your peers or can be made available to the world. Here are four examples of the levels available to you:

1. *Students to students*—creating work to exhibit to other students. This could be in the form of sharing papers through peer editing, group discussions, oral presentations, or activities that allow students access to one another's work.

2. *Students to university/college community*—sharing work with the wider university/college community. You could participate in forums or debates, organize a conference, or publish your work in the school newspaper or literary journals.

3. *Students to wider community*—sharing work with the wider community. You could step off your campus and organize a conference that the community is invited to attend, or work with a local museum and create a museum exhibit.

4. *Students to the world*—reaching the world through telecommunication capabilities. You could create a website as a class or individually to share your work. You could work as a group and develop an ezine (online magazine) to share with others.

The possibilities are endless. Whatever you do in your academic activities can be transformed into something to share with others. Remember, it is the application and dissemination of your learning that is most important.

STUDENT TO STUDENT—LEARNING MOSAIC   10.1

This project gives you an opportunity to articulate, as a group, what aspect of the course represents a significant concept, idea, skill, or insight you gained this semester. You will create a class learning mosaic.

Follow these steps:

1. Form groups of three or four students.

2. Each group will create one puzzle piece.

3. Puzzle pieces will be approximately one foot square.

4. Each puzzle piece must do the following:

   A. Be a *visual* representation of what you have learned

   B. Include a short *explanation* of what you have learned

   C. Have a *label* or *title* that summarizes what the puzzle piece depicts.

5. Fit the puzzle pieces together, and exhibit the mosaic on a wall to show the class the collection of individual learning that took place.

ACTIVITY

CREATIVITY

Not feeling particularly creative? Sometimes we are stuck in a box—and sometimes this box isn't even of our own making! For years you have put the final touch on your learning by writing a paper, doing an oral presentation, or taking an exam. Moving beyond these traditional modes takes a bit of a reach, especially if you haven't had practice doing so. The following list of tasks and questions might help you formulate a plan for sharing your scholarship with others:

I learned three important things in college—to use a library, to memorize quickly and visually, to drop asleep at any given time given a horizontal surface and fifteen minutes. What I could not learn was to think creatively on schedule.

AGNES DE MILLE

1. *Do you know your objective?* In other words, define your ideas in your own words. Ask yourself, "What do I have to do to communicate my ideas well?"

2. *Did you formulate a strategy for disseminating your ideas?* Do you know the message you have to offer? What do you want to communicate to others? Do you have a new perspective? New information?

3. *Do you know enough about what you are trying to share to share it?* Maybe you should make a list of everything you know that is related to your topic. Brainstorm. Take your list of ideas and expand on them.

4. *Go outside of your own knowledge base to get more ideas of how to exhibit your work.* Talk to people. Use a dictionary. Look at visuals, magazine ads, paintings, book covers, pictures, anything. Listen to other people talk about their work.

5. *If none of this works, change directions.* Try new ways of approaching your subject. Analyze movies, books, or designs to figure out how their creators might have come up with their ideas.

6. *Trust yourself.* Run with your ideas. If your intuition says yes, go with it. If you can't draw, write. If you can't write, paint. If you can't create music, dance. If you can't sing, take a picture.

7. *Finally, ask yourself if your designs reflect your objectives.* Does the strategy you have chosen adequately tell the story you are trying to tell? Are the spirit and the concept connected?

WRITING

Student to University/ College Community

Student newspapers include editorials, articles on campus news and sometimes world news, cartoons, advice columns, ads, sports reports, and other sections quite similar to a daily newspaper. Imagine, for a moment, that your school newspaper actually had an entire section devoted to learning, a place where students could contribute what they had learned that month, semester, or year. This contribution could be in the form of an editorial, a short story, an essay, an article, and so forth.

For this writing assignment, assume that this section exists in your school newspaper. Think of something you have learned this semester that you could share with other students and teachers on your campus. Write in a style that is readable and accessible for all. Make it interesting. Remember the demographics of your audience.

Include the following in your contribution to this imaginary section of your school paper:

1. A catchy title that describes your learning
2. An introductory paragraph making it completely clear what you are about to describe
3. A description of the learning that took place and that you want to share
4. A reflection on what the learning means to you
5. A conclusion on what this kind of learning might mean to others

STUDENTS TO WIDER COMMUNITY—MUSEUMS

You have probably been to several kinds of museums in your lifetime. Most likely, you have been to a zoo, a children's museum, perhaps a museum of natural history, and an art museum. If not, you have seen pictures of museums, talked about them in school, and maybe even seen specials about museums on television.

Have you ever contemplated that museums house knowledge in various forms? From the original copy of the Declaration of Independence to vases from the Chinese Ming dynasty, museums are the repositories of our history, our ideas, the things that inhabit the earth, our dreams, our inventions, and more.

When you think about museums, understand that the displays you view have at least five different objectives. First, there are *contemplative* displays. These are the ones with pretty things on display—a collection of jewelry, fashions, paintings. Second, some museum exhibits are *didactic*. Their intent is to tell a story or to teach something to the museum patron. Third, some displays are *reconstructive*. Quite often you see this kind in a museum of natural history representing imaginary scenes from the past, such as a desert terrain with dinosaurs. Fourth, at times a museum will decide to *group* items together for an exhibit, forming a collection of objects usually from a certain time period or a particular location. Finally, museums have exhibits for *discovery*. These are the ones you probably like most—the hands-on science museums, places where you can discover for yourself how gravity works or how a pendulum swings.

Each of these kinds of exhibits is meant to offer information in some visual form to the viewer. Behind the scenes are dozens of scientists, anthropologists, experts in art restoration, and many other museum experts. Well schooled in various fields of study, these people take knowledge and offer it to the wider community through very carefully planned exhibits.

10.2   CREATING A MUSEUM EXHIBIT

One of the ways you can contribute your scholarship to the wider community is by deciding as a class to take something you have studied and create an exhibit. Working with your local museum is usually quite simple because museums are very interested in collaborating to serve the community. If you decide to pursue this kind of project, keep in mind the kinds of displays that are possible and then ask the following questions as you design your exhibit:

1. What will the exhibit look like (color/smell/sound)?

2. How will we make it (handmade/machine made)?

3. What is it made for (function of exhibit/object)?

4. Is it well designed (nice to look at/decorative)?

5. What is it worth (to others/to yourself)?

Journal Entry 25

My brain is a great gift. Using all of it increases its value.

Anne Wilson Schaef

For this journal entry, think back on your first month in college. Draw images, jot down words, and write out scenarios while trying to capture the essence of your first month. Remember the first time you saw your roommate? What about the food you were served in the dining room? How about getting lost on the way to your first class? Experiencing the freedom? Finding a washer and dryer?

The reach of your contributions is not limited to your local community. With the possibilities afforded you by the new communication technologies, you can share your learning with people all around the world. You can create an individual website and disseminate information, or you can get together as a group and create an artifact to be displayed on the Internet for others to use. Either way, the Internet does make it possible for you to take your work outside of your immediate neighborhood easily.

Project:

1. Look at magazines and jot down the variety of items you find. Obviously, you'll find articles, advertisements, and pictures, but what else? Once you've gotten a list together, share it with the class.

2. Get together in groups, and make lists of all the aspects of a first-year experience that you included in your journals.

3. Individually, choose a topic and then discuss how it could be best displayed in an electronic magazine. For instance, if you choose dorm life as your topic, you might want to do a picture essay of a "day in the life of a freshman." Or, if you are interested in the complexities of finding one's way around campus, perhaps you could do a cartoon series.

4. Create your individual contribution to the electronic magazine by drawing, writing, creating art, doing a column, or developing an advertisement.

5. With the help of your instructor, divide the production tasks among the members of your group. You will need editors, design coordinators, layout people, those who know the technological side, and so forth.

READING

Many people have used their college education creatively, not always exactly in their field of graduation. They have contributed in a manner that transcends the particulars of their majors. Read the following newspaper article to see how some very successful people translated their education into their work lives.

Is an MBA a Ticket to Success?

Adrienne Lewis, USA Today

"Many of nation's top CEOs say 'not necessarily'."

George Bush may be the first president with an MBA degree, but U. S. business is run by CEOs with a hodgepodge of degrees in everything from atmospheric physics to French literature.

Hewlett-Packard CEO Carly Fiorina, a medieval history and philosophy major (Stanford '76), says her curiosity about the transformation from the Middle Ages to the Renaissance folds neatly into the digital awakening that she must now address.

"A century of sustained and enduring human achievement" long ago leaves her confident that "we have, in fact, seen nothing yet," Fiorina says.

Walt Disney CEO Michael Eisner never took a single business course as he earned a double major in English and theater (Denison '64). He has nudged his three sons into liberal arts. He was reminded of a favorite English professor, Dominic Consolo, when reading the script for "Dead Poets Society," a movie about a passionate poetry teacher starring Robin Williams. Eisner considers it to be one of the best movies Disney has made.

"Literature is unbelievably helpful because no matter what business you are in, you are dealing with interpersonal relationships," Eisner says. "It gives you an appreciation of what makes people tick."

Ambitious college grads peddling offbeat degrees in a job market gone sour can take heart that such success stories are far from rare. One-third of CEOs running the nation's largest 1,000 companies have master's of business administration degrees, according to executive search firm Spencer Stuart; many others do not.

Certainly, many CEOs take a more conventional educational path: Cisco's John Chambers added an MBA to his law degree, and Enron CEO Kenneth Lay added a Ph.D. in economics to his MBA. But for every CEO who takes a businesslike approach, there are those who follow pure interests and trample practicality on the way to the top.

No one disputes that there is a place for the traditional MBA. Miramar Systems just hired a Harvard MBA for business development. But CEO Neal Rabin, who majored in creative writing (UCLA '80), says chief executives who learn at the knee of Harvard case studies know too many ways that companies fail. They find themselves paralyzed by fear, he says.

Michael Dell, founder and CEO of Dell Computer, was a pre-med biology major at the University of Texas before dropping out after his freshman year.

"I took one course that was remotely related to business: macroeconomics," Dell says. "One of the things that really helped me is not approaching the world in a conventional sense. There are plenty of conventional thinkers out there."

Microsoft Chairman Bill Gates also left college without earning a degree—Harvard's most famous dropout had been studying computer science. More typical, however, are executives who completed school but whose course of study now seems irrelevant.

These CEOs say their offbeat majors have been anything but irrelevant. Some say they still apply the knowledge learned in pursuing those degrees in making day-to-day business decisions.

Others say the degrees helped launch their careers where economics, finance or business may have not.

Any good education would have been enough to get a foot in Corning's door 37 years ago, says CEO John Loose. But it's unlikely he would have been chosen for his first big international assignment without a degree in East Asian history (Earlham '64).

"To have an understanding of the history and culture of Koreans, Japanese, Indians and Chinese was invaluable," says Loose. Even today, Corning continues to court Asia as a rare bright spot in the depressed fiber-optic market.

Likewise Sue Kronick, now group president of Federated Department Stores, majored in Asian studies (Connecticut College '73).

Her rise from a Bloomingdale's buyer was helped by understanding India's economic system so well that she found ways to slash the cost of imports.

"My background served me well," Kronick says. "You tend to get more narrow in point of view as time marches on. Liberal arts is about approaching problems from a different point of view."

Unlike President Bush (MBA Harvard '75; BA history Yale '68), 87 percent of Fortune 300 CEOs did not attend an Ivy League school, according to Spencer Stuart's Route to the Top survey last year. Corning's Loose got his degree from Earlham College, a 1,200-student school founded by Quakers in Richmond, Ind. Denison University, attended by both Eisner and history major Terry Jones ('70),

CEO of Sabre Group/Travelocity.com, is a 2,100-student college in Granville, Ohio.

Offbeat routes to the top are not restricted to CEOs with liberal arts degrees. After earning a master's ('71) and Ph.D. ('73) in chemical engineering from Drexel University, Ramani Ayer accepted an entry-level job with Hartford Financial Services Group.

"My professors thought I was nuts," Ayer says. Today, he is Hartford's CEO.

"The mathematical ways of looking at the world are very transferable from engineering to insurance," Ayer says. Those who rise to the top know why things happen the way they do, he says. "Engineering is very good training for knowing why."

An industrial engineering degree (North Carolina State '71) eventually landed Gordon Harton, president of jean company Lee, into the fashion world. "I wouldn't be the person you'd want to select the hottest colors for next spring," he says. "And I can't remember using calculus in any marketing decisions."

Harton worked 15 years in operations, doing plant layout, scheduling and capacity planning, but discovered he was more interested in marketing and fashion.

Engineering teaches that the best solution is usually the most simple—a principle Lee applied when its marketers were quick to spot the trend for baggy fitting jeans simply by talking to boys who rode skateboards.

Upoc CEO Gordon Gould says his environmental studies degree (Pitzer College '92) has transferred easily to computer systems and helped him understand how a computer virus might spread. Upoc is a service that lets teens and young adults get tailored information and exchange messages on mobile phones and pagers.

Blue Shield of California CEO Bruce Bodaken has a bachelor's (Colorado State '72) and a master's (Colorado '75) degree in philosophy and once taught an introduction to ethics course.

"Philosophy teaches you to ask deeper questions, how to think through a tough problem," Bodaken says.

Journal Entry 26

Never mistake knowledge for wisdom. One helps you make a living;
the other helps you make a life.

Sandra Carey

Do a survey of at least 10 people you know in your family and neighborhood regarding the kinds of college degrees they have. List the degrees they have and their current job. Then ask them what they think they took with them from their college degree that helps them in their current career.

Write a reflection on both the *USA Today* article and the information you gathered. What seems to be the most obvious message? Think about this carefully as you read the following section on internships.

INTERNSHIPS/APPRENTICESHIPS

The term "internship" is commonly used to cover a wide variety of experiential learning opportunities. The primary purpose of an internship is to provide practical perspectives on the academic concepts and theories you have studied. An internship prepares you for future employment by giving you the opportunity to apply the skills you have learned in a vocational setting. Thus, an internship is a great way for you to extend your education, gain meaningful career contacts, and create a significant, differentiating advantage for yourself in the job market.

Internships include a wide variety of activities—practicums, summer jobs, external research—and can be full-time or part-time and occur any time during your college experience. They can be a required part of your curriculum, such as a practicum in social work or student teaching for a degree in education, or they can be volunteer or paid. Even applying for an internship gives you valuable experience in the process of applying for a job.

Each internship should be accompanied by learning goals, which you can set for yourself. Ask yourself what you want to gain from the experience. Here are some suggested goals:

- Experience in a professional work environment
- Increased marketability for yourself
- A clear sense of your career goals
- Creation of a network of contacts and references
- Better understanding of your field of interest

Both you and the employer who takes you on as an intern will benefit. You will make significant contributions to your employer's operations through your insights and work, and you will gain from the experience and opportunity to discover more about the application of what you have learned in college. Throughout your internship, you will actively apply previously acquired knowledge in meeting the expectations of your position. You will demonstrate interpersonal and communication skills, all the while honing your oral and written abilities. You will exercise decision-making and problem-solving skills as you are given self-directed assignments. Finally, you will be able to assess your own career plans and aspirations in relation to what you are experiencing. Is this what you want to do? Are you in your best arena for success? What else could you learn to do better? Where else might your skills fit?

Sometimes, doing an internship might put you off the four-year schedule for graduating from college. If you can afford the time and finances, do it. If you can't, try to find a summer internship. No matter how you include an internship in your college career, the benefits and learning derived from the experience are invaluable.

To see how useful an internship might be, try a day of job shadowing. Because you are at the beginning of your college career, you may not be at all certain about what you want "to be when you grow up." That's OK. Pick a profession that mildly interests you. Check with family and friends to find someone who works in that profession. Chances are that you won't have too much trouble finding someone who would welcome your shadowing their day at work. Take the following steps:

1. Think of a profession you would like to know more about.
2. Find a person who is doing the work that interests you.
3. Contact this person and tell them you are looking for a one-day experience that mirrors their work.
4. Set up an appointment to spend a day "shadowing" what the person does.
5. Convince the person that you will not interfere, but that you are extremely interested in just observing "a day in the life of . . ."
6. Take a notepad and jot down what the person does as well as how you felt and your ideas, reactions, and responses to what you observed.

Journal Entry 27

Education is what you get from reading the fine print. Experience is what you get from not reading it.

Unknown

Go over your observations from the "day in the life" activity. Draw a mind map of what your day looked like; then write a story about what occurred during your day. This can be a simple description of the day. Include as many details as you can about people, activities, your reactions, and your thoughts about what transpired.

   When you have completed both the mind map and the story, reflect on what you learned. Make a list of these items, both positive and negative. It is quite possible that one of the things you learned was that "this job is boring!" But, if you say this kind of thing in your reflection, take the time to explain what you mean by boring and why it might be boring to you.

CASH IN ON EDUCATION

Ginny Latta
Family nurse practitioner

Let's give some thought as to how we have "cashed in" by obtaining a bachelor's degree. Four or five years is such a long time. Why not just go to college for two years, get an associate degree, and be done with it? Get it over with quickly? Such is the thinking of many young people who are anxious to try their wings in the "real world" and start making post-McDonald's wages. Speaking of money, a lot would be saved by paying two years less tuition, right? You are not alone if you take this view, but what a short-sighted view it is.

Money. Now that's "cashing in" for sure. Think how brief is the time in college, however, related to your overall career. Spending some money up front on additional courses will increase your income exponentially over the first few years out of college. Not to mention, the opportunities in a company are many times first offered to someone who has already "gone the distance." They know your dedication and ability to complete a project are proven as a college graduate.

Bringing in a good income is only a very small part of "cashing in," in my view. Doing what you enjoy, doing what gives you satisfaction, doing what gives back to the community in which you live, that is really cashing in. And to accomplish all these goals, you must be prepared. I have had people tell me, "You have just been lucky to have had a 38-year career in nursing where you could do patient care, teaching, research, and management." Yes, sometimes there is a factor of luck, and I have been blessed to have worked at what I love. If you define "luck," however, as "preparation meeting opportunity," you will begin to see why an education is so important.

Earlier I mentioned associate degree programs. Do not take my meaning wrong—they do provide a good education. However, it was apparent after I completed my A.D. that there was tremendous benefit to additional learning and being prepared for opportunities when they presented themselves. For example, my family has lived in many areas of the country. With each move, positions in my specialty were not always available. Earning a bachelor's degree and eventually a master's degree opened up many more job possibilities than you can imagine.

Learning can occur on a formal level or through life experience. You can "cash in" on both of these as you proceed toward a bachelor's degree. Where in your community will you meet a more highly educated, varied group of people than on a college or university campus? This is a place you can learn from professors who have studied and lived their disciplines. This is a place you can learn from people who have come from other countries and backgrounds. This is a safe place for you to grow and become more confident. This is a place where you can become a better person, able to make your way in the world, make your dreams come true, and have a career you love. It is a time in your life when you can learn from other cultures, from different academic disciplines, and most importantly, begin to respect other points of view. A bachelor's program opens your world. Today's world asks us to think bigger, think broader, think smarter, and think outside our small vision.

I have believed, lived, and found joy in what an anonymous person wrote, "The truly educated never graduate."

CHAPTER ELEVEN

Service Learning

Objectives

- to learn the definition of service learning
- to create goals for service learning
- to review the possibilities of service to the community

"And that bright ribbon up ahead, Underneath the cloudy sky, . . ."

When I first got started, I was very excited. Since I first heard about it, I was looking forward to being involved in something that would make a difference for the community. Back in high school, I had joined organizations that interacted with young children. I was glad I could continue service work with the RAP (first year learning community) program. When I first met my student, Aliikai, we talked for a little bit. He was really quiet but talked when I asked him questions about himself. I felt it was important to establish security between us first.

After we talked for a little bit, I read two books to him. I was really ecstatic because the books were some I had read and enjoyed very much as a child. I put as much "color" in the readings as I could by using different tones and sounds. Along the way, I also paused and asked him questions about what he thought about the story. He was always very attentive when it came to the pictures. After we finished, I talked to him some more. I asked him what books he liked in particular and suggested that he bring books he liked the next time we met. He said he didn't care, but I figured it would be easier for me to pick books. It was a pretty good first meeting.

Afterward, I didn't see him for a while. The next time, his class went on a field trip, so I ended helping Tina make flash cards with sounds of the alphabet as primers for the smaller kids. The next time, class ended early, so I helped at the book fair in the library. I liked watching the kids get so excited with books like *Harry Potter* and other stories. I remember I was just like them when I was a child. It's good that schools have book fairs because it emphasizes reading. So even if I wasn't reading to my student, I was still helping in some other way with reading.

The next meetings were all right. I read two books to him each meeting and tried to associate the stories in the book with school, his friends, and so forth. I wanted him to stay interested, because sometimes he got distracted. Today, we read some stories about family. I thought it would be relevant because Thanksgiving is around the corner. This is all that has happened to this point. This is pretty much a typical day at the work site. However, I'd like to make some changes and have Aliikai read next time.

I like the whole idea of grouping college students with younger children. Overall, I've always liked the concept of community service. The fact that we are in college and giving a small amount of time to a good cause is a great thing. We are helping education progress by contributing our efforts. Education in particular needs all the attention it can get. There are all the issues surrounding how we should deal with funding, special education, and teacher's wages, but there should be more focus on how the student is doing. I believe that in

elementary school, children's education is critical, because their minds are open to new things. By starting early in their acquiring of knowledge, it will get easier to keep learning. By giving even a half hour of our time, we benefit the children. The saying that "one person makes a difference" applies to what we are doing. We're all serving children in hopes of fostering their learning.

The way others see this volunteering, in my opinion, is that we are probably good people for wanting to give back to the community. However, I believe it is the person's heart, more than anything else, that makes "service", actual service. I can say that this volunteering effort is more than just a grade; it is a learning experience as well as a sharing one. Some of the kids probably don't get much attention from home. Some come from big families, and the parents don't always have time to focus their attention on each individual. This is where we come in and provide the student with that extra help.

I am glad to see Aliikai every week. Each time, I am hoping he grows more comfortable so he can speak up more. I also hope that he is getting something good out of our work together. For example, by listening to me read, he may want to volunteer to read aloud in class frequently. I believe that children are looking for role models all the time, and showing how much you care about their learning makes them feel important.

I don't think there is such a thing as a perfect volunteer. It depends on a person's willingness and desire. The label of "volunteer" does not exist by itself. Volunteering is caring, serving, and effort. It also involves understanding and patience. To see improvement in a child's literacy takes time, but every little contribution counts. To know that you had even a tiny impact on the child means that you've helped him take a step further. It doesn't matter how much you've done but that you wanted to do it.

I have learned so far that each child is different. Each has a different learning style. The trick is to focus on each child's best way of learning so that your reading sessions are productive. I have also learned that most children really love school. They love being in the classroom, reading, and writing. I believe that the development of literacy in the early stages of a child's life is extremely important in how the child will learn in the future.

I heard a quote saying that "to lead is to serve." It was the motto of one of the clubs I was involved in during high school. At first I didn't understand it, but now I can make a connection with the RAP readers program. By serving children's educational needs, we are becoming leaders to and for them. We are leading the leaders of the future. So in a way, we are all leaders when we give something of ourselves.

—*Shirley Calpito*

TRAVEL ESSENTIAL

Information Literacy and Service Learning

Service learning is a laboratory for practicing all the elements of being information literate. Service learning provides an experience in which we can view our own stories in the context of the stories of others. We might be working at an animal shelter helping people to select animals for their household. We could be reading to children in a local library. We might work in a legislator's office helping to prepare documents. How is our experience of these situations relating to our own lives and learning?

Service learning provides an opportunity to ask, "What is going on here?" "Why is this important?" "What are the problems here?" "Is this the best way to do this?" We are able to step back a bit as students in a service learning situation and observe the actions around us and why they might be happening. Our experience and observation in service learning produce questions. Those questions can lead us to use our information-finding skills to discover what others have learned about the service learning situation we are in. This discovery process focuses on authority as a way of knowing. We examine the discourse on the subject, learn what questions researchers have asked, and in that process learn more questions. We assess the credibility and validity of our sources to see how well they can be incorporated into our own story of the service learning situation.

Through reflection, we integrate all the elements of the service learning situation to better understand the relationship between our own perspectives and the perspectives of others. This creates a new story that is personal yet informed.

SERVICE LEARNING

The fundamental assumption underlying the inclusion of service learning in higher education is that the practice of service, and of other forms of experiential learning, will allow the student to develop a better understanding and appreciation of academic material. In other words, you will be able to put the material learned in your courses to work in your own life as well as in the lives of others.

You learned earlier in this text that one of the missions of higher education is to foster learning, discovery, discussion, and the gathering of information about the world. It does seem that in order to do this, students should spend some time in the world outside the classroom. Your time in college should not be divorced from the wider community; it should be integrated. Students learn best when given the opportunity to address problems that interest them. Thus, linking issues of importance to students' service learning experiences makes sense. It is important to develop thoughtful citizens who contribute time to their communities. Service learning will help you see the relationship between what you learn and how you live. Thus, it is another way to bridge the gap between theory and practice. It is also a call for practical experience to enhance learning as well as reinforce moral and civic values.

If you can't locate the other, how are you to locate yourself?

TRINH MINH-HA

Additionally, service learning offers you the ability to go outside the classroom; learn about "others"; find out about their lives, thoughts, and struggles; reflect on what your presence in their lives might mean; and, finally, discover who you are. Putting experiences together, yours and theirs, is what brings insight. You may learn about your own learning styles more clearly. Your experiences may raise your self-esteem, build character, empower you to see yourself as a integral player within your community, help you visualize yourself as someone with a lifelong commitment to your community, and lead you to become a responsible and engaged adult.

Service learning differs from the experiences you might have as an intern, but many of its outcomes are similar. Service learning is a form of experiential learning, in which you engage in activities over the course of a semester that address human and community needs. The benefits to both the student and the community are enormous, creating a definite win-win situation.

GOALS OF SERVICE LEARNING

Service learning is both a unique way to learn and a vehicle for achieving academic goals and objectives. It provides a structured time for you to obtain learning experiences that include the use of your academic skills, such as reading, writing, listening, communicating, and so forth. It also gives you the opportunity to devel-

Never doubt that a small group of thoughtful committed citizens can change the world: indeed, it's the only thing that ever has.

MARGARET MEAD

op empathy, personal values, an awareness of things beyond the realm of your personal experiences, self-esteem, confidence, and a sense of responsibility. Your learning reinforces the service in which you participate, and the service reinforces your learning.

The general goals of service learning are to:

- Provide opportunities to integrate theory and practice
- Sharpen problem-solving strategies
- Develop critical thinking skills
- Awaken awareness of social responsibility
- Create a greater sense of obligation to one's own learning

Thus, you are being given more than just an opportunity for hands-on experiences. You also are encountering diverse viewpoints on the cause of social problems. You will confront the main question—what is knowledge for?—and thus will seek out a context for all of your academic learning.

Pulitzer Prize–winning author Robert Coles is a researcher and teacher of psychiatry at Harvard University who is considered one of the world's most respected experts on the inner lives of children. Coles recognizes that service learning is an excellent way to introduce students to their own communities, to connect theory with practice, and to offer experiential learning. Read the following essay, "Satisfactions," and see why Coles thinks that volunteering within a community regenerates the spirit.

Satisfactions

Robert Coles

The first civil rights activist and SNCC member I met did not belong to the "office group," as some called it, who worked out of Atlanta, but was a young black student, Dion Diamond, who had taken leave from the University of Wisconsin to work in Louisiana, where he had relatives. A black New Orleans lawyer, A. P. Tureau, had become a friend of mine; he was the NAACP Legal Defense Fund's representative in Louisiana, and he knew well the four black children who initiated school desegregation and with whom I was talking twice a week. I met Dion at Tureau's home and later in a Baton Rouge prison, where Dion had been jailed on grounds of "disturbing the peace"—for attempting to have lunch at a restaurant that wanted no part of black customers. I was to testify on his behalf. Curiously, the local prosecutor had decided to call him "unstable" and possessed of an "anti-social personality," hence his lawyer's decision to ask me to interview him and later tell the court what I thought of his "personality."

As I sat in the prison's visiting room and heard the tall, thoughtful, sensitive, hard-working man tell of the extreme danger he'd been facing, voluntarily, in hopes of seeing an end to segregation in Louisiana, I wondered, first to myself and then out loud, what gave him the strength to keep going. He was in constant danger, and in 1962 there wasn't the national backing and attention that coalesced behind the Mississippi Summer Project of 1964. Often he was working alone, and there was a distinct possibility that one day he'd be found alone and dead.

The psychiatrist in me was posing questions to him, for I knew that in court similar questions would be posed. I said, "Dion, your ideals and values apart, I'm wondering why you keep at this, given the danger and the obstacles." In fact, I had a lengthier wind-up to the question, because I didn't want him to think I was insinuating that there was anything psychologically wrong with his choice of activity—the line of reasoning that the county prosecutor was pursuing. I knew that even in friendly hands, a question about motivation can be regarded as an implied judgment: Hey, you, what *is* your problem, why *do* you behave this way, do these things? (Not everyone is prepared to turn the tables on the questioner: Hey, you, what is *your* problem, always asking people things, always wanting to know why *they* do as they do?)

In any event, I was stopped in my well-meaning tracks by the young man's three-word reply: "The satisfaction, man." I'm afraid my imagination then was rather limited. I could think of few possible satisfactions for him. Dion had been telling me about how tough his work was, how lonely at times, how frightening at other times, and, worst of all, how discouraging—the suspicion he encountered from black people, who knew well the dangers of trying to integrate a lunch counter or a motel and who were not reluctant to be psychologically skeptical of him: Why *are* you here among us, urging us to do what might eventually mean that we get shot at or arrested?

When I asked him about those "satisfactions," he said, "I'm meeting some really fine people. I'm listening to them tell me a lot about their lives. I'm hearing them stop and think about what they're willing to do to change this world here in

Louisiana. Isn't that enough—isn't that a good reason to feel satisfied? If you can spend some of your life doing work like this, then you're lucky! There may be a sheriff out there waiting for me with a gun, but if he gets me, I'll die thinking: Dion, you actually *did* something—you were part of something much bigger than yourself, and you saw people beginning to change, right before your eyes, and that was a real achievement, and that's what I mean by 'satisfaction.'"

Something Done, Someone Reached

To this day I go back to that young man's appraisal of himself and others—of a volunteer effort and its satisfactions. Dion kept telling me what he was trying to *do;* he kept describing for me the various individuals he was getting to know—the lives he was affecting, even as his own life had already been deeply affected. I wanted to know about his earlier life. I asked about any "troubles" he may have had, any brushes with the law (or with my kind of doctor); about the ways he was handling the terrible stresses of being, in essence, a front-line warrior, taking on tough, sometimes murderous, local and state power. He was polite, even deferential, but also determined to let me know how he spent his time and willing, in his quiet, unassuming manner, to ask me to become a student of his. Several times he asked whether I would be interested in visiting the communities where he had been working, meeting "the folks," as he called them.

I felt that he was trying to divert me from his "problems," his "attitudes," his "feelings," his "mood," his "thought content," in favor of his "daily rounds," as he called them. I wasn't averse to hearing about those rounds, but I wanted to know why he chose such a clinical word: were a lot of the people he visited sick in some way? He laughed, told me he didn't think his friends were any sicker than "the rest of the people in Louisiana." He wondered whether anyone had studied, psychiatrically, the segregationists, the people to whom he was *persona non grata*—the sheriffs and their deputies, the officials who ran the schools and the voter registration offices, the businessmen and the professional people in the country. "They're all ready to call me nuts at the drop of a hat, and now they have me in jail, and they're pushing the judge to call me a sociopath or something, a first-class screwball, maybe, but no one is looking at *them!* What's wrong with *their* heads? They're full of hate and prejudice, and they say awful things about anyone who doesn't look like them and belong to their race and their class!"

I was beginning to crumble inside, to share his grave doubts about how my profession is used to sort people, judge them, even condemn them. But for a while I tried to put up the solid exterior of the friendly and interested doctor who nevertheless was firmly rooted in the "reality principle," as it is put in psychiatry. I pointed out that those country officials whose sanity he questioned were people of power—indeed, they had him in jail—and I suggested we try to be rid of them, make a winning case against them, rather than try to confront them as he wished to do. Anyway, I noted, I doubted that they would agree to subject themselves to the kind of psychiatric scrutiny he wanted.

He agreed, though he clearly was interested intellectually in challenging my mind—which, I only gradually realized, *he* was "evaluating" and, in his quiet fashion, trying to strip down to its bare-bones, class-connected and race-connected assumptions. He did, however, graciously let me press my conventional psychiatric questions (the taking of a "history"), and waited until I was evidently finished to resume his suggestion, variously tendered, that I spend some time with him as a civil rights "field secretary"—see what he was doing, and with whom.

Eventually I testified in court, as did others, and he was let free—with a warning from the bench that he would do well to return to Wisconsin and college life. Shortly afterward, I took Dion up on his suggestion to accompany him. Our visits to the rural homes of the "folks" he had mentioned were not easy ones to make. I left my car in Baton Rouge and went with him in his car—followed, almost always, by a police car. I knew the police were looking for any excuse to arrest him again. He made light of it, called them "my friends." He drove so circumspectly that I became aware of every road sign and of the speed he was maintaining, however low. He kept looking in his rear-view mirror, smiling. When he signaled a coming turn with his left arm and hand, I had the feeling he was trying hard to be the obliging child to fiercely punitive parents, ever ready to take out the strap—or their pistols.

He was also turning the whole exercise into a parody, but not a joke; he was the "suspect," and they were his pursuers, constantly on his trail. He also told me how lucky he was to have me with him: "They know you from the trial. They think of you as a New Orleans doctor, and they'll not want to bother me while you're around." I smiled, but he zeroed in directly on the ultimate humiliation of all this. "They watch their step with you, and even with me—the 'Wisconsin by,' they call me—but they'd shoot a Negro here anytime; they've told me that! The Negroes tell me that, too—and when they do, I feel so ashamed for everyone, for the United States and for all the Negro people here in Louisiana, who have to live with the knowledge that their lives have no meaning at all legally: they are noncitizens. I'd even say nonpeople, to the police, to the sheriff and his deputies, the ones who supposedly are 'the law.'"

Nevertheless, Dion was only occasionally given to such grim, melancholy, and penetrating critiques—to a barely suppressed moral indignation, which used irony, and again, parody, most of the time for its expression. As we went into the unsubstantial (sometimes all too flimsy) homes of these small-town and country people, I noticed his face light up. These families, a number of them tenant farmers, were nearly penniless, living hand to mouth. Because of our escort, the police, we brought along plenty of fear and anxiety—as if those folks didn't already have enough to worry about with the daily insults and threats that constituted their experience of "law and order" in that segregationist world.

Yet in no time, as we sat and nursed our Cokes and Pepsis and 7-Ups and orange sodas ("Now, Mister Doctor, what can we do you with . . ."), I began to see legs stretching, arms folding or falling back in relaxation, facial muscles constructing smiles; I began to hear jokes and stories and laughter—some of it the sharp, dry, bitter laughter of people who didn't know whether to be amused by their difficult lives or cry out their hearts on that account. I also began to hear music: people singing, strumming guitars, hitting old upright pianos. I began to hear, finally, plenty of exhortation: the Old and New Testaments summoned lest, as one field hand put it, "we forget all those who knew pain before we were ever even near being born." The biblical themes of exile and return, of suffering and redemption, of mystery and revelation, and the biblical view of the powerful as suspect, the lowly as destined to sit close to God, in His kingdom—these were subjects close to the heart of men, women, and children caught in the most unpromising of earthly lives.

As we went from home to home—it was summer, the weather was hot and humid, and there were no air conditioners to help out—I began to understand how much this young activist from up North meant to the people receiving us and, conversely, how much they meant to him. I also learned to appreciate what he meant when he spoke from deep within himself.

"I tell you, this is a real *privilege;* I am doing something useful with people who are the salt of the earth! Every day I thank my lucky stars—I thank God—for the good fortune to be here, going from home to home, sitting and listening to these folks tell their stories, being fed by them, being taught by them. You asked me yesterday why I do this, and I could recite the civil rights line, and I believe it—that our people aren't free, and that we have to fight for our freedom, especially here in the segregated South. To be absolutely honest, I came here to spend a month working on a voter registration project, but I've stayed here because I love what happens when I go visit these folks. Every day I learn something from them—about gospel music, about how to put in a good vegetable garden, about the history of the Mississippi Delta and upstate Louisiana, about all the tricks of the local whites, and remember, the Negroes here know *everything:* they have eyes and ears in every white home, and the reports come filtering back every night.

"It's why I get accomplished, the people I reach and who get to me: that's why I'm here. We have a growing movement here of men and women who really want to work together to break the back of the whole segregationist power structure. They meet in the basement of a church, and they sing and pray—and they also talk hard, rough politics. 'It's your baby,' one of the men said to me, about the 'club,' they call it, 'the freedom club.' Talk about why I do this work! I'll have to leave—but I'll never really leave for good. The way I see it, this is the most important educational experience I'll ever have. People say, 'Hey, man, you're into fighting with cops.' I answer, If you don't take on the cops, then you're into something else: surrendering to cops! So we're for sticking to our original purpose here—getting more and more people to become voters—and I'm staying because I get the satisfaction of seeing the baby grow and being with all the folks, a huge family.

"You know what? You look at those cops now—they've begun to respect us! They don't give us that big belly laugh anymore, they don't spit at us or sneer at us. They look real serious when they follow us around. And the other day, I couldn't believe it, one of them, he nodded at me and two of my buddies when we came out of the store. It was as if—well, hey, we sure do know each other! I thought I saw just the beginning of a smile on his face—just the start of one. You want to know why I do this work? To see that look on that cop's face!"

Over the years I have heard his sentiments echoed many times—the enthusiasm and pleasure, the exhilaration that accompany action taken, and the consequences of such action: deeds done, people very much touched, and in return, quite eager to return the favor, through dozens of reciprocal gestures, remarks, initiatives.

Moral Purpose

In a modest, unselfconscious way, Dion was regarding himself and that policeman as historical figures: a pair of protagonists worthy of a moment of notice—each of them a witness to social change as well as a participant in it. As I listened to him, I remembered reading *Middlemarch* and *War and Peace* in college—the effort of George Eliot and Tolstoy to render a time, a place, a series of events, through the concreteness of character portrayal, through narrative attention to ordinary people, as well as to the exceptional ones, those with money, power, privilege. Here were two minor figures in an unfolding national drama—yet each of them intuitively knew well what was happening not only to themselves, but countless others: a smile marking a crack in what hitherto had been called "a way of life." No question that for many volunteers the considerable satisfaction that goes with making a connection with a fellow human being is enhanced by the overall context of the service being rendered. They have sought, found, and fulfilled a moral purpose. For this young political activist, the moral purpose was obvious: he was engaged in a struggle against the tyranny of segregation. But all service is directly or indirectly ethical activity a reply to a moral call within, one that answers a moral need in the world.

The manner in which a moral purpose is worked into a particular volunteer's life will vary enormously. Some volunteers are at pains to insist (to themselves, let alone others) that what they are doing *is* a moral effort and that what they get from their actions is a kind of moral satisfaction or peace—a moral hunger assuaged. Others wave aside the moral underpinnings of their actions, emphasizing instead the friendships they have made, the boredom overcome. Even when pressed about the good they are doing, they demur, as did Gary, a college student who became a Big Brother to a youngster whose family had recently arrived from the Dominican Republic.

"I enjoy leaving this place [a college community] and I love going to the neighborhood where he lives—the sights and sounds and smells. I suppose some people would want me to wear my heart on my sleeve and to say I feel sorry for all the people there and I'm trying to help them—but I don't like that word 'help,' I really don't. When people tell me they admire what I'm doing, I go ballistic; I say they should compliment my friends Juan and his family for being nice enough to put up with me! They let me come visit them. They feed me. They help me with my Spanish. I get to shoot baskets; I learn all about a neighborhood—who makes money doing this or doing that. I know where to place bets. I know where to buy the best food, and where the best places to eat are. When I go to visit Juan, I learn by walking, listening to him and his friends, seeing all there is to see though his eyes and though my own."

Gary also acknowledged the boy's problems and indicated that Juan had an angry, sullen side that could flare up unexpectedly. Once that admission is made, more can be allowed. A volunteer who has insisted on presenting himself as a grateful recipient of the personal cultural largesse of theirs changes tack, reluctantly it seems, tells of the darker side of his experiences, even as that narration, ironically, enables him to get nearer to the very real breakthroughs he has witnessed as an older friend to someone who has needed almost desperately what a relaxed but thoughtful student has provided.

"We take walks—that's the best. He acts like he owns the whole world. He points out everything to me—it's better than a lecture here. But all of a sudden, he'll see someone, or he'll notice something in a store window, and he becomes a different person. He looks so grim! He doesn't talk, he just stares ahead. Then I try to draw him out. I talk. *I* start pointing things out. I ask him questions—anything to get him, get us out of this mood. It works, but it takes a lot out of me. It's then that I begin to realize how hard this kid's life is. I know that the man he calls Dad is his stepfather, and he beats him up *really* badly; that his mother is a heavy drinker, and she tunes out, to the point that they all don't know what to do with her. It sounds like she goes into a trance and then, all of a sudden, she clears, and she's back to normal. His sister is sleeping around at fifteen, having dropped out of school; and a younger brother has epilepsy, the serious kind. Not a pretty picture!

"I'll be honest—I'm surprised at myself some days, because I'll hear me giving Juan a really strong lecture. I'll tell him that he's fighting for his life and that if he doesn't watch out, he'll end up drowning. You may think I'm stepping outside my bounds; I'm only nineteen years old, and I'm a history major, and I've never even taken a psychology course, so what do I know! But when you see someone floundering, and you're afraid he's going to go under, then you sure try your damnedest to throw out every lifesaver you can think of!

"I have been trying to be a friend to Juan, and I've tried to give him some direction. I don't mean that I preach sermons, rant and rave. I wouldn't last a minute with him or his neighborhood friends, if I *told* him what to do, told them. But I play basketball with him and his friends, and there are times when we just stand around after some serious playing, shooting the breeze, and it's then that I show my hand. I start in casually, talking about how you've got to realize that you either take responsibility for your life and try to find some direction you're headed for or, if you don't, you'll be at the mercy of other people, and believe me, if *they're* going to be deciding what you're going to do—then *forget it!*

"The gist of my message is that you either get pushed and pulled by all these other folks, or you take charge yourself. That's what I keep hitting Juan with, and he does listen. The more I talk, the more I realize *I'm* listening, too! A lot of what I'll tell him and his buddies—it's what my dad told me, and my mom, and her dad. Basically I'm trying to connect those kids with the middle-class world I come from. I don't say it the way I heard it at home, but the heart and soul of my own values, that's what I'm advocating. I have no illusion that I'm this kid's savior. I'm only one person who can save him—that's what I keep hammering away at. When I come at him like that, Juan listens. He even nods his head. I feel a little optimistic. But hell, I know the odds, and the more I come to see him, the better I know the odds.

"When I'm through, and we've had our pizza or something, and I'm ready to say good-bye, I look him right in the eye, and I say, 'Keep trucking, man'; and he says, 'Yeah.' Once in a while he'll say, 'I will.' That makes my day—my week! I feel I've actually done something with my life—for someone else, not just me, me, me: the big me that we all celebrate in this place!

"I don't know how you persuade someone who is a stranger, except for an hour or two a week, to dream about a different life and then go to work to try to get there. But *underneath it all,* that's what should be happening between Juan and me. It's my voice that might be of help—that's the conviction I have to feel. I've got to be as sensitive as can be—as *clever.* I don't mean to sound like a con artist, but you have to figure out how to do an end run around all the enemies—everything that is pulling down, down, down on this kid's life, and to do that, as they say, 'ain't easy, man.' I haven't found the way—but I have found, I think, a general direction. I keep say-

ing my piece, even if I sound like the boring professor who repeats himself every lecture.

"The more I say what I think, what I believe—well, the more I really *do* believe it! That's the big irony, and I'm afraid to mention it even: that all of this volunteering, this 'do-good work,' one of my cynical friends calls it, will end up being a big boost for my morale and my life. That same guy says, 'You're doing that for your brag-sheet.' I get really furious at him, but I don't give him the pleasure of seeing how I feel. It's true—sure, it'll be nice to list this on my CV; but damn it, I could just go through the motions here. I could show up every week— every *other* week, every third week—and buy my way out by going to a pool hall with Juan and playing pool, or playing cards, or just having a Coke, and pretty soon I could say, 'I have to go, Juan, so have a nice week.' I'd have my community service record for the CV. Maybe that's part of what motivates us [to do such work], but it doesn't take too long (I'll speak for myself, and I'm not bragging, I'm *worrying,* actually), it doesn't take too long for something else to get going: what I've been talking about. You become a link for these kids, but you become self-conscious about it, and that means you're putting yourself on the ropes, asking yourself the big questions, so you'll be able to do the same with your Little Brother."

Gary kept addressing the irony that he himself was the moral beneficiary of an involvement with a Little Brother. He was looking intensely inward, groping hard to clarify his own beliefs and values so that he could try to stand by them in his conversations with Juan, and so that he could speak not just out of self-knowledge and a common sense that is, actually, fate's, luck's gift to him, but out of a sincere conviction, a moral earnestness, the expression of which he had come to realize might well be his main chance, his only hope, of reaching, of persuading Juan: "Somehow I think I'm trying to get to him, so he'll pick my values, when he's facing a choice, rather than those he gets from the street and, I hate to say it, at home. That's a tall order. I don't mean to put it like that—we're back to this ego thing: a big temptation. But there's a conflict, a struggle in everyone: what do you decide about all sorts of things? I just hope Juan picks up some of the determination I picked up from my parents, picks it up through our time together. I try to tell him what I believe, and I've even told him that when I talk with him, it helps me because I realize that what I believe is important!"

As I've listened to this student of mine I've learned how much stronger he has become as a Big

Brother, a tutor, an older friend to Juan. (He would eventually earn a doctorate in education and help teach in an undergraduate course I offer.) It is as if the weekly meetings, often two or so hours long, enable in each of the two another kind of coming together than that of a shared activity, even a shared conversation. The volunteer, on his own, is given pause: what does he uphold to himself, and why? If he is to be a convincing friend and teacher and guide it is such a question he will have to answer—hence the moral introspection he pursues. Juan's need for a kind of moral purpose that will carry him through any number of critical moments becomes for his older friend, who lives across the proverbial railroad tracks, a reason to locate more explicitly and consolidate his own moral purpose as a prelude to sharing it, however gingerly and indirectly.

Naturally, guile always matters in moral exchanges: how do you get something across without souring the entire enterprise by stirring up annoyance, irritation, resentment? That question, too, haunted this young volunteer—how should he "deliver" moral energy to another person? The longer he struggled to convey his moral strength to Juan, the more solid his sense of his own purpose in life became. This gift surprised him, even embarrassed him, but he had to learn to accept it if he was to keep at it with Juan. He did indeed persist with the boy, much to the benefit of both of them.

Personal Affirmation

Not all people who work with or on behalf of others become moralists (in the nonpejorative sense). For many volunteers there is obviously a moral purpose at work. Yet those people do not find themselves morally challenged as they do their volunteer work, do not think of it as bringing a moral bonus. Many even make a contrast between the obvious moral nature of their work and their own sense that they are getting "quite a bargain," as one middle-aged suburban hospital volunteer put it.

"I go to the hospital because I enjoy doing the work there. I love the nurses and the doctors, and I love the patients. I feel lucky to be able to spend part of my week that way. I hesitate to say I'm there because I feel I *should* be there. I don't deny that if I were a different person, with other values than the kind I have—we should be useful to others!—I probably would be elsewhere: maybe playing golf all spring, summer, autumn, like some of my friends do. But I have to be honest: I don't really judge someone playing golf or tennis, which I love to play, as doing something any less worthy of my time and energy than working as a hospital volunteer. I don't

mean to sound selfish, but if you asked me what it means to me to do my work—why do it—I'd have to say that I do it because I enjoy the world there, and, frankly, it's a tremendous educational experience. Not a day goes by that I don't learn something from the doctors, listening to them, and from the patients I meet.

"I was always interested in medicine anyway; if I could have done the premed work, I'd have tried to go to medical school. The next thing I knew I was married, and then I had two children to bring up. My husband's career is hard for me to understand; he's a tax lawyer. If there was some way for me to do volunteer work that connected with his work, I'd have done it. It's just as well, though; he's very much in favor of what I do, and he loves to hear my stories after I come home from the hospital! He said to me a few weeks ago, This job is really helping you learn how *much* you can do—and I said I think that's true.

"I used to think I was weak; I had a slight anemia, and my thyroid was on the low side. But since I've learned the ropes there at the hospital, I find myself really pitching in—until the next thing I know, people are telling me it's time to go home! I'm glad to leave, but I'm glad to come back in a day or two. I have to say it: I *miss* the hospital. There's a sense of excitement—lives are at stake! For me, it's a place where I feel myself needed and where I can live up to the expectations of others. Now this job is a big part of my life. I put a lot of myself into it; but I get back so much more. The people I meet who are struggling with pain and uncertainty—they help me realize that you can take things for granted until you get sick, and then you stop and think about what life really means."

What she was saying was not all that surprising. At times she came across as the slightly restless suburban housewife whose service smacked of condescension toward those who have fallen into sickness—their suffering an excuse for her to count her blessings! But when I watched her in the hospital or heard her recounting a most active, exhausting, giving day, it was certainly possible to overlook what she said and remember what she did week after week, often with great tact and sensitivity.

She was perhaps speaking most accurately when she emphasized the discoveries her work offered—all the people she met, all the stories she heard. "I remember what I hear in the evening; I talk to my husband about what I hear, and he says it's changed me a lot, what I do there on those wards." Interestingly, she avoided saying she had changed for the better, nor did her husband mount that claim—a certain modesty in people who were not always able to sustain humility.

Modesty—like arrogance—is no one's exclusive property by virtue of class or race. A woman from a quite genteel world, on her knees cleaning up after a patient who had fallen and then vomited, took the experience to heart and became quieter, less self-regarding, more reflective, more modest. Thirty miles away a tough working-class man, who never pretended to be soft-spoken or self-effacing, found a way to cope with disappointment when his son was born with Down syndrome. To make ends meet, he worked long hours as an automobile mechanic, then pumped gas at night. When his son was first born, a boy at last after five girls, he was not sad, anxious, or self-pitying, only angry.

His wife understood her husband well. "He's always been a man's man—he has his buddies, and they drink a lot of beer on Fridays. Otherwise, he's sober and very hard-working—two jobs, and never more than six hours' sleep. He's been a good husband and a good father: he loves those girls! But I'd be lying if I told you he didn't want a son. Oh, he was crazy for a boy, and when we decided to give it one last chance and he kept telling me he knew we'd have a sixth girl, he knew it, I knew something myself—how much he wanted a boy.

"Then I delivered, and we all were in ecstasy because it was a boy. Then came the news there was something wrong, that the boy, Ben, wasn't so good, and he wasn't passing the tests these doctors have when they examine babies. The rest—it's a nightmare. I don't know how to tell it—all we went through, but especially him."

Soon after Ben was declared retarded ("modestly" so, the doctors said) the parents had to decide whether they could take care of the boy themselves or would have to entrust him to others. They had no real money, so "others" meant a public institution. The father's dreams of raising a son had to be surrendered. The mother, trained as a practical nurse before a busy family life caused her to abandon thoughts of a career, related the gradual changes in her husband, the slow but finally steep decline in his spirits, in his entire way of being.

"He used to be full of energy, and now he's lost a lot of it. He used to jump out of bed, and he'd be ready for the day, even if it was five in the morning and dark, in coldest winter. These days he's sleeping hard, and the alarm goes off, and he wants to go back to sleep. Now, it's me—I'm the one who has to nudge him out of bed. He'll even fight with me; he'll accuse me of pushing him. I don't. Sure, we'd be broke if he stopped working. I keep quiet, though. I never defend myself when he starts being accusing toward me. He'll stop pretty fast—he sees I'm just letting him go on, and he decides it's no use to be like that. He must feel terrible—really guilty, because he's a decent guy ordinarily.

"That's the trouble, this is not an ordinary time! He's heartbroken. We both are, only I seem to be taking it much better. I say a dozen times to myself: God's will. If the good Lord wanted to send a retarded child here, and a boy, then that's His decision. For me the church is a big help. You know something? When he was at his lowest, he even stopped going [to church]. I said, 'It's bad enough, our troubles, and now you're going to send yourself to hell?' He looked at me, and you know what he said? He said, 'I'm already in hell.' I was ready to throw a glass at the wall when I heard that! I thought to myself, I'm fed up with all this feeling sorry for yourself that's coming out of his mouth! I just grabbed my raincoat and I left the house, and I slammed that door so hard I was afraid the roof would cave in. Then I realized I'd forgotten my pocketbook, so I ran back in and I grabbed it and ran out, and I slammed the door again, even harder, if that was possible! The only thing was, I saw out of the corner of my eye that he was crying, that he was wiping his eyes with a handkerchief.

"I was in the car, and I was ready to go, and then I said to myself, Hey, stop a minute. What's more important—to go to church and sit there and fume and ask Jesus to feel sorry for you and to condemn your husband or to skip church and go back inside and sit with him and hope he'll really break down and cry and cry, so all that disappointment in him will come out, and then he can talk with me, and we can try to figure out a way that we can pick up from here."

She chose to go home and take the chance that her husband would resolve his growing desperation—his disappointments, as she kept calling them, which were struggling to "express themselves," as she put it. She went into the kitchen and busied herself with his favorites, and said nothing. Finally he began to sob openly, and they began to talk.

"He didn't need to say much. All he needed to do was show me what he was feeling—I guess you could say show *himself*, because he'd been biting his lip and pushing himself like mad, as though there was nothing eating away at him, when everything he did showed that in a while there'd be nothing left of him at the rate he was going! I just sat there—I was relieved. Funny thing, I thought I'd start crying myself; but I didn't—I was almost happy. I knew this was a turning point.

"All of a sudden, I broke my silence, and I said, 'Honey, you're as busy as anyone in the world can be, I know, but you've got to find some time for yourself, not for me and the kids, as much as we want you and need you. You've got to find some way of doing something that will give you some peace.' He looked up at me, and I could see he knew what I was saying, but he was helpless; he didn't know what to do. I was going to tell him to talk with the priest, but I thought better of it. I knew he wouldn't talk with his friends—he's Mr. Confidence and Mr. Keep Busy with them. I racked my brains, and then I thought, Why not a doctor? I just blurted it out, the name of the pediatrician. I didn't say anything else, I just said his name. I didn't have to go further, or maybe I was afraid to, or I didn't know what words to use."

A week later he and the pediatrician had a long talk. The doctor took the lead, told his patient's father that he needed to become part of Ben's life and that one way to do so was to work with older retarded children. That way, when the boy was no longer a baby, the father would have some experience with children who needed special education. A month later, with the doctor's help, this father began volunteering on weekends at a state school for retarded and disabled children.

"I was 'slow' myself: I was 'disabled,'" he would recall a year later. He was also anxious, frightened, ready to give up and flee or to break down and cry. But he also wanted "some way out of the trap" he'd built for himself. He intuitively knew that his tears were a kind of grief, evidence of a mind in mourning. "I've been crying for all the hopes and dreams I once had—they're not going to happen. It's only gradually occurring to me that the only way out of this corner I'm in—like I keep saying, it's a trap, and I've made it myself—the only way out is for me to find some other place to go, some new hopes for myself."

By then he had already begun to build up some "hopes"—not for himself or, least of all, his son, but for the three or four youngsters he was learning to engage with, challenge to activities, help restrain and excite to action. Pretty soon he and his boys were quite a team—in sports and games and cleanup activities, in doing routines and assisting the staff with other children. Pretty soon he began to figure out ways to connect with his own son, to show the boy and his mother and sisters that there was a lot this busy mechanic could do to fix the way a home was running.

He didn't lose his wistfulness about what might have been. Rather, he let those thoughts ignite in him the fierce willfulness he had always possessed as a worker. Once the sight of boys playing in a Little League game had been unbearable. The time would come when he would organize his own son's Little League team. When a neighbor once called the team "special," he flinched. "I didn't like the way he used that word. I felt myself getting weak. I was a little teary for a second, and my knees felt as though if someone just touched me, I'd fall over. But in another second I was up for anything. I said, 'You bet we're special.' I meant it. Me and the kids, we were doing great, and we'd show him, we'd be thrilled to show him! It was then I knew I'd crossed some big street, and I was walking on the other side and my head was up, not down, and it was working with those kids that did it. They're the ones who got me across to the other side—do you see?"

I nodded, grateful to a man who had shown what it can mean to fall down, then pick himself up, not through hours of psychological talk or the support of a "group," and not even through the healing that time itself offers. In the end, his willfulness responded to his wife's loyalty and affection and to a doctor's sensible suggestion. But in the end, also, his pain responded to the visible, concrete opportunities a few children offered him. The gifts he brought on their birthdays and at Christmas signaled not only what these children had come to mean to him, but what they had enabled him to find and affirm in himself. They walked him "across," to a place where he was able to manage on his own. He became once again the assertive, capable, resourceful person he'd been before his setback, a setback that was followed by a breakthrough. As I heard him talk about the "choice" he had made, as I heard him remember "wishing" with each visit to that state school for the strength to make the best of his time with those children, I remembered the Latin I had learned many years earlier: the very root of the word "volunteer," *voluntas*—a choice—comes from *velle*, to wish.

Stoic Endurance

Some people exert themselves in a manner less directly personal than the man described above. In many years of work among poor families in Boston and Cambridge, I have met individuals who have wondered why they engage in volunteer work, and to what effect. They may imply that they do what they do—but for no particular reason that they care to spell out and with no particular personal consequences. They claim no affirmation for themselves, though an outsider, watching them in action and overhearing what they say, might disagree. They don't even assert the restricted satisfaction of friendships. Sometimes they acknowledge a motivation that does scant credit to their depth of commitment. An aside such as "I just get a kick out of it" hardly conveys the satisfaction achieved from a voluntary obligation taken on with great seriousness.

In Roxbury I met a middle-aged black mother who did her fair share of listening to children. She worked as a bus driver, taking children to and from school every weekday. After her husband died of a stroke at the age of forty-four, she was tempted to immerse herself in the troubled lives of her two daughters and their four children. She had encouraged both daughters to finish high school and take courses at a nearby community college to become nurses or computer programmers or teachers, whatever might catch their interest. The daughters adamantly refused: they wanted no more school, even though they were not always happy as mothers. One went dancing a lot (her boyfriend, the father of her one son, had left her and gone to the West Coast). The other, who had three children, moved in and out of serious depressive states, even as she tried occasionally to work in a fast-food chain. Her husband had been hurt in an automobile accident but received no compensation because he had been drinking and was responsible for the crash. The other driver had walked away without injuries fortunately. There was no real reason why this man couldn't go to work—at least work that didn't require heavy manual effort. But he was mostly unemployed, and he continued to drink.

In these unpromising family circumstances this bus-driving mother and grandmother went out of her way to keep an eye on many of the children whom she transported to school. She volunteered at an elementary school as a teacher's assistant, and even on the bus she did far more than drive. I first heard about her from a mother whose son and daughter I was getting to know. She told me that her children's bus driver "taught" her charges all the way to school and all the way back. A month or so later I was introduced to this woman at a school meeting and told again of her unusual vocation. We agreed to meet, and we did, many times. I became another of her students. I was at times overwhelmed by her memories of specific instances in which children had learned a lesson or two on the bus or at the school where she did her "aiding."

Once I took the liberty of inquiring about her reasons for doing this teaching. She warmed to the question but wasn't sure she knew how to answer. "I wish I could tell you more," she said almost plaintively. Then she said, "I want to see these kids make it in life. I want to see them survive." As she spoke,

I thought she was also expressing her own persistence, her capacity for stoic survival. She was a wise woman, earthy and intelligent and determined with regard to those children she tried to assist.

What follows are some highlights from several long, intense, taped interviews I did with her a few days after her fiftieth birthday. She had been getting chest pains and needed no doctor to tell her that her heart was ailing. She had arranged a medical appointment and, almost in preparation for the bad news she expected, was anxious to concentrate on what she called "the good side" of her life. No doubt that half-century mark had prodded her to become more than usually reflective, though she had occasionally been outspokenly introspective in the two years I had known her.

"I had an aunt who would come and help us out, she was a maiden lady, my momma called her. This aunt, Josephine, would sing gospel music, and she'd start her declaring. She'd tell us that we had to do something God would notice, or else we'd just get lost in the big shuffle! I can still hear her saying that now. I can still see myself staring at her and getting more and more worried by the second! What would happen to me if God just overlooked me while He was paying attention to some others, who'd been smart enough to make sure they captured His attention? Why, I'd end up in one of those big fires 'down there' that don't get put out by any men with hoses shooting out water!

"So I'd try to figure out how to get His attention, and I had some ideas. One, I'd go to church *alone* sometimes, and that way He'd see me being loyal, and He'd remember me from all the others. Two, if I did something, got a job, I'd try to do it a little better and different from other folks; that way the Lord up there would spot me, or maybe He'd hear from others what I was doing. Three, I'd try to go the extra mile so I could show Him that I'm not just running with the crowd. That's the worst, my aunt used to tell us, when you just sit there and let yourself be traveling like the other folks around you.

"When I'm driving the bus, I call some kids to be up there near me, sitting, and I've done my homework—I've checked into *their* homework!— and I'm ready for them. I'll quiz them. I'll try to give them hints about how to do better in school. I'll teach them about obeying and keeping quiet and speaking out at the right time. If they're doing good, I reach into my bag, and I give them a chocolate bar—and it's extra good, not just the five-and-dime-store kind! 'Made in England' is what it says on the wrapper—and I get them to read it.

"The teachers have called me an 'honorary' one, and that's fine. I go to school and sit there in a class, and try to get those kids to pay attention and study as hard as they can. When a kid does well, I feel great! It's my reward—and I hope the good Lord is taking it all down. A lot of times, though, I don't get my hopes too high—about the kids or about myself, either. A lot of times I'm saying to myself that I've seen so much trouble hereabouts, and it's not getting the slightest better, and sometimes it's worse. So if a kid learns to spell a little bit better, and he does his figuring, his arithmetic a little better, and he writes his sentences right, it still won't prove much down the road, because there's a trap he'll fall into—drugs, or a bullet that hits him even if it's meant for someone else, or sickness.

"A lot of our kids, they fall sick, and there's no good doctors here to see them. A lot of our mothers, they're not taking the care of their babies that they should. I know! I could start being upset. I could raise my fists and pound them. But I've learned some lessons from life. I've learned that we've been walking before God, all of us, since He first turned us loose down here; and there must be some reason for all this, but it's not any of us, no matter all the schools you've gone to and the subjects you've studied—it's not one of us who can find out what the Lord was hoping to do when He got all this going down here. Once you know that, you can begin to sit back and be sincere, and continue your work, and do all the good you can—but not be thinking you're going to lift the world up and change everything upside down."

Such a mix of continuing energy, spent generously on children, and a stoic endurance that forswears self-importance or even a conviction of one's significance in the lives of others is not altogether rare in certain older volunteers, even if they don't attribute their condition to the Lord's presence (a threatened presence?) in their lives. This woman took great pleasure in asking children to do a lot and yet not expecting a world-shattering miracle as a consequence of what happened between her and them. She hoped (and prayed daily) for a "touch of wisdom" - a quiet acceptance of what would be. She did hope to contribute to what would be, yet she had a sense of history that was almost Tolstoyan in nature: she was mindful of all the forces that conspire to make us turn out as we do.

Her exertions, her hard everyday labor, most certainly helped shape the minds of many children. Still, there was much else going on, as she noted like a sociologist, if not a theologian: she knew the power of "the streets," the role of chance in the "tricks of the world," and finally, of course, "God and what He might decide to do."

I think of that bus driver when I watch several older people visit sick children in a pediatric ward or when I watch schoolchildren visiting the elderly in a nursing home not far from an urban middle school. Some of the older are not unlike that bus-driving woman: energetic and forceful, yet glad to feel detached. They try to help others even though they themselves are ailing a bit.

"I couldn't do this work if I was too involved with those children," one woman remarked to me. "I've learned that if you exhaust yourself, if you over-commit yourself, you lose rather than win. The children pull back—and why shouldn't they! You have to learn just the right attitude with them, and when you've got it, then you really can enjoy this work. It doesn't become a chore or a burden, and yet you do get close to the kids. It's a matter of tone you could say: you know enough to persist, but not feel the world hangs on your every word!"

Some professional people—doctors, lawyers, teachers—also work hard to remain aroused and interested but somewhat detached; then they find themselves better able to enjoy the work they do. A lawyer much involved in legal defense cases for the poor explained that both for the sake of his clients and for his own sake he had to learn how to keep some distance, or perspective, without losing his personal commitment to the work and to those with whom he was working. He was eager not to lose that commitment; he wanted to remain enthusiastic, full of dedication, and even passion. Not least, he wanted to feel a kind of excitement and fulfillment.

"I've been doing this kind of law long enough to know that it can be enjoyable only if you've adjusted your head in a certain way. I don't have any formulas. I think each person has to find his or her own momentum and speed. But you can't think it all hangs on you. You can't go around with the idea that if you come at the cast full speed ahead, all guns blazing, then there will be a legal action and then a victory—or a defeat—and that will be that. You've got to understand that out here, doing this kind of law, there are lots of complications that can make even what seems like an easy case, destined for success, come crashing down. You never really know whether people are going to want to sustain their involvement with you, and if they don't, why.

"Of course, what I said can apply to any client—but here there's a lot of fear, and people appear, then disappear, or they change their minds, and they're not going to tell you why. I'm at my best when I've got a clear idea of what I'm trying to do, and when

I've made my best try to work closely and efficiently with my clients. But I'm not sitting there expecting the world to change for them, for us; quite the contrary, I've resigned myself to the realization that this may be a win, or it may be a loss, but at least we're here, giving it a real try, and that's an important step right there. When my head is 'on' that way, I'm feeling right about things, and I won't fall flat on my face if we lose or go into orbit if we win—neither would be justified."

That "resignation" or acceptance of God's will is what Kierkegaard explored in *Fear and Trembling*—not a surrender of personal initiative, not an apathy, not a descent into gloom or despair, but a thoughtful acknowledgment of what can and cannot be done. For Kierkegaard such resignation was a believer's step: I await what the Lord decides. For this lawyer there was a world of obstacles to face, only some of which would yield to his strenuous exertions. He used the word "resigned" in a thoughtful, unsentimental exploration of the possible, the not so possible, and the quite likely impossible (but one never knows).

A Boost to Success

For a person to remain committed to service despite the outcome, he or she must have felt a prior sense of accomplishment. Some people who work at community service or enlist in privately sponsored or government service programs are also anxious to help launch a career. They hope to become doctors or lawyers or to enter the world of business or to teach. They look ahead to applications, interviews, committee evaluations and decisions. The ladder upward beckons toward college or graduate school, toward a hospital appointment, law clerkship, business or teaching position. It is not easy to understand the complex mixture of ideas, concerns, and motives that informs the decisions of such volunteers. Any discussion of the satisfactions of service ought to mention the dilemmas many students feel as they balance their idealistic motivations with the practicalities required as they contemplate their future occupation or profession.

Not all young volunteers are as forthcoming—as relentlessly able and willing to enter into self-scrutiny and share the results—as one young man who as a Harvard undergraduate worked for two years tutoring children in the Roxbury section of Boston. He worked hard to earn the children's trust, but he still felt he was "on trial."

"A month ago, one child suddenly shot this question at me: 'Hey, what's in it for you?' At first I wasn't sure what he meant—what 'it' was supposed to be. He saw me trying to figure out what I was being asked, how to ask for some kind of clarification. So he expanded his question. 'You come out here a lot, and you're nice to us, and a few of us were wondering, Why does he come here, and what will he get out of it?' I didn't answer right away. I could have spouted a big line: how much it means to me to be able to have helped others, and the tremendous satisfaction I get when I see someone improving in school, and my parents' Christian beliefs that you give to others, try to do the best you can to share what you have with people who are in need. Then I could have added that I have *fun,* that I like coming here and meeting people, and we have a good time, and I feel better, frankly, when I return because I have a sense of accomplishment, and I've enjoyed being with friends, and I remember the stories I've heard, and the jokes.

"Instead I sat there, and I guess I was silent *too* long, because a couple of kids laughed nervously, and one kid said I didn't have to answer the question. 'Besides,' she added, 'we like you, and we don't care what your reasons are for coming here.' I was relieved to hear that! It was as if I did have these deep, dark, ulterior reasons, but they were willing to give me a break and forget the whole thing. No sooner did I think that when another thought came to me: you're being too defensive and suspicious yourself. Just answer the question—be brief and cool! But I couldn't, and now it was too late. I'd hesitated so long that I was the one who turned it all into a big deal!

"Finally I said the truth; I said that it was a real hard one to put to me, what they'd asked. I said, 'Look, I like coming here—you've become friends of mine, I hope, and I hope you feel the same way, that I'm a friend of yours. I love getting a pizza and bowling, and I love trying to help out with your work so you can do better, just the way certain teachers helped me out in high school, and before that too.' I said, 'If you can see someone doing better and better in school, and you've been able to be part of that—of the person improving in English or math—then you feel good, or at least I do.' Then I tried to be honest, to level with them. I said, 'Hey, I can't deny that it helps me to come out here. I like doing it and feel proud to be able to be with you and make friends and do the teaching. But yes, I wouldn't want to deny it, I'll put this down on my record, what I've done here, and that will help me—people like to see that, admissions people. I won't deny it!'

"That's about it, word for word, what I said. I was grabbing hard for words, and I was afraid that I was falling down and making a mess of everything! But they were very nice to me. They told me to forget it, and they told me I was cool, and they told me it was time to go get one of those pizzas, since I just mentioned them. That's what we did—we broke off the talk. Frankly, I was torn. Part of me thought we really should stay there and talk some more—this was pay dirt we were hitting: how do you learn to trust someone, if you ever do? But I was also relieved to have the subject changed. I felt a little like a hypocrite, and I was afraid some of them felt that way about me. Later, when we were eating our pizzas, and everyone was talking about other things, my mind was still on that question I'd been asked, and what the right answer to it is, and how you phrase your answer."

He was certainly not alone in the moral quandary he expressed. He spent a long time trying to settle in his mind exactly what he was doing in Roxbury as a tutor and what his reasons and expectations were. Some others who did similar community service, he felt, were "crudely opportunistic." What I asked him to explain, he was terser than usual. "They want to list their community service work on their CV." Then he added, after a very short pause, "So do I. It's self-servicing for me to distinguish myself from them—me the good guy, they the clever frauds. It's so damn complicated. I don't know how to begin to look at all this—what our motives are."

We discussed the issue for a long time, and we took it up on other occasions. I mentioned that everything he did—his intellectual and athletic interests, his church activities—could also be placed under the "cloud of suspicion" he occasionally summoned in his mind as he contemplated his community service work. He had turned that youth's question into an excuse for a far-reaching kind of self-arraignment, I began to realize. In a later chapter, I scrutinize how this moral preoccupation can be a prelude to depression and despair. Here it is important to note under the rubric of satisfactions the unquestionable pleasure many young men and women have taken, not only in the value to others of their community service work, but in the value it can have for themselves as well.

That value is not only a moral one (so much learned from others in tutoring them) but also a personal one, as this young man said quite pointedly: "This work I do will help me, I sometimes think, more than it will help the kids. I guess I ought to say that the work will give a boost to my success, and that I know it, and that when you ask me about the satisfactions I get from this kind of work—well, if I left that out, I'd be leaving something out that's part of the picture!"

His expression was singularly candid and quite telling. He worked all of the ironies and complexities, really, of a privileged life into a few sentences: the satisfactions of doing community service work and the additional satisfaction that went with knowing that his work would no doubt advance the further work he hoped to do as a lawyer or businessman (he hadn't yet settled that question). In our many further talks devoted to this matter, we brought in other students to ponder the awkward yet important implications of a quite human ethical issue first given shape (speaking of irony) by the question of a boy in a ghetto school who was having an exceedingly hard time of it educationally.

Those who took part in this discussion were outspokenly idealistic and at the same time self-critically assertive of their rights and needs—a rather tense and complicated attitude. Again and again I heard comments that were apologetically self-serving—sinners proclaiming with melancholy insistence their necessary wrong-doing!

"I live in a world where you have to play all the angles," a young woman announced, and than she denounced such an imperative with considerable vehemence. "I'd like to work at public-interest law, but first I have to get into law school, and so if I work at helping public interest lawyers now, I'll have a better chance of becoming one later." Minutes afterward, those words prompted her conscience to rebel: such talk was "sleazy," she wanted it known, and she didn't so much ask for forgiveness as hope that "one day there will be an end to it [the kind of remarks she'd just made], at least for me. Maybe they [on the admissions committee] see through all this. Maybe they remember this own chicanery." Her good work as a teacher of needy children had now become a manifest confidence trick, at least with respect to what she had intended when she began the service work. Still, the work had its own worth, most of these ambitious, able young men and women remembered, and their tutees would agree.

READING

The following essay was written by a first-year student in response to his reading of Robert Coles's article. Ryan Lee has an interesting perspective as he relates the reading to his own experiences.

The Eyes Search for Something

Ryan Lee

"Satisfactions" blends human accomplishment with emotional satisfaction. It is a collection of stories made to motivate lives, turn gears, and regenerate a spirit for giving and receiving. The total emotional baggage is heavy enough to cause one to resort to action. Have you ever read a tear-jerker? Or a feel-good story? These are the stories that change lives. A desire builds and builds, climbing to the epitome of human emotional ecstasy. And what is this desire, what is this great ecstasy? To find out you must read on.

I'm going to start with a story, not a touching story, not a tear-jerker, just a plain story. John is a boy that I see once a week at my volunteer work. Once a week, Monday's from 2:30 to 4:30 I go to this school and play with kids. John didn't stand out in my eye. He didn't hug me like the little girls. He didn't have something impressive to show me, like when Nathan learned to tie his shoes. He was just a dark-skinned, dirty boy. I didn't even look forward to playing with him.

Often times he'd come to me with red eyes and speaking through a small mouth, "Wuss your name?" A boy of medium stature, soft spoken, and yet possessed two of the firmest eyes I've seen. I'd answer him. The next week he'd ask me the same, "Wuss you name?" Never did I lose my patience. I always answered the same. And he'd probe into my eyes, standing in front of me already with an answer but still unblinkingly firm in his gaze. He didn't move, didn't speak, just stared into my eyes. I felt like I could not leave his. I felt during these moments an obligation to allow him the contact. Those eyes, they were searching for something, I just knew it. His lips were red and his eyes were red, red as fire.

Picking teams in kick ball made me angry. It always hurt one pitiful kid. The last one picked cried, as the kids rushed out into the field forgetting even to say, "Okay we'll take Dana . . ." She was left there, the last player available and a forgotten child. She cried profusely until I explained to her that she was needed by the fielding team. Sometimes kids like to feel needed. Dana's tears soon dried upon her face and she joined in as part of children at play. Too many young hearts are carelessly handled because they are put in the hands of children who scantily know the difference between standing in Dana's shoes or their own. They forget the feeling of standing alone, the last pick, looking out through glassy eyes at a majority. They forget until the group one day says, "This time you are not good enough to play." Only then does the cycle of pain and education begin to work in the lives of youth. Every day hearts are broken and it breaks my heart to have to watch these fragile kids get torn apart from a simple game of kick ball.

Along comes John, late with a frown, but eager to play. He never did smile much. I told him to go and get a partner and he did. I said, "Okay everybody, John's going to be on this team and you guys get Michael." A sudden, "No!! We don't want John on our team!!" and then from the other end of the gym, "We don't want him either!!" Now could you imagine the hurt. I saw it in his red eyes. He looked one way at one team for some sort of acceptance, then at the other. He was not a poor player, in fact no worse than Michael. Why then? Why the rejection from every player in the gym? At that moment he looked around with red eyes, he hadn't a single friend in the room. Instead of sorrow a fire set aflame John's rage.

He played hard, and when Reno yelled at him for dropping a catch, John pushed him. A fight started between the larger Reno and medium sized John. I once again looked into John's eyes. His eyes always told the story. This time was like every other time, John wanted to beat the living crap out of every person on earth, but he knew he couldn't do it. With every fight, John walked away with his tail between his legs. The fire within him blazed profusely. One day it will explode in a magnificently disgusting display of total and uninhibited rage upon unlucky kids. I took John and tried to explain to him that fighting never solves the problem. I tried to be a mentor. Not for myself but for John. I see a danger that possibly nobody else may see. I am desperately seeking an answer. Like I said, one day he will explode. He'll kill somebody, or get killed. His red eyes, his red lips, no other breathes a fire so young and potent.

If you ever visit this school, John will be there. Take a good look at him, search his soul. What you will find is an opportunity for yourself; you will feel a strong desire to change his life. The same desire felt in the blood of a lone white man willing to die for Negro rights in the 1960's. The same desire brewing in the soul of a man trying to reach out, be a big brother, and save one kid from turning to the lifestyle offered on the streets. The same desire that keeps a bus driver working to direct her kids to a good life.

This story I just told is real. There is an urgency to love these children. What is this story all about? It says something about the education system and the home. The fifth grade teacher can say, "Why didn't Johnny learn that in the fourth grade?" and the fourth grade teacher can say, "Why didn't Johnny learn that in the third grade?" and the third grade teacher can say, "Why didn't Johnny learn this in kindergarten?" I ask you, How do you expect Johnny to know anything if he isn't being taught right in the home? It all comes down to what is taught in the home. Families are the most crucial institution in the lives of our children today. And I see too many kids who come to school gazing into my eyes, searching for something like John does. Something which in many cases the home does not provide them so they come to school and learn hard lessons on loneliness and rejection. They walk home thinking nobody cares. And it brings tears to my eyes to watch the lives of our youth slowly deteriorate because of a lack of love. Kids like John and Dana look to us for love. Children like to feel needed. Kids helping kids, teachers learning about students, students learning about teachers, this is what school is all about. If there is one lesson to be taken from all of this it is to become a friend to these kids. Once your eyes meet in a warm moment of need you will realize that satisfaction is secondary to giving love to life.

WRITING

More Satisfaction

You've now read both Robert Coles's perspective on service within the community and one student's account and reflection on the work he was doing in a school with children. Both sources reveal knowing you can make a difference produces great satisfaction. There is also frustration that whatever you can do is never quite enough. However, much learning occurs whether you are satisfied or not.

For this paper, you will explore how others have responded to their work within the community. Take the following steps:

1. Find at least three people in the community who are involved in service. These can be volunteers in national organizations, such as the American Heart Association and the American Cancer Society, or smaller community-based organizations, such as spouse-abuse shelters, foster care facilities, or a local food bank.

2. Develop a questionnaire of at least 10 questions that you will use to interview your three volunteers. These questions should focus on what they do, how they view their work, and what satisfactions and frustrations they have felt.

3. Ask these people to take a moment out of their day to talk with you about their work in the organization.

4. Write a paper describing your volunteers, their work, and their organizations. Inform your reading audience about the learning that occurs for these volunteers. Include references they might make to their frustrations and concerns.

5. Write a final reflection on what kinds of learning might be relevant in your college education to help you view their stories with some insight. In other words, is it important to know something about the sociology behind the homeless? Perhaps you need to understand a particular culture better to understand their behavior?

The purpose of this paper is for you both to make contact with people serving the community and to begin articulating for yourself what kinds of academic learning help you understand your community.

Journal Entry 28

Too many have dispensed with generosity in order to practice charity.
Albert Camus

The best way to find yourself is to lose yourself in the service of others.
"Mahatma" Mohandas Karamchard Gandhi

Reflect on the above quotes and then write a few paragraphs explaining their meaning.

CASH IN ON EDUCATION

Thomas Taylor Watts
Attorney, Kemper and Watts

My four-year stint in college ended more than 30 years ago, but I remember it clearly. The faces and the feelings, the ideas and the sounds were all fixed in my memory by the emotions of the time. To this day, when I hear certain songs, I am immediately transported back to parties, protest rallies, football games, and friends.

To my surprise, I also remember certain facts and ideas learned in class, facts and ideas I have never once needed to know how to live my subsequent life: Light travels at 186,000 miles per second. Formal religions were "invented" as a means for societies to unify warring tribes.

If I had a chance to do it again, I would attend every concert and special lecture. I would take classes on the fishes of the Arctic Ocean and the peoples of the Western Sahara. And I would take every opportunity to discuss the things I discovered with teachers and friends, and even family. Because I now realize, but didn't at the time, that the experiences and the process are more important than the subject.

It is the skills you acquire rather than the facts you learn that allow you to cash in on your education, as my life well shows: I went to college to become an astrophysicist. Somewhere in the middle of quantum mechanics, I discovered I was a terrible physicist. But my professors, and my fellow students, taught me how to think about the world in an educated way. In classes on government and psychology and even physics, I learned how to gather information, analyze it, ask questions about it, and draw conclusions. It is those skills, constantly practiced, and improved over time, that have provided the means to achieve success and satisfaction.

I'm a lawyer. When I analyze the facts of a new case, when I cross-examine a witness, when I argue for a particular result on behalf of my client, I am using the skills first learned in History 101. And although my clients are amused to discover I graduated with a degree in physics, I don't feel that I wasted my time. Physics taught me how to analyze and solve problems, a skill that I employ to this very day.

SOUVENIR:

My Own Reflection

One of my employees took care to copy snippets of papers written by my students. Over the years, we have had many moments of laughter and delight by these. She called them "Out of the Mouths of Baby Ruths," and I'd like to share a few of them with you. These are excerpts from student papers that obviously had some problems with context and spelling.

> After the ceremony, all your friends and family come and see you. They all give all kinds of flowers and leis. I was covered all over until my forehead, I almost couldn't **breed** because it was so heavy. . . .
>
> Many of our elders scowl and say that we worship **satin** or are constantly thinking evil thoughts just because we are into the color black. . . .
>
> She was gorgeous. Blond hair, beautiful brown eyes and the **sexist** legs . . .
>
> I want to **expose myself** with other people of different ethnic groups. . . .
>
> Most beginners or part time users will be **coma toast**. . . .

Then there are those who just have trouble with spelling:

pedestool, egsajerated, quarteroise, valid victorian

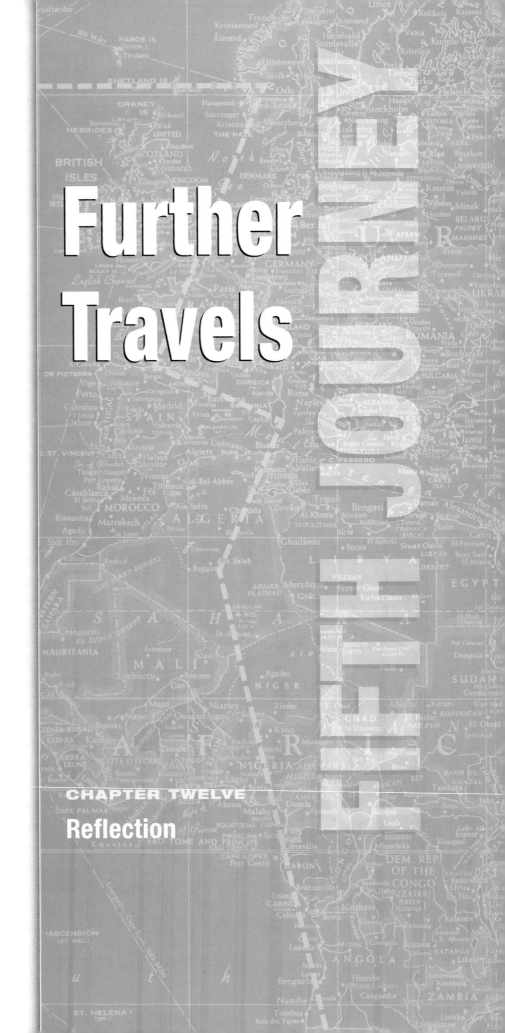

Further Travels

FIFTH JOURNEY

CHAPTER TWELVE

Reflection

Introduction to the Fifth Journey

This text began with you the student; it now ends in the same manner. What you bring to your educational experience is the most important element in making meaning from learning. You have discovered why and how scholarship is created, what connection you have to this knowledge, and how you can contribute to scholarship. You should accept that being accountable and taking responsibility for your own education will in turn contribute to the quality of your life. Additionally, by engaging in service learning opportunities, you should now have a better understanding of why your contributions are so vital.

Evaluation of one's own work and assessment of it by others are integral components of any learning experience. Certainly, it does not belong solely at the end of a book as though it has no relationship to anything that went on before. Your journals, writing assignments, and other classroom activities have been designed to help you become aware of how you are thinking, what you have accomplished, which ideas you now comprehend, and what you need to keep making sense out of learning.

This last journey is a reminder that taking the time to reflect on your academic development is crucial. You have to look back on the path you have chosen, see what transpired, and then illuminate it for yourself. Interpret your experiences in new ways, and see how well you make connections between what you knew before coming to college, what you know now, and what you might experience in the future. In other words, by reflecting, evaluating, and analyzing what's gone before, you can give shape to your future educational experiences.

The Fifth Journey suggests further travels. This means that you will soon move into uncharted territory. In order to do this well, you must take a moment to gather your thoughts about what has transpired until now.

Don't forget that learning is about the personal. You bring your history to college with you—your educational, family, social, economic, cultural, and gender-based experiences make up this history. Your experiences in college are influenced by this history; your experiences in life continue to create it. Whatever knowledge you acquire is at once molded by who you are. Do you know this? Do you know who you are? Are you aware of your growth and expanded sense of scholarship? Have you changed over the semester? If so, why? How?

The last chapter is titled "Reflection" because this activity will bring together ideas, concepts, understanding, and meaning for you on a personal level.

Of course, my favorite has always been the bibliographic entry at the end of one paper I received. It looked like this:

Ricky Lake or Jenny Jones. Don't know which. Don't know when.

These are funny, no doubt. However, after reflecting on these kinds of mistakes and simply straightforward misinformation I've received from students, I began to notice something very important. Students were making these mistakes because they were never really paying attention. This was a little like the National Anthem. Do we really know the words? Have we ever really paid attention? And if not, why not?

These mistakes may reflect a lack of experience in reading, writing bibliographies, or using words such as "pedestal." But even more significant is that they tell me that the students haven't been engaged in their own educations. This is one more reason that this book focuses on personal narratives at the beginning and end, with a look at evaluation and reflection. The more you can connect with your education and learning, the less careless you become about your work.

Your learning needs to have meaning. The rest follows.

It also is intended to show you that your journey never ends. The road you've made so far is one full of experiences and learning. It is time to reflect on these experiences, be changed by them, evaluate them and, then, continue your walk.

COMPASS

Service reveals a large portion of what life is, and it moves us and supports us in realizing this important vision . . . helping others is a vehicle for working on yourself. After working with others, one begins to realize that unity of humans is more real than believing that people are separate and alone.

—First-year student

Engaging in community service is a form of experiential learning. Over the course of a semester or year, students engage in activities that address human and community needs. Although the activity itself is vastly meaningful, reflection is really the key to this component of your education.

This last chapter discusses one way of knowing—reflection. Service learning is based on the pedagogical principle that learning and development do not necessarily occur as a result of the direct experience but, rather, as a result of the reflective component of the experience. What does this mean? It means that you develop a greater sense of belonging and responsibility as a member of the larger community when you find the work you do has meaning. However, the meaning of time spent in a service project is not always perfectly clear. Therefore, you must take time to actively reflect on the experiences and in this way tie what you saw, heard, and felt (experienced, observed) and what you may have learned from others (authority) to what you begin to understand as a result of reflective thinking and writing.

Reflection

Objectives

- to view reflection as a way of knowing

- to gather thoughts about the course

- to evaluate one's own work

"Is giving us tomorrow,
The gift is you and I."

In conclusion, you can't force anybody to want to learn. You can't make them remember how much they liked to when they were a child. You can write articles for years and they might reach anybody. You may even publish a book that tackles this issue on the nose and nobody may be affected by it. It is up to the students to want to learn themselves. Success begins with an "s," which also stands for self. For you to truly be successful and really want to learn, then it can only begin with your . . . **self.**

—*Kendis Leeburg*

TRAVEL ESSENTIAL

Information Literacy and Reflection

Information literacy is, by definition, personal. Although information-literate people share common attributes, the value you give to information and your perspective on using, finding, and evaluating information are yours to create. Information literacy has to become part of the story you are telling about your relationship to learning and to your ways of knowing about the world around you. When is it most important to seek information in your own life?

How do you decide when an information source is credible? What evidence needs to be presented for you to consider information valid? When do you decide to use more than the Internet for information? How do you decide? How many different perspectives are needed before you are confident that you have an accurate context for your story? Do you have all the skills you need to find information efficiently and thoroughly? These questions, when answered, constitute your definition of information literacy.

Take a minute or two to think about your own answers to these questions. Are there other questions you need to ask yourself in order to make your own definition of information literacy? Deciding what you are going to do and how you are going to change is the connection between information literacy and evaluation. Evaluation is assessment and action.

If you need to change something about your curent definition of information literacy and the definition you want to have for yourself, what will you do to make that happen? Will you spend more time learning how to search the Web? Will you take an information literacy course? Will you think about how to better determine credibility and validity for your sources? Will you learn how to use databases better? Will you practice asking more questions about your research? What will you do to become an information-literate person?

Journal Entry 29

We must find a way or make one.

Hannibal

The title of this book is *College: We Make the Road by Walking*. Now that you are near the end of the book, what do you make of the title?

First, take a moment and draw the meaning of the book in the blank space provided in your journal pages.

Second, write a paragraph explaining the meaning of the title to you.

Third, come up with a new title for the book. *Make it your own.*

REFLECTION

Reflection actually should be structured as an official part of your course work. It involves taking the time to review, think about, and analyze an experience—be it a reading, a lecture, a discussion, or a field trip—in order to gain deeper under-

---

No journey carries one far unless, as it extends into the world around us, it goes an equal distance into the world within.

LILLIAN SMITH

standing. It provides you an opportunity to think about the knowledge you have gained and how your attitudes and views might have changed.

The reflective process has three elements:

1. Examination of new knowledge and skills, new information, and alternative ways of knowing or perceiving the world around you

2. Affective reflection, in which you examine what you feel in response to your new knowledge or experience (this involves emotions and attitudes and perspectives)

3. Examination of what you have learned in light of the process involved

How many times have you complained about boring lectures or readings? How often have you lost interest in a discussion or group project? Sometimes this happens if you take on a passive role and allow yourself to be fed the knowledge, expecting the learning to just happen. On the other hand, if you take the time, with the support of your instructors, to do some critical reflective thinking, you might engage with the subject matter more deeply.

In the next reading, Leo Buscaglia comments on how interconnected we are as humans. As you read his essay, reflect on the concept of connections. Think about how the concepts and ideas you learned throughout this text might be interconnected. Reflect on your life, and consider all the ways your experiences have been intertwined.

The Role of Connectiveness

Leo F. Buscaglia

No man is an island of itself. Each is a piece of the continent a part of the main.

—John Donne

Just as fully functioning persons write the script of their own lives, they also respect the connectiveness of all things along the way. They realize that the self is only the self in that it has a world, a structure of which it is a part—a part, yet apart. We are a community of persons and a world of things. We are what we are because birds exist, plants grow, bees pollinate, winds blow, tides change, rains fall, and accidents happen. Nothing occurs in the world that in some way does not affect us all. Even the most insignificant act we perform will have some effect upon the world.

Philosophers talk of all of us being caught up and moving in a single stream of life. We all originated from the source but are not ourselves the source. We arise as a special quality of the source and pass on into it again while the true source itself remains. We will run our unique way, over rapids, peaceful ponds, fiercely at times, calmly at others. We will join other streams and rivers along the way, gaining strength, being propelled or momentarily falling aside in muddy, stagnant pools. But no matter how quickly or slowly or quietly or passionately we move, we all come eventually to the same end in the same sea. We have returned to the source from which we rose. We therefore at one time or another, the beginning, the end, as well as the way, but are permanently never any of them. We are an important

part of the dynamic process, but we, like everything else, are only passing through. We are each a singular person but we are each a universal person as well. Both are equally important. We are born provincial, egocentric, limited. The more we become, the more universal the person we are. We finally come to realize that most human conflicts arise through our provincialism, our concern for our personal problems, our selfish interests, our own conflicts.

Most of us define a good day as one in which all things have gone our way. We see the good life as one in which our personal dreams have been realized. It is not our concern if thousands go to bed each night hungry and in despair, as long as they keep out of sight and leave us alone. It doesn't matter to us if the world's children are being battered or not being educated properly. Our children are fully grown and doing well, and we have no responsibility for the others. It is only when we are mugged by the hungry children or brutalized or terrorized in our home that we realize the connectiveness of all things. There is no place to hide. No one is guilty. We are all innocents in an ever changing stream for which each of us is responsible. It is a fantasy to believe that peace comes without all of us moving together with the stream in unity, joy, wonder and love. An English poet, Francis Thompson once wrote that he could not pick a flower without troubling a star.

A bush grows. The blowing wind, gliding birds and busy insects gather the pollen to sow it again miles from the original flowering plant. We pass, unsuspecting, on a morning's stroll. We, too, gather the pollen on our clothes and unsuspectingly carry the plant to spread its life beauty to new uncharted areas. The flower is born from the same source, journeys along the same path, momentarily uses our nurturing and understanding to continue on its way. Without us it would pass into oblivion, and we would deny all who follow the comfort and wisdom of the flowers.

In some way, however small and secret, we are all dependent one upon the other. Fully functioning persons recognize this power and know that it stems from the source which is able to create light or produce darkness. A word, an act, an expressed feeling can reverberate in wide circles in the pond—touching unsuspecting travelers. Our mood at the start of a day can affect all those with whom we will come into contact. The river runs its course. We cannot escape moving together and affecting whatever we encounter. The collective actualization of the trip is put into jeopardy by even one person's nonbeing.

WRITING

The Connectiveness of Knowledge

Reading Leo Buscaglia's article should remind you once again that you are part of a whole and that your actions and thoughts are indeed connected to the world in which you live.

Now, take the time to reflect on this past semester and all that you learned—in and out of the classroom. Are you able to see any connections between your life and what you learned? Can you find any similarities between some of the topics covered in your classes? Can you find a theme that runs through most of what you learned? Implicitly or explicitly?

For this paper, choose one or two concepts that you learned this year. Write a paragraph about each concept explaining what you learned. Then sit back and think about each concept and whether the concepts are connected in some way. When you have figured this out, go back and add two paragraphs to the paper explaining the connections.

When finished, take the time again to figure out what this learning might mean to your next semester in college. Write a paragraph or two explaining what meaning your new knowledge has and how you think it will relate to your future learning.

This is reflective writing.

Before beginning to make the box, fill in the squares numbered 1 to 4 with words that you think have helped you with learning. What does it take to learn? What are the necessary pieces?

Begin the box:

1. Fold your sheet along the line marked **B** and **J**.
2. Fold your sheet along the line marked **C** and **K**.
3. Fold your sheet along the line marked **E** and **F**.
4. Fold your sheet along the line market **G** and **H**.

You should now have a piece of paper with four folds. You can begin to create your origami box. There are four corners that you now must crease on a diagonal.

5. Fold the corner matching up **E** and **B**. Do the same for **C** and **F**, then for **G** and **J**, and again for **H** and **K**.

Once you have done this, you can easily see the way this will finally be put into the shape of a box. Begin at one end of the paper, and fold in the two corners, pushing the extra paper into the middle and folding the outer edge over them to secure the box. Do this by folding inward: A1, D2, I3, L4. Do the same at the other end, and you should have a box that can stand up on its own.

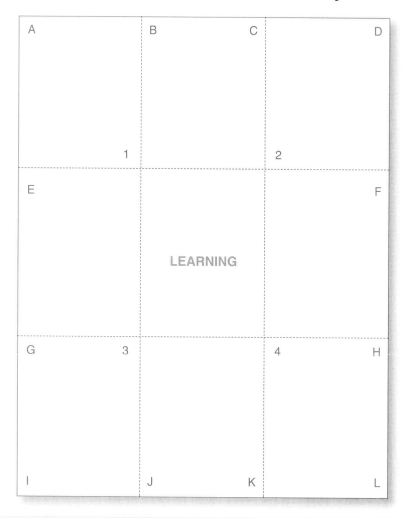

The following article examines the kind of reflection that can be accomplished in response to service learning activities. These reflections are, in fact, no different than reflecting on any kind of experience or learning activity you might engage in. Read this excerpt and think about the amazing insight these students have gained about themselves.

Students' Reflections about the Self

Robert A. Rhoads

Some of the students who worked with homeless citizens in the D.C. project shared their reflections about how they thought of themselves as people and where they might be heading. In general, students found their work with the homeless to challenge their sense of self on a number of fronts. For example, some students were emotionally challenged by what they experienced, as the following comments reveal: "I found that working with homeless people was much harder on me than I'd expected. I found the work somewhat difficult and a bit discouraging. I think that I was shocked emotionally and that I need to think about how I can deal with the harsh reality of their lives and where I fit in all of this." A second student also talked about the emotional nature of the D.C. project: "I found it extremely difficult to say good-bye on the last day. I wondered if I would ever see any of those people again. Maybe I shouldn't have allowed myself to get so close to some of them, but I guess that's part of why I came."

A student from Michigan State University spoke of learning that some students deal with their emotions by complaining. She described her experiences on a trip to New York City and a project working with homeless citizens: "Some of the other students on the trip didn't have experience with a lot of issues related to homelessness. They have different family backgrounds and experiences. Some aren't very tolerant. I learned how people deal with their emotions. We had to shower in a decaying basement, and some of the students reacted very negatively—'Oh, how

gross!' It was hard for me to hear their complaining. My attitude is 'Just deal with it.'"

One student from the Johns Island project pondered questions regarding learning about oneself: "What did I learn? Good question. The first thing is I've learned that I'm not as afraid of heights as I thought I was [she had to climb a ladder to do roof repairs]. Second, I learned that it's okay to be fearful of major life changes. And third, I've learned more about myself. I've got another piece into my personality jigsaw puzzle. I know I like to help, and to do good for others. I like to have fun, too—to get the most out of life that I can. And the quest for knowledge of the world of fiction and the world around me is important also." A senior in wildlife management who also participated in the Johns Island project learned the following about herself: "Many of my beliefs are not like those held by the majority of the volunteers on this trip; I'm somewhat conservative, yet I had an easier time accepting these differences than they did. The experience taught me that I'm more firm in my beliefs than I thought I was and that it's hard being the one who's different, but not impossible."

A graduate student offered the following thoughts concerning his personal challenge to learn to be more patient and how working in community service settings had helped him: "I guess I have a tendency to be impatient and I think I still need to work on it . . . I found myself in situations when in the past I would have reacted differently. But this time I kept my thoughts to myself, and instead of ruining everybody's fun I kept quiet. I guess I was more patient and prudent with my reactions." Another student from the Johns Island project discussed what she discovered about herself: "I'm usually very shy, but on this trip I was much more open than usual and I learned that people will accept me if I'm comfortable with myself. I felt comfortable and accepted, and I think it might have something to do with the fact that we are all here for the same reason—we all have a common bond. Everyone paid to come here and help someone and for no reward other than feeling good about yourself."

Other students also seemed to be using their experience of community service to work through personal issues. One student mentioned, "I'm learning that I move more by momentum than I thought I did . . . When I was a little kid I was a perfectionist. And it kind of got to the point that it got in the way, but now I'm getting better . . . Now I see things on a bigger scale." Another student talked about her personal growth: "I have to distance myself because I tend to get very emotional. When I learned about the concentration camp in seventh grade, I couldn't eat. I have to work through my emotions in order to help. So I've made this conscious effort to distance myself so I can contribute . . . I have to conquer things that prohibit me from helping: I've got to mitigate that somehow. I think these kinds of experiences are helping me to conquer my fears. I'm also learning about another culture—a lifestyle that is different from mine. And that is helping me to understand others better."

For a number of students, involvement in community service contributed to their sense of self as a spiritual person. Several students in this study saw strong connections between their faith and their commitment to serving others. A junior majoring in health education had this to say: "For me, service work always leads to a spiritual awakening. Service challenges me to face the deeper meanings of life—things that I typically try to ignore." Another student who participated in the Yonges Island project also commented on her spiritual growth: "I'm a spiritual person, but I'm not a Christian and I'm not a Catholic. I just have to look a little harder for a religion that suits me. Or maybe no religion at all . . . These kinds of experiences help me to think about what it means to be spiritual and to ask questions about why we should care for others." Some students talked about the spirituality they experienced from those they worked to serve:

"It's fascinating, the level of spirituality here [Yonges Island]. It's a neat feeling to listen to the people here and to see their relationship with God. They're so emotional. . . . I feel it too. . . . You learn a lot about yourself when you're here." Another student talked about the residents of Johns Island: "People here have a deep faith. I think that's really cool, given the hardships they live with, the way they face life. They need their faith."

Now all the learning experiences pertaining to self-understanding pleased students. For example, one student noted that she felt very uncomfortable when she was around African American homeless citizens: "I felt the gap between Black and White people. I felt very uncomfortable at times." She was not pleased with her discomfort and hoped to figure out how she could grow from it. "I have to take this feeling and see if I can't learn from it. I don't think of myself as a racist, and yet why was I so uncomfortable?" Three other students talked about things they learned about themselves from which they would like to grow:

I learned that I am not nearly as good a person as I had thought. I learned that I still have some personal issues related to accepting others to deal with. Compared to some of the people I met, my life seems trivial and uninspired. I will resolve to do better.

My work as a volunteer has really helped me to see that I have more I have to understand about myself in order to grow. I'm still on the journey and have a long ways to go.

I think this week has helped me to recognize that I truly don't know much about myself. I've also learned that I'm not good at talking during group sharing. Everybody talks about all the things they have done this week, but I can't really explain the moments we've experienced. I guess I can't really do them justice.

The students in this section highlight how community service provides a context for extensive learning about and understanding of one's self. Sometimes their experiences helped students to find answers to their identity struggles, whereas at other times important questions arose. In both cases, the self was reconfigured through the ongoing interaction that characterizes service founded on mutuality.

Remember, this text has been based on the concept of being on a journey through known and unknown territory. This activity will help you go back and *reflect* on your writing to see if you have learned anything, changed in any way, and gained new perspectives.

Gather together all of the writing you have done in this course over the past semester. Include in-class writing assignments, informal and formal papers, and your journal entries.

Read all of your writing carefully, and then answer the following questions:

1. How do you feel about your work?

2. Did you work hard or not? Did you accomplish anything?

3. What kinds of things were frustrating? Difficult?

4. What are you proud of?

5. What can you learn from your own writing?

6. What bits of your writing stick in your mind?

7. Are there any particular phrases or sentences you have written that you feel really good about? What are they?

continued

Now, go back through your writing again, read it, and answer the next 10 questions:

1. How often did I take the time to back up my opinions and statements?

2. Did I make generalizations all of the time?

3. To what extend did I oversimplify my responses to ideas?

4. Was I unwilling to take the trouble to really think about what I was writing and therefore had little or no substance to my work?

5. Did I ever jump to conclusions and write a paper without giving alternative ideas any thought?

6. Is my perspective the same or has it changed?

7. How is my writing now? Has it improved?

8. Did I give all the writing my best effort? Why or why not?

9. How could I improve my work?

10. Did I enjoy any particular part of the writing?

WRITING

Purpose of Schooling

If you are a typical student, you have spent about three-quarters of your daily life in school. Have you ever reflected on your life in school and on what the purpose might be for all this time spent there?

Write a thoughtful reflection on your memory of school, and try to answer as many of the following questions as you can. Base your answers and narrative on your own experiences in both elementary and high school.

- What was your reaction to school and learning in elementary school?

- Did you like school?

- Do you remember how you felt about yourself as a student?

- Do you remember a particularly remarkable teacher or grade level or educational experience in the classroom?

- What made a teacher or a year more remarkable than others?

- What do you think is the purpose of an elementary school education?

- Relate all of the above questions to your middle and high school years.
- What did you learn about yourself as a student or learner in your later years in school?

- What is the purpose of a high school education?

John Taylor Gatto received the state teacher of the year award in New York. He wrote the following speech for accepting the award. He taught school for over 30 years and was obviously an excellent teacher. However, you will see from this speech, he has a very negative attitude toward what happens in school.

As you read his speech, reflect on your experiences while using this text. Have you been taught confusion? Been ignored? Are you indifferent? Dependent on others for ideas or your self-esteem? Or do you feel empowered to embark on the remainder of your educational journey?

The Seven-Lesson Schoolteacher

John Taylor Gatto

Call me Mr. Gatto, please. Twenty-six years ago, having nothing better to do with myself at the time, I tried my hand at schoolteaching. The license I have certifies that I am an instructor of English language and English literature, but that isn't what I do at all. I don't teach English, I teach school—and I win awards doing it.

Teaching means different things in different places, but seven lessons are universally taught from Harlem to Hollywood Hills. They constitute a national curriculum you pay for in more ways than you can imagine, so you might as well know what it is. You are at liberty, of course, to regard these lessons any way you like, but believe me when I say I intend no irony in this presentation. These are the things I teach, these are the things you pay me to teach. Make of them what you will.

1. Confusion

A lady named Kathy wrote this to me from Dubois, Indiana the other day:

> What big ideas are important to little kids? Well, the biggest idea I think they need is that what they are learning isn't idiosyncratic—that there is some system to it all and it's not just raining down on them as they helplessly absorb. That's the task, to understand, to make coherent.

Kathy has it wrong. *The first lesson I teach is confusion. Everything* I teach is out of context. I teach the un-relating of everything. I teach dis-connections. I teach too much: the orbiting of planets, the law of large numbers, slavery, adjectives, architectural drawing, dance, gymnasium, choral singing, assemblies, surprise guests, fire drills, computer languages, parents' nights, staff-development days, pull-out programs, guidance with strangers my students may never see again, standardized tests, age-segregation unlike anything seen in the outside world . . . What do any of these things have to do with each other?

Even in the best schools a close examination of curriculum and its sequences turns up a lack of coherence, full of internal contradictions. Fortunately the children have no words to define the panic and anger they feel *at constant violations of natural order and sequence* fobbed off on them as quality in education. The logic of the school-mind is that it is better to leave school with a tool kit of superficial jargon derived from economics, sociology, natural science, and so on, than with one genuine enthusiasm. But quality in education entails learning about something in depth. Confusion is thrust upon kids by too many strange adults, each working alone with only the thinnest relationship with each other, pretending, for the most part, to an expertise they do not possess.

Meaning, not disconnected facts, is what sane human beings seek, and education is a set of codes for processing raw data into meaning. Behind the patchwork quilt of school sequences and the school obsession with facts and theories, the age-old human search for meaning lies well concealed. This is harder to see in elementary school where the hierarchy of school experience seems to make better sense because the good-natured simple relationship between "let's do this" and "let's do that" is just assumed to mean something and the clientele has not yet consciously discerned how little substance is behind the play and pretense.

Think of the great natural sequences—like learning to walk and learning to talk; the progression of light from sunrise to sunset; the ancient procedures of a farmer, a smithy, or a shoemaker; or the preparation of a Thanksgiving feast—all of the parts are in perfect harmony with each other, each action justifies itself and illuminates the past and the future. School sequences aren't like that, not inside a single class and not among the total menu of daily classes. School sequences are crazy. There is no particular reason for any of them, nothing that bears close scrutiny. Few teachers would dare to teach the tools whereby dogmas of a school or a teacher could be criticized, since everything must be accepted. School subjects are learned, if they *can* be learned, like children learn the catechism or memorize the Thirty-nine Articles of Anglicanism.

I teach the un-relating of everything, an infinite fragmentation the opposite of cohesion; what I do is more related to television programming than to making a scheme of order. In a world where home is only a ghost, because both parents work, or because of too many moves or too many job changes or too much ambition, or because something else has left everybody too confused to maintain a family relation, I teach you how to accept confusion as your destiny. That's the first lesson I teach.

2. Class Position

The second lesson I teach is class position. I teach that students must stay in the class where they belong. I don't know who decides my kids belong there but that's not my business. The children are numbered so that if any get away they can be returned to the right class. Over the years the variety of ways children are numbered by schools has increased dramatically, until it is hard to see the human beings plainly under the weight of numbers they carry. Numbering children is a big and very profitable undertaking, though what the strategy is designed to accomplish is elusive. I don't even know why parents would, without a fight, allow it to be done to their kids.

In any case, that's not my business. My job is to make them like being locked together with children who bear numbers like their own. Or at the least to endure it like good sports. If I do my job well, the kids can't even *imagine* themselves somewhere else, because I've shown them how to envy and fear the better classes and how to have contempt for the dumb classes. Under this efficient discipline the class mostly polices itself into good marching order. That's the real lesson of any rigged competition like school. You come to know your place.

In spite of the overall class blueprint, which assumes that ninety-nine percent of the kids are in their class to stay, I nevertheless make a public effort to exhort children to higher levels of test scores, hinting at eventual transfer from the lower class as a reward. I frequently insinuate the day will come when an employer will hire them on the basis of test scores and grades, even though my own experience is that employers are rightly indifferent to such things. I never lie outright, but I've come to see that truth and schoolteaching are at bottom, incompatible, just as Socrates said thousands of years ago. The lesson of numbered classes is that everyone has a proper place in the pyramid and there is no way out of your class except by number magic. Failing that, you must stay where you are put.

3. Indifference

The third lesson I teach is indifference. I teach children not to care too much about anything, even though they want to make it appear that they do. How I do this is very subtle. I do it by demanding that they become totally involved in my lessons, jumping up and down in their seats with anticipation, competing vigorously with each other for my favor. It's heartwarming when they do that; it impresses everyone, even me. When I'm at my best I plan lessons very carefully in order to produce this show of enthusiasm. But when the bell rings I insist they drop whatever it is we have been doing and proceed quickly to the next work station. They must turn on and off like a light switch. Nothing important is ever finished in my class nor in any class I know of. Students never have a complete experience except on the installment plan.

Indeed, the lesson of bells is that no work is worth finishing, so why care too deeply about anything? Years of bells will condition all but the strongest to a world that can no longer offer important work to do. Bells are the secret logic of schooltime; their logic is inexorable. Bells destroy the past and future, rendering every interval the same as any other, as the abstraction of a map renders every living mountain and river the same, even though they are not. Bells inoculate each undertaking with indifference.

4. Emotional Dependency

The fourth lesson I teach is emotional dependency. By stars and red checks, smiles and frowns, prizes, honors, and disgraces, I teach kids to surrender their will to the predestinated chain of command. Rights may be granted or withheld by any authority without appeal, because rights do not exist inside a school—not even the right of free speech, as the Supreme Court has ruled—unless school authorities say they do. As a schoolteacher, I intervene in many personal decisions, issuing a pass for those I deem legitimate, or initiating a disciplinary confrontation for behavior that threatens my control. Individuality is constantly trying to assert itself among children and teenagers, so my judgments come thick and fast. Individuality is a contradiction of class theory, a curse to all systems of classification.

Here are some common ways it shows up: children sneak away for a private moment in the toilet on the pretext of moving their bowels, or they steal a private instant in the hallway on the grounds they need water. I know they don't but I allow them to "deceive" me because this conditions them to depend on my favors. Sometimes free will appears right in front of me in pockets of children angry, depressed, or happy about things outside my ken; rights in such matters cannot be recognized by schoolteachers, only privileges that can be withdrawn, hostages to good behavior.

5. Intellectual Dependency

The fifth lesson I teach is intellectual dependency. Good students wait for a teacher to tell them what to do. It is the most important lesson, that we must wait for other people, better trained than ourselves, to make the meanings of our lives. The expert makes all the important choices; only I, the teacher, can determine what my kids must study, or rather, only the people who pay me can make those decisions, which I then enforce. If I'm told that evolution is a fact instead of a theory, I transmit that as ordered, punishing deviants who resist what I have been told to tell them to think. This power to control what children will think lets me separate successful students from failures very easily.

Successful children do the thinking I assign them with a minimum of resistance and a decent show of enthusiasm. Of the millions of things of value to study, I decide what few we have time for, or actually it is decided by my faceless employers.

The choices are theirs, why should I argue? Curiosity has no important place in my work, only conformity.

Bad kids fight this, of course, even though they lack the concepts to know what they are fighting, struggling to make decisions for themselves about what they will learn and when they will learn it. How can we allow that and survive as schoolteachers? Fortunately there are tested procedures to break the will of those who resist; it is more difficult, naturally, if the kids have respectable parents who come to their aid, but that happens less and less in spite of the bad reputation of schools. No middle-class parents I have ever met actually believe that *their* kid's school is one of the bad ones. Not one single parent in twenty-six years of teaching. That's amazing, and probably the best testimony to what happens to families when mother and father have been well-schooled themselves, learning the seven lessons.

Good people wait for an expert to tell them what to do. It is hardly an exaggeration to say that our entire economy depends upon this lesson being learned. Think of what might fall apart if children weren't trained to be dependent; the social services could hardly survive; they would vanish, I think, into the recent historical limbo out of which they arose. Counselors and therapists would look on in horror as the supply of psychic invalids vanished. Commercial entertainment of all sorts, including television, would wither as people learned again how to make their own fun. Restaurants, the prepared-food industry, and a whole host of other assorted food services would be drastically down-sized if people returned to making their own meals rather than depending on strangers to plant, pick, chop, and cook for them. Much of modern law, medicine, and engineering would go too, the clothing business and schoolteaching as well, unless a guaranteed supply of helpless people continued to pour out of our schools each year.

Don't be too quick to vote for radical school reform if you want to continue getting a paycheck. We've built a way of life that depends on people doing what they are told because they don't know how to tell *themselves* what to do. It's one of the biggest lessons I teach.

6. Provisional Self-Esteem

The sixth lesson I teach is provisional self-esteem. If you've ever tried to wrestle into line kids whose parents have convinced them to believe they'll be loved in spite of anything, you know how impossible it is to make self-confident spirits conform. Our world wouldn't survive a flood of confident people very long, so I teach that a kid's self-respect should depend on expert opinion. My kids are constantly evaluated and judged.

A monthly report, impressive in its provision, is sent into a student's home to elicit approval or mark exactly, down to a single percentage point, how dissatisfied with the child a parent should be. The ecology of "good" schooling depends on perpetuating dissatisfaction, just as the commercial economy depends on the same fertilizer. Although some people might be surprised how little time or reflection goes into making up these mathematical records, the cumulative weight of these objective-seeming documents establishes a profile that compels children to arrive at certain decisions about themselves and their futures based on the casual judgment of strangers. Self-evaluation, the staple of every major philosophical system that ever appeared on the planet, is never considered a factor. The lesson of report cards, grades, and tests is that children should not trust themselves or their parents but should instead rely on the evaluation of certified officials. People need to be told what they are worth.

7. One Can't Hide

The seventh lesson I teach is that one can't hide. I teach students they are always watched, that each is under constant surveillance by myself and my colleagues. There are no private spaces for children, there is no private time. Class change lasts exactly three hundred seconds to keep promiscuous fraternization at low levels. Students are encouraged to tattle on each other or even to tattle on their own parents. Of course, I encourage parents to file reports about their own child's waywardness too. A family trained to snitch on itself isn't likely to conceal any dangerous secrets.

I assign a type of extended schooling called "homework," so that the effect of surveillance, if not that surveillance itself, travels into private households, where students might otherwise use free time to learn something unauthorized from a father or mother, by exploration, or by apprenticing to some wise person in the neighborhood. Disloyalty to the idea of schooling is a devil always ready to find work for idle hands.

The meaning of constant surveillance and denial of privacy is that no one can be trusted, that privacy is not legitimate. Surveillance is an ancient imperative, espoused by certain influential thinkers, a central prescription set down in *The Republic,* in *The City of God,* in the *Institutes of the Christian Religion,* in *New Atlantis,* in *Leviathan,* and in a host of other places. All these childless men who wrote these books discovered the same thing: children must be closely watched if you want to keep society under tight central control. Children will follow a private drummer if you can't get them into a uniformed marching band.

Journal Entry 30

I touch the future. I teach.

Christa McAuliffe

After reading "The Seven-Lesson Schoolteacher," compare your educational experiences in the classroom with those described by Gatto. In what ways can you relate to his essay? Can you agree with the points he made? Which ones? Why or why not? In what ways do you differ with him? Has your idea of the purpose of education been altered at all by what you just read? How about by your experiences "making this road"? Did you find your experiences in higher education to be significantly different? Enough so that Gatto's seven lessons are not relevant any longer?

Be not afraid of growing slowly, be afraid only of standing still.

—Chinese Proverb

As a final project for this course, you will design a map of your learning. In an earlier journal entry, you were asked to respond to this book's title and then to come up with your own. For purposes of this assignment, use your own title.

- Write down the *title* you created for this book.

  _____

  _____

- Make a complete *list* of what you have learned. Divide this list into such categories as skills, lessons, ideas, theories, behaviors, content, and so forth.

  _____

  _____

  _____

  _____

  _____

- Once you have these lists, *put them in order* from the most important things learned to the least important (if this is not possible, then you can put some items side by side).

  _____

  _____

  _____

  _____

  _____

- Now *visualize* for yourself how this journey might look. Would it be a maze? A straight path? A cobble stone street? A river? A skateboard ramp? Maybe a roller coaster? Or a huge tree with many branches? Perhaps it would be a patchwork quilt or a ladder? A comic strip? Be creative and try to match your experience to some visual representation.

- Make a *sketch* of your "picture of learning," and put some of the words on your list in strategic places.

- Write a *reflection* of several pages describing how your picture/collage/painting/photograph/sculpture/rendition of your learning captures the journey you have taken. Link your picture to your personal title.

Cashing In on Your Own Education

YOUR ROAD MAP

Index

Occupations, computer search and, 163
O'Donnell, Rosie, 115
Olmstead, Frederick, 20
"One Liar's Beginnings," 42–43
Open-mindedness, 8
Opium War, 21
Oral presentation, 48, 49–50
Origami, 266
Orita, Wendy, 58
Outline of History, 20
Outsider, being an, 94–95, 96
Outward journey, 11–12

Passion, lack of, 214
Pathfinder, 210
"Pedagogical Sights/Sites: Producing Colonialism and Practicing Art in the Pacific," 174
Pentagon, 85
Perceptions, 142
    male vs. female, 88, 89–90
"Perplexing Lessons," 66–69
Personal:
    narrative, 151, 157
    sketch/story, 47–48
Perspective:
    cultural, 172
    historical, 103
Perspectives, 80–86
    expanding, 8
    information literacy and, 79
Persuading, 82
Philosophy, 109–112, 116, 264
Picasso, Pablo, 177
Plagiarism, 208
Plains Indians, 2–3
Plato, 28, 109–112, 116, 175
Point of view, 79
    articulating your, 3
Position, class, 273
Power, as purpose for knowledge, 133
Prediction research, 193
Presentation:
    oral, 48, 49–50
    visual, 48–49
Principles, 79
Private pleas, 39
Problems, internalizing, 173
Problem-solving, 237

Projects, group, 2–3
Project Zero, 71
Prompts, writing, 53–54
Public:
    requests, 39
    speaking, 48, 49–50
Puerto Rican, 90–91
Purpose:
    moral, 241–243
    of knowledge, 132, 133

Question:
    analysis, 177
    significance of, 199
Questions:
    answering, 178
    as basis for research, 191
    as key to answers, 170
    asking, 176
    as stimulus for thinking, 175
    journalists', 191
    to stimulate writing, 52–54
Quezon, Justin, 23

Ranking, group, 81
RAP, 235–236
Reading, service learning and, 234–235
Real vs. artificial, 123
Reality, 104, 105–124
    information literacy and, 107
    television, 114–115
Rebuttals, 203
Recombinant DNA, 134–137
Reconstructive exhibits, 222
Red China, 21–22
Reference books, 178
Reflection:
    as way of knowing, 127, 128, 143, 258–277
    by students, 267–268
    information literacy and, 261
    process of, 263
    writing and, 210
Relationships, identifying through research, 193
Republic, The, 109, 275
Requests, public, 39
Research, 103, 154–160, 189–210
    action, 194
    defined, 192
    descriptive, 193

doing, 198–208
explanatory, 193
exploration, 191, 193
indexes and, 186
information literacy and, 191
kinds of, 193–194
locating sources, 201
methodology, 192–194
picking a topic, 198–199
prediction, 193
scientific method and, 194
value-free, 194
verifiable, 194
and World Wide Web, 204
writing and, 172
Resolving differences, 213
Responsibility, civic, 213
Reunion, college, 188
Rhoads, Robert A., 267–268
Ride, Sally, 13
Ritz, Mary Kaye, 114–115
Rogers, J.A., 20
"Role of Connectiveness, The," 264–265
Rukeyser, Muriel, 154

Santos, Linda, 124
"Satisfactions," 238–249
Satisfaction, seeking through volunteering, 252
Schaef, Anne Wilson, 223
Scholarly:
    narrative, 149, 151, 157, 159
    and personal, 143
Scholarship (*see also* Knowledge):
    contributing to, 212–214
    information literacy and, 217
    understanding, 166–168
Schooling, purpose of, 271 (*see also* College, Education)
Schubert, Gary, 128
Science, hazards of, 134–137
Scientific:
    inquiry, 104
    method, 128, 194
    truth, 137
Search:
    commands, 155
    computer, 162–164
    database, 155–158
    doing, 157
    engines, 162, 163